MMPI
INTERPRETATION MANUAL FOR COUNSELORS AND CLINICIANS

Second Edition

Jane C. Duckworth, Ph.D.

Professor of Psychology—Counseling
Department of Counseling Psychology
and Guidance Services
Ball State University

INCORPORATED

Accelerated Development Inc.
2515 West Jackson
P.O. Box 667
Muncie, IN 47305
Tel. (317) 284-7511

Library of Congress Catalog Card Number: 79—64500

International Standard Book Number: 0—915202—22—0

Editors: Cindy Lyons
Linda Davis

Graphic Artist: Mary Blizzard

Printed in the United States of America
First Edition March 1975
Second Edition September 1979

For Additional Copies order from

INCORPORATED

Accelerated Development Inc.
2515 West Jackson, P.O. Box 667
Muncie, IN 47305
Tel. (317) 284-7511

PREFACE

The second edition of the **MMPI Interpretation Manual for Counselors and Clinicians** *represents four years of thinking and reflection concerning the first edition of the book. As a consequence of this thinking, the original book has been revised the following ways:*

1. *The Validity and Clinical scales sections include the most recent research on the scales and summary tables at the end of each scale reflect new thinking concerning these scales. Most changes have come in the moderate elevation and low point sections of the tables. In addition to these changes in the summary tables, references to the New scales when appropriate, have been added to the Clinical scale summaries. These additions have been made to help the user become more aware of how the New scales may be used to refine or clarify the Clinical scale interpretations.*

2. *The New scale section has been greatly enlarged by the addition of more information on the interpretation of these scales. Dr. Wayne Anderson, Professor of Counseling Psychology at the University of Missouri and the person who taught me the MMPI, graciously agreed to help with this section and has added many of the new insights about these scales. I feel his contributions have enhanced the book greatly.*

3. *A new chapter on interpreting the MMPI has been added to assist those practitioners who would like to know how to do MMPI interpretations incorporating the New scales. Dr. Anderson also assisted with this chapter by contributing a section on how he does MMPI interpretations so that you have two approaches to MMPI interpretations, Dr. Anderson's and mine.*

4. *Two new references have been added to the acknowledgment section following the preface. I have found the book* The MMPI: A Practical Guide *by John Graham to be extremely useful, especially concerning two point combinations. The other new reference is an article by Kunce and Anderson (the same Anderson who helped*

write the New scale and Interpretation chapters). The article is entitled "Normalizing the MMPI" and suggests interpretations for the Clinical scales when they are in the 60-70 T score range. You will find both of these references used thoughout this book.

I would like to conclude by using material from the preface of the original book published in 1975. I feel the points in this preface are still valid.

This book concerning the MMPI is designed for use by graduate students and practitioners (psychologists, social workers, and physicians) who counsel with university students and mental health center out-patients. As with other authors who write books of this type, I feel major gaps exist in works presently available concerning these populations and the MMPI. Also, as with other authors, I have been frustrated in my attempts to find a suitable text on the MMPI for my graduate students. Consequently, I felt it would be helpful to have a simplified reference work on the MMPI available for myself, my students, and other practitioners; a work which could be used easily while performing the day-to-day chores involved in counseling and therapy. Thus, I have written this book on the MMPI to fulfill several purposes.

The first purpose is to present MMPI information for practitioners whose clients are basically normal. By normal I mean those clients who typically do not require hospitalization and in most instances can be helped without extensive alteration of the personality. By normal I do not mean that the clients do not have problems because they are seeking some kind of help.

I do have a few psychotics and neurotics in the counseling center and mental health center populations, of course; but mainly, the largest number of problems with which I am concerned arise from situational stresses rather than from long term personal inadequacies.

Most current books available on the MMPI are useful primarily for practitioners working in hospitals with confined or out-patient clients. This book, as mentioned previously, is designed for use with basically normal populations. However,

IV

certain information from hospital populations is relevant to the college counseling center and mental health center populations and has been included in this book.

My second purpose for this book is to collect from various sources the information concerning the MMPI which would be useful for work with these normal, non-hospitalized populations. My experience has been that this information is scattered throughout many books and journal articles, and as such is not readily accessible in any one place.

My third purpose for this book is to present information about and interpretations for the New Scales, (A, R, Es, Lb, Ca, Dy, Do, Re, Pr, St, and Cn), printed by some computer scoring services. I have found most of these New Scales to be particularly helpful in working with normal populations, but the scales usually have been, I feel, inadequately presented or even omitted in other books. A chapter of this book is devoted to the New scales with the hope that others will be encouraged to start using them in their interpretations. The items included in the New Scales are presented in the Appendices.

The fourth purpose for this book is to present the material in such a way as to be accessible easily and quickly. To this end I have used a combination of an outline format and a written paragraph form.

The fifth purpose is to use vocabulary which would describe the behavior and thoughts of people with various MMPI high and low points, avoiding as much as possible using clinical labels or emotionally laden words. My experience, particularly with students, has been that they tend to cling to clinical lables and to over-react to emotionally-laden terminology.

This book is designed to be an efficient reference for practitioners and a usable text for MMPI teachers and students. In order to determine how these goals have been met, I encourage you to send comments to me about the book so that I may improve future editions of it by retaining strengths and modifying weaknesses. Therefore, I have included a tear-out page at the end of this manual for your comments.

June 1979   Jane Duckworth

ACKNOWLEDGMENTS

The selecting, rewording, and editing of the material in this book have been based primarily upon my use of the MMPI and experience as a practitioner and teacher. However, I have drawn heavily from several sources. Therefore, I acknowledge my special indebtedness to the following authors and their works:

Butcher, J. (Ed.). *MMPI: Research developments and clinical applications.* New York: McGraw-Hill, 1969. (Of special help was the article by R.C. Carson in Appendix A.)

Carkhuff, R.R., Barnett, L., and McCall, J.N. *The counselor's handbook: Scale and profile interpretation of the MMPI.* Urbana, IL: R.W. Parkinson and Assoc., 1965.

Dahlstrom, W.G., and Welsh, G.S. *An MMPI handbook: A guide to use in clinical practice and research.* Minneapolis: University of Minnesota Press, 1960.

Dahlstrom, W.G., Welsh, G., and Dahlstrom, L. *An MMPI handbook: Volume I. Clinical Interpretation.* Minneapolis: University of Minnesota Press, 1972.

Drake, L.E., and Oetting, E.R. *An MMPI codebook for counselors.* Minneapolis: University of Minnesota Press, 1959.

Gilberstadt, H., and Duker, J. *A handbook for clinical and actuarial MMPI interpretation.* Philadelphia: W.B. Saunders, 1965.

Graham, J. *The MMPI: A practical guide.* NY; Oxford Press, 1972.

Gynther, M., Altman, H., and Sletten, I. Replicated correlates of MMPI two-point code types: The Missouri Actuarial System. *Journal of Clinical Psychology,* 1973, 29, 263-289.

Hovey, H.B., and Lewis, E.G. Semi-automatic interpretation of the MMPI. *Journal of Clinical Psychology,* 1967, 23, 123-134.

Kunce, J. and Anderson, W. Normalizing the MMPI. *Journal of Clinical Psychology*, 1976, 32, 776-780.

Marks, P., and Seeman, W. *The actuarial description of abnormal Personality*. Baltimore: The Williams and Wilkins Co., 1963.

Marks, P., Seeman, W., and Haller, D. *The actuarial use of the MMPI with adolescents and adults*. Baltimore: The Williams and Wilkins Co., 1974.

I also owe a large debt of gratitude to Alex Caldwell for materials gathered from his talks at the annual MMPI conferences. I have tried to acknowledge his contributions wherever they occur, but there may be instances where an idea I feel is my own has been given to me by him.

Finally, I want to thank all of you who took the time to send the feedback sheets to me. Your suggestions and comments have been most appreciated.

Muncie, Indiana   Jane Duckworth
June, 1979

TABLE OF CONTENTS

X

LIST OF FIGURES

chapter 1

INTRODUCTION

This MMPI book has been written primarily for counselors and clinicians who work with two types of populations: university counseling center clients and mental health clinic clients. These populations are not usually psychotic or neurotic but are likely to be people who are functioning adequately in their world but having problems in one or two areas. These problems may be longstanding ones, but more usually they are the result of situational pressures and stresses. These pressures may range from mild (such as selecting an academic major) to severe (such as divorce or death in the family).

The MMPI was developed in the 1930's and 1940's as a complex psychological instrument designed to diagnose mental patients into different categories of neuroses and psychoses. Since that time its use has extended to all kinds of settings, including employment agencies, university counseling centers, mental health clinics, schools, and industry. Its use also has been expanded to include research and screening. Most importantly, its diagnostic origins have been expanded to include a person's behavior, attitudes, thought patterns, and strengths; data which are extremely useful to the practicing counselor and therapist.

The MMPI as originally constructed had eight Clinical scales (scales 1 through 4 and 6 through 9). Two additional scales, 5 and 0, have since been added to the Clinical scales. Originally the MMPI Clinical scales were intended to place persons into various diagnostic categories. Designers expected that people taking the test would have an elevation on one scale which would then indicate the diagnosis for that person such as schizophrenic, hypochondriac, and so forth. It was soon discovered that this was a very limited approach, and consequently, three major developments occurred.

First, MMPI interpreters began describing the behavior associated with the various elevations instead of just placing people into diagnostic categories. This development provided information useful to the counselor and clinician in the treatment of the person.

The second development was to use the varying scale elevations to differentiate intensity of behavior and thinking. For example, scale 2, which was originally only interpreted as depression, is now used to differentiate between people who are feeling "blue" (lower elevations) from those who are severely depressed (higher elevations).

The third major interpretative development of the MMPI was the use of the whole profile for analysis, rather than only one, two, or three high points. This approach has added subtlety and richness to the interpretations.

An initial improvement of the MMPI, occurring soon after it was developed, was the addition of four Validity scales to the Clinical scales to measure the test-taking attitude of the person. This addition is one of the major strengths of the MMPI. These Validity scales note the number of items omitted (? scale), the amount of obvious social virtues claimed by the person (L scale), the amount of "different" or bad experiences the client is reporting (F scale), and the amount of good feelings the person is reporting (K scale). No other psychological instrument, to my knowledge, is so thorough in attempting to determine the client's mental set at the time of test administration. These Validity scales are typically shown first on the MMPI profile so that the test-taking attitude of the person can be taken into account in interpreting the Clinical scales which appear in the second section of the profile.

In addition to these two sets of scales, over 450 experimental scales have been developed to measure such diverse areas as alcoholism, ego strength, dominance, anxiety, and status needs. Many computer services include eleven of these experimental scales in their reports. These eleven scales are termed the New scales and as such form the third section of the MMPI profile. I have found most of these eleven New scales to be extremely useful in my MMPI interpretations and have included a section on them in this book.

2

One of the difficulties some people have in using the New scales is getting them scored so that they can be interpreted. However, as mentioned previously, many computer scoring services do report the New scales, and I would suggest using such a scoring service. If the MMPI is scored manually, the keys for the New scales are listed as an appendix to this book. These keys also are available from Psychological Assessment Resources, Inc., P.O. Box 98 Odessa, FL 33556. When scoring MMPI's manually, I have found the profile sheets provided by National Computer Systems, 4401 W. 76th St., Minneapolis, MN, extremely useful for plotting the profiles because they do include the New scales as well as the Validity and Clinical scales.

Thus the MMPI, as used in this book, has three sets of scales: the Validity scales, the Clinical scales, and the New scales. I tend to use these three sets of scales in the following way. I look at the Validity scales *for the mood and/or test-taking attitude of the person.* Then I look at the Clinical scale elevations *for problem areas* (except for scale 5 where an elevation may not be a problem) and finally I note the New scales *for additional problem areas as well as some areas of strength.* The use of these scales is explained more completely in the introduction to each set of scales.

FORMAT AND USE OF THIS MANUAL

The following format is used in this book in presenting the chapters on the Validity, Clinical and New scales. First, an introduction and general information about the scale is presented, then high score interpretations are given, usually divided into moderate elevations (60 thru 70 T score points) and marked elevations (70 T score points or above). These interpretations are followed by the low score interpretations (usually 45 T score points or below). Combinations of scales are then noted and the interpretations for them are given. All Clinical scales in the combinations are at a T score of 70 or above, unless otherwise noted and are listed in order from the highest to the lowest peaks. Validity and New scale combinations use scales at a T score of 60 or above. If a scale in a combination is lower than a T of 50, the symbol "—" above the scale number is used, for example 5̄ in 4-5̄.

At times a scale score may fit in more than one interpretive category. For example, a Clinical scale score of 70 could be

3

interpreted as a moderate elevation (T = 60 thru 70) or a marked elevation (T = 70 or above). When this happens, use whichever interpretation seems to fit the situation.

Information should be gathered from the chapters concerning the Validity, Clinical, and New scales according to the high and low points present in the profile to be interpreted. The T score range between 45 and 60 is not usually interpreted for the Validity and Clinical scales but is in some cases for the New scales. A profile may be interpreted using only the high and low score sections or it may be interpreted using combinations (with or without the information in the high and low score sections) if the profile scales are high enough to be in a combination (above 70 T score points for the Clinical scale combinations or above 60 T score points for the Validity or New scale combinations).

For the reader who is new to interpreting the MMPI, the best way to become acquainted with the various scales is to read the introductory remarks for each of the scales. As one works with the MMPI, the more detailed information listed under the high and low points of the scales becomes useful. Finally, as one becomes yet more skilled in the usage of the test, the combinations with their more intricate interpretations become useful. A word of caution is necessary about the Clinical scale combinations. Only the highest two or three scales above 70 T score points are considered as a combination. The other Clinical scales above 70 should be interpreted by referring to the respective high point sections of the scales involved.

Also included is a chapter on interpreting the MMPI (Chapter V) that the reader may find useful in helping to develop his or her own interpretation skills.

I recommend that the whole book be read through first in order to get the total picture of the MMPI I am presenting. After the overview, separate sections can be used as needed.

chapter 2

VALIDITY SCALES

Of primary consideration in the interpretation of any inventory is the attitude of the person taking the test. Most inventories either have no way to check this attitude or have a simplistic approach to the problem. The MMPI is unique in this area. Four separate scales have been developed to measure the test-taking attitude of the subject, the **?**, **L**, **F**, and **K** scales. Of these scales, two (**L** and **K**) were designed to measure the person's trying to look better on the test than he or she really is, and one (the **F** scale) was designed to measure the person's trying to look worse on the test than he or she really is. The **?** scale measures how many questions the client left unanswered on the test, and thus can show the person's resistance to the test, confusion, or the fact that he or she did not have time to finish. These Validity scales can be interpreted either individually or in combinations.

In reality, the **?** scale does not usually have to be interpreted because it rarely has enough raw score points to be scored on the profile sheet. Similarly, the **L** scale is only rarely above a T score of 45, therefore the interpretation of this scale usually uses only the low end of the scale (the person is not trying to look good on the test). Only the **F** and **K** scales vary considerably therefore the various interpretations of them are considered carefully.

"?" SCALE
(Cannot Say Scale)

The ? scale raw score is simply the number of items the client has left unanswered. Omission of items is largely dependent upon the subject's response set, which in turn is usually influenced by the instructions given. If the instructions call for all items to be answered, they usually are. MMPI's are usually given with these instructions, and most people leave few, if any, questions unanswered.

The usual number of items omitted is from 0 thru 6, with a mode of zero and a median of one. It may be of interest, when more than six items are not answered, to look at the items omitted to see if a pattern exists. If a pattern occurs, it may indicate an area which the client does not want to consider, or about which confusion exists. This knowledge can be useful in counseling the person.

Elevations on this scale are rare. As a matter of fact, the omission of more than twelve items is very unusual. In the last 1000 profiles processed, only two persons omitted a substantial number of items. One person omitted the last 100 items because she was stopped before she had finished. The second person omitted 57 items without knowing it because he was mentally confused. In no other situation were more than 12 items omitted.

GENERAL INFORMATION

1. The ? scale raw score is the number of test questions a person does not answer.

2. Normal people decline few items on the MMPI (Butcher & Tellegen, 1966; Gravitz, 1971; Rankin, 1968). Thus, this scale

tends to be highly skewed, with 0-6 being the usual number of unanswered items. The modal value for this scale is zero, and the median value is one question unanswered.

3. The number of items omitted is largely dependent upon the subject's response set, which is usually influenced by the testing instructions given (Carkhuff, Barnette, & McCall, 1965). If the instructions are for all items to be answered, they usually are.

   Dahlstrom, Welsh, and Dahlstrom (1972) feel that some problems may result from giving the instruction to answer all items because people may resent having to answer all of the questions. I have found this rarely to be the case.

4. Most researchers feel this scale should not be considered or interpreted until a raw score of 30 (T = 50) or more is obtained. I feel however that even when fewer than this number are left unanswered, it might be useful to see if a certain pattern exists to the unanswered items, that is, they may all be related to a certain area such as sex or family.

5. The reason people leave items unanswered may range from lack of knowledge about a subject to defensiveness. See the high score section of this scale for the various reasons for omissions.

6. The effect of a high ? score (T = 70 or above), if the omissions are scattered throughout the test, can be a general lowering of the entire profile without much distortion of the pattern, except for the women's scale **5**. For this one scale, the more items that are omitted, the higher the T score becomes (Carkhuff et al., 1965).

   The presence of a high ? scale score however does not always mean that the profile is too low to interpret, because the motivations leading the subject to omit items also may lead him or her to choose an unusual number of deviant responses (Dahlstrom et al., 1972).

7. Considerable consistency over time is prevalent for this scale. That is, a person will have approximately the same score on it if the test should be given a second time (Dahlstrom et al., 1972).

?   8

HIGH SCORES
(T = 60 or Above)

1. High scores may indicate the following:

   a. Indecision or obsession with the "right" answer.
   b. Defensiveness (wanting to look good). These people do not know what answer would be the most favorable one for them to choose. Therefore, they do not answer the question.
   c. Not wanting to answer the question, but also not wanting to say "no" to the tester. Therefore, the client takes the test but leaves many questions unanswered.
   d. Distrust of the tester's motives.
   e. Lack of ability to read or comprehend all items.
   f. Not enough time to finish the test as would be shown when only items toward the end of the test are omitted. This situation may occur because an obsessive compulsive person might take a considerable amount of time to answer each item.
   g. A seriously depressed patient who finds the items beyond his or her capacity for decision (Carkhuff et al., 1965).
   h. Aggression toward the test or tester.
   i. Mental confusion whereby the person does not realize he or she has omitted questions.

2. In some research studies, MMPI tests with a **?** scale T score above 70 are considered invalid (Feldman, 1952; Meehl, 1946).

LOW SCORES
(T = 50 or Below)

1. Low scores are more likely to be obtained when the testing instructions call for answering all the items.

2. Even when only 6 items are omitted, a review of the omissions may reveal a pattern.

3. People may not answer questions in certain areas for the following reasons:

   a. Because they are not sure what they feel or believe about an area.
   b. Because they cannot face their feelings about an area.

?

c. Because they do not trust the counselor to keep the test answers confidential.

d. Because the items pertain to one or more areas of life that these people have not experienced.

COMBINATIONS

The Validity scales, ?, L, F, and K, in these combinations are at a T score of 60 or above, whereas the Clinical scales, 1 through 0, are at a T score of 70 or above and are the highest Clinical scales on the profile.

?-L

1. The person may be trying to place himself or herself in a highly favorable light but is using rather crude methods to distort the test record (Dahlstrom et al., 1972).

?-L-F-K

1. When all the Validity scales are elevated, intense and highly generalized negativism is suggested (Carkhuff et al., 1965).

?-F

1. The profile may be invalid because of mental confusion or reading difficulties. Further testing may be necessary to distinguish which of these two hypotheses is correct.

?-K

1. The person may be very defensive (Hovey & Lewis, 1967).

?-5

See the 5-? combination, p. 126.

SUMMARY OF ? SCALE INTERPRETATIONS

Number of Items Omitted	Interpretations
0 thru 6	This is the typical number of items omitted.
7 thru 12	The subject would prefer not answering questions about one or more areas.
13 thru 67	Scores in this range are rarely seen. Reasons for scores in this range may be in the categories above (7 thru 12) or below (67 or above).
67 or above	Scores in this range may indicate lack of time to complete the test, indecision, defensiveness, not wanting to answer the questions, distrust, lack of reading ability, aggression, depression, or confusion.

— **NOTES** —

L SCALE
(Lie Scale)

This scale is usually measuring the degree to which a person is trying to look good in an obvious way. The higher the scale, the more the individual is claiming socially correct behavior. The lower the scale, the more the person is willing to own up to general human weaknesses.

My experience indicates that the L scale is nearly always below a T of 50 and is rarely above a T of 60. People scoring at a T of 55 or above on this scale may be presenting themselves as morally righteous, although this in fact may not be true. Job applicants, for example, tend to have an elevated L, because they wish to impress the person doing the hiring.

In mental health centers, an elevation on this scale frequently indicates a rather naive person who has not thought deeply about human behavior, particularly his or her own. In a college setting, an elevated L, particularly with a slightly elevated 3 scale, frequently indicates people who like to look on the bright side of life and do not like to think bad thoughts about themselves or others. Thus, the exact inference to be construed from an elevated L depends upon the person's background, setting, and purpose for taking the inventory.

Scores at the low end of this scale indicate a person who is not socially naive, at least to the extent of claiming social virtues he or she does not have.

GENERAL INFORMATION

1. The 15 items of the L scale attempt to identify people who will not admit to human foibles, such as telling white lies or not

reading newspaper editorials. Such persons may wish to be seen as perfectionistic (Carson, 1969), or they may be naive.

2. The **L** scale items are seen as positive attributes in our culture. However, most people, excepting the most conscientious or naive, do not see such attributes as being true of themselves (Carson, 1969).

3. This **L** scale may indicate:

   a. The way the person actually sees himself or herself, that is, as morally straight.
   b. The degree to which a person may be attempting to "look good" by choosing the response that is more socially acceptable.
   c. The person's tendency to cover up and deny undesirable personal faults.

4. Caldwell (1977) believed this scale may measure a person's fears of shame and moral judgment. If a person has these fears, he/she will deny moral fault and therefore score high on this scale.

5. This **L** scale is not a subtle scale. The items are seen by most people to be fairly obvious "trap" items, and elevations on this scale above a T score of 50 are infrequent. See the high score section of this scale for the types of people who score in this direction.

6. The mean raw score for this scale is close to zero, and the modal raw score is 4.

7. Test-retest reliabilities vary considerably. These variable correlations may be an artifact of the brevity of the scale (15 items) (Dahlstrom & Welsh, 1960).

8. Although most people do not score high on this scale, in a recent study (Gravitz, 1970b) some normal subjects did. In this study using normal subjects, four items of this scale were endorsed in the scorable direction by more than half of the subjects, while just under one-half answered four other items in the scorable direction. Thus, eight of the 15 items in this scale were answered in the scorable direction by almost one-half of the subjects.

9. Under instructions to present oneself in the most favorable light, the **L** scale tends to elevate (Gloye & Zimmerman, 1967; Grayson & Olinger, 1957; Hiner, Ogren, & Baxter, 1969; Lanyon, 1967).

Under these instructions, the tendency is for the **L** and **K** scales to be between a T score of 60 and 70 and for the **F** scale to be near 50. These three scales thus form a "V." See Figure 8, page 46.

10. The **L** scale is negatively correlated with education. That is, the more education the subject has, the more likely the **L** scale is to be low (Lebovits & Ostfeld, 1967).

HIGH SCORES
(T = 55 or Above)

Moderate and Marked Elevations

1. Persons who score high on this scale may actually see themselves as virtuous, scrupulous, conforming, and self-controlled (Hovey & Lewis, 1967).

2. High **L** scores also may indicate

   a. Naive people.
   b. People who repress or deny unfavorable traits in themselves (Good & Brantner, 1961).
   c. People applying for jobs who want to look good on the test.
   d. People with below average intelligence.
   e. People with only elementary school education.
   f. People with rural backgrounds.
   g. Ministers or people with strict moral principles (Cottle, 1953).
   h. People with socioeconomic or cultural deprivation—ghetto or ethnic minority backgrounds (Dahlstrom et al., 1972).

3. A high **L** score may indicate that the Clinical scales are depressed. This fact should be taken into account in reading this profile.

L

LOW SCORES
(T = 45 or Below)

1. Low scores indicate an ability to acknowledge general human weaknesses (Hovey & Lewis, 1967).

2. The person who scores low may see himself or herself as non-righteous and relaxed (Hovey & Lewis, 1967).

3. Low scores are typical of the college population. However, a socially sophisticated and/or educated person may score low on **L** and still be trying to "look good." In this instance, the **K** score may be elevated.

COMBINATIONS

The Validity scales, **?**, **L**, **F**, and **K**, in these combinations are at a T score of 60 or above, whereas the Clinical scales, **1** through **0**, are at a T score of 70 or above and are the highest Clinical scales on the profile.

See also the **L-F-K** profiles, pp. 45-47.

L-?   See the **?-L** combination, p. 10.

L-?-F-K   See the **?-L-F-K** combination, p. 10.

L-F

See also the **L-F-K** profiles, pp. 45-47,
the **F-L** combination, p. 29.

1. The discrepancy shown in this combination between defensiveness, such as denying socially disapproved actions and thoughts (high **L**), acknowledgment of a number of unusual, bizarre, or atypical experiences (high **F**) may be manifested by a person exhibiting different behavior in different contexts (Dahlstrom et al., 1972; Wilson, 1965).

L

a. A person with this combination may be defensive in a personal interview but may show unusual experiences and thoughts in projective testing where he or she is not aware of what is being revealed.

b. The discrepancy between defensiveness and bizarreness may be the result of poor psychological integration, which characterizes some disturbed, naive people.

L-K

See also the L-F-K profiles, pp. 45-47.

1. A person with this combination may be repressing and denying unfavorable traits (Blazer, 1965a).

2. This pattern may indicate deliberate faking good on the test, because high scores have been obtained in numerous studies where subjects have been asked to present themselves in the most favorable light possible (Gloye & Zimmerman, 1967; Hiner et al., 1969; Lanyon, 1967).

3. Marks, Seeman, and Haller (1974) noted that this Validity scale pattern occurs with their 1-3/3-1 pattern and also with their K+ pattern. See the 1-3 pattern, p. 60, and the K+ pattern, point 5, p. 38.

L-F-K

See also the L-F-K profiles, pp. 45-47,
the F-L-K combination, p. 29.

1. This pattern may be produced by answering all questions "false." This is called the all-false or negative response set. See Figure 1, the all-false response profile, p. 18.

L-K-3

1. This combination may be found in highly defensive normal people. They may not even be aware of their great defensiveness.

L-1-2-3-$\overline{5}$ See the 1-2-3-$\overline{5}$-L combination, p. 59.

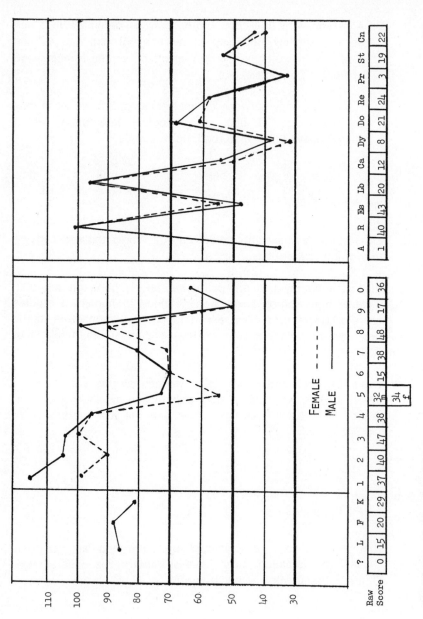

Figure 1. All-false response set.

18

SUMMARY OF L SCALE INTERPRETATIONS*

T Score	Interpretations
50 or below*	These people are willing to admit to general human faults.
50 thru 60*	These people are presenting themselves as, or may actually be, virtuous, conforming, and self-controlled.
60 or above*	Scores in this range may indicate naive people, people who repress or deny unfavorable traits, or people applying for jobs who want to make a favorable impression.

*Where T scores are listed in two categories (i.e., 50 or below and 50 thru 60) and a score is obtained that is listed for two categories, use whichever interpretation seems to be most appropriate for the individual.

L

— NOTES —

F SCALE
(Frequency or Confusion Scale)

Experience with mental health clinic and college counseling populations suggests that the **F** scale is nearly always measuring the degree to which a person's thoughts are different from those of the general population. Only rarely is an elevated **F** indicative of purposeful faking-bad. As the elevation increases, subjects seem to be reporting an increasing number of unusual thoughts and experiences. With a college population or with creative people, different thoughts, to a mild degree, are not uncommon, and an **F** of 65 may be quite typical. When people become involved intensely in unusual religious, political, or social groups, they frequently have elevations on the scale as high as 75. However, when elevations go beyond 75, usually the person is using the **F** scale to request help by reporting many unusual thoughts and happenings.

In a mental health setting, the elevations do not have to be as high as 75 for the request-for-help interpretation to be made. For example, a T of 65 in this population may indicate that the person is having difficulty in some one area of life. As the elevation increases, the person tends to report an increasing number of problem areas and a greater degree of severity of the problems.

Elevations above 100 in either population limit the profile as an instrument for diagnosis. With an elevation above 100 on **F**, usually an elevation occurs on all of the Clinical scales. Such a profile generally indicates that the person is unable to pinpoint any one area of concern and is reacting to everything.

Low **F** scores usually indicate a person who feels he or she is relatively free from stresses and problems.

GENERAL INFORMATION

1. The **F** scale consists of 64 questions not answered in the scored direction by 90 percent of the people.

2. As the **F** scale becomes elevated, the person is saying more unusual things about himself or herself. This action may be for many different reasons. See the high score section for the various interpretations.

3. Special comparisons are usually made with the **K** scale for diagnostic clarification. See the **F-K** Index, pp. 49-50.

4. Test-retest reliabilities are only fair. The scale is particularly sensitive to fluctuations in a person's psychological state or to treatment (Carkhuff et al., 1965).

5. Blacks tend to score high on this scale (Gynther, 1961; Gynther, 1972).

6. The **F** scale score tends to decrease with age for low and high IQ subjects but remains relatively constant for average IQ subjects (Gynther & Shimkunas, 1965a).

HIGH SCORES

Moderate Elevations (T = 60 thru 70)

1. Scores in this range may indicate one special area of concern, for example, family problems, religious problems, or health problems (Dahlstrom et al., 1972).

2. People who think differently than the general population score in this range (creative people, some college students).

3. Very compulsive people who are trying hard to be frank may score in this range (Good & Brantner, 1974).

4. The following people tend to have **F** scores in this range:

   a. Emotionally disturbed and deliquent girls (Stone & Rowley, 1963).

b. Prisoners and heroin addicts (Sutker, 1971).

c. Normal homosexual males (Loney, 1971).

d. Socialized delinquents (Tsubouchi & Jenkins, 1969).

e. People with behavior disorders (Gynther, 1961).

5. Social protest or emotional commitment to a different-thinking religious and/or political movement also may lead to elevations in this range. If the elevation on the F scale is for this reason, the Clinical scales tend not to be extraordinarily high (Carson, 1969; Dahlstrom et al., 1972).

Marked Elevations (T = 70 or Above)

T = 70 thru 80

See also the F-K Index, pp. 49-50.

1. These elevations may be indicative of unusual or markedly unconventional thinking as a way of life, especially for some college students.

2. Occasionally people who are intensely anxious and want to be helped score in this range. They also may score above 80 T score points.

3. Another cause for elevation of this scale is difficulty in reading or interpreting test statements because of poor reading ability or emotional interference. Because some of the more difficult items to read on the MMPI are on the F scale, it is possible for a poor reader to get an elevation on this scale (Dahlstrom et al., 1972).

4. Young people struggling with problems of identity frequently score in this range.

T = 80 thru 90

See also the F-K Index, pp. 49-50.

1. Before the profile can be considered valid, it must be determined whether or not the person (1) was out of contact with reality, (2) had a low reading level, or (3) was purposely malingering (Dahlstrom et al., 1972).

   a. Once the interpreter is satisfied that these causes are not operating, profiles with this high an **F** score can be read and interpreted (Gynther, 1961; Gynther & Shimkunas, 1965a, 1965b; Kanun & Monachesi, 1960).

b. In situations where elevated **F** scale scores can be interpreted, the person's problems are such that he or she truly may have very atypical experiences which are reported in the **F** scale items (Dahlstrom et al., 1972). Occasionally people with these atypical experiences will score as high as T = 100 or above and still have a valid profile.

2. Scores this high may occur because of a "cry for help."

3. People who are severely disturbed and uncooperative subjects with behavior problems may score in this range.

4. The person may want to appear unconventional. This desire is not unusual for adolescents (Carson, 1972).

5. Male psychiatric patients with this elevation tend to show aggressive acting out behavior (Gynther, 1961; Gynther & Shimkunas, 1965a, 1965b; Rice, 1968).

$$T = 90 \text{ thru } 100$$

See the **F-K** Index, pp. 49-50.

1. Scores in this range may indicate a random marking of the test. This random marking may be purposeful or the result of the fact that the person is illiterate and does not want to admit it. The person also may be confused, have a psychological disorder, or have brain damage (Carson, 1969). See the random response profile, Figure 2, p. 25.

2. Scores in this range also may indicate a person whose problems are such that he or she truly has very atypical experiences which are reported in the **F** scale items (Dahlstrom et al., 1972).

$$T = 100 \text{ or Above}$$

See the **F-K** Index, pp. 49-50.

1. Scores of 100 or above may show confusion on the client's part in marking the items.

F

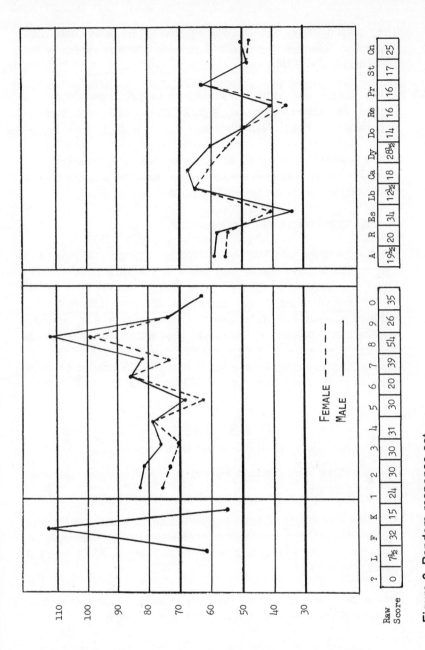

Figure 2. Random response set.

2. The person may be deliberately trying to look bad. See Figures 2, 3, and 4, the random, all-X, and all-true response set profiles, pp. 25; 27-28.

3. These scores may reflect the severity of psychopathology the person is experiencing or highly specialized and atypical experiences in the individual's life.

4. When **L** and **K** are low (T = 45 or below), a **F** elevation of T = 100 or above may indicate an all-true response set. See Figure 4, the all-true response set profile, p. 28.

5. These scores may reflect scoring errors.

6. Gynther, Altman, and Warbin (1973a) and Gynther, Altman, and Sletten (1973) have found that white psychiatric patients with raw **F** scores greater than 26 (T = 100 or above) have higher scores on withdrawal, poor judgment, thought disorders, and reduced speech than other patients. The phrase that best describes these patients is "confused psychotic." These terms do not apply to patients generating obviously faked MMPI's. For Blacks, those scoring above an **F** score of 26 raw score were seen as no different from Blacks with scores below an **F** of 26.

LOW SCORES
(T = 45 or Below)

1. These scores may indicate normal persons who are relatively free from stress.

2. Adjectives which have been suggested to describe low scorers are sincere, calm, dependable, honest, simple, conventional, moderate, and/or having narrow interests (Carson, 1969; Hovey & Lewis, 1967).

3. Low scores tend to indicate honestly reported records in college samples (Exner, McDowell, Stockman, & Kirk, 1963).

4. The **F** scale score tends to reach to this range after therapy (Cottle, 1953).

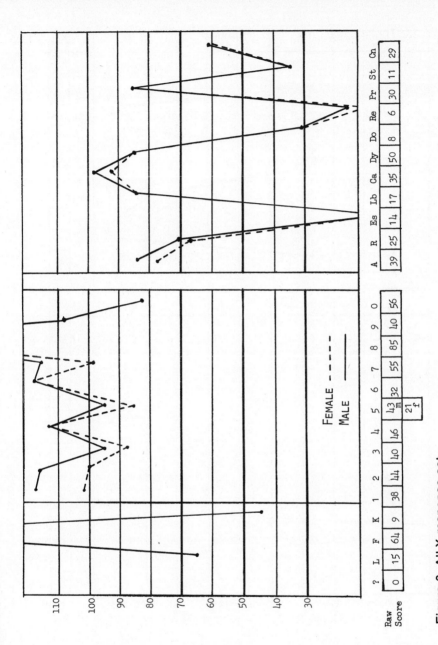

	?	L	F	K	1	2	3	4	5	6	7	8	9	0		A	R	Es	Lb	Ca	Dy	Do	Re	Pr	St	Cn
Raw Score	0	15	64	9	38	44	40	46	43 m / 21 f	32	55	85	40	56		39	25	14	17	35	50	8	6	30	11	29

FEMALE - - - - -
MALE ————

Figure 3. All-X response set.

27

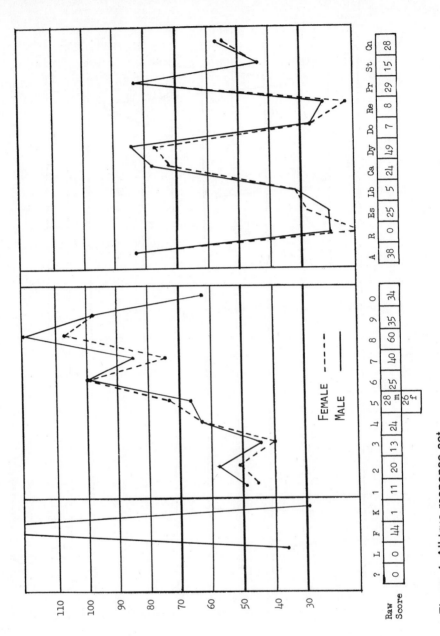

Figure 4. All-true response set.

28

COMBINATIONS

The Validity scales, **?**, **L**, **F**, and **K**, in these combinations are at a T score of 60 or above, whereas, the Clinical scales, **1** through **0**, are at a T score of 70 or above and are the highest Clinical scales on the profile.

F >25 Raw Score Points

1. If the **F** scale elevation is not the result of random marking or low reading level, the client who has this elevation usually appears to be confused. There may also be impaired judgment and delusions of reference and hallucinations (Gynther et al., 1973).

F-?   See the ?-F combination, p. 10.

F-?-L-K   See the ?-L-F-K combination, p. 10.

F-L

See also the **L-F** combination, p. 16,
    the **L-F-K** profiles, pp. 45-47.

1. This combination suggests the response set pattern where the person selects the most deviant answers (Blazer, 1965b). See Figure 3, the all-X response set profile, p. 27.

F-L-K

See also the **L-F-K** combination, p. 17,
    the **L-F-K** profiles, pp. 45-47.

1. When the **L** and **K** are moderately elevated and the **F** is markedly elevated, a random marking of the test may be indicated (Dahlstrom et al., 1972). See Figure 2, the random response set profile, p. 25.

F-K

See also the **F-K** Index, pp. 49-50,
    the **L-F-K** profiles, pp. 45-47.

F

1. This combination involves a contradiction in that the person reports self-enhancement and self-depreciation at the same time. This contradiction seems to be the result of lack of insight, confusion, or difficulties in grasping the nature of the test (Dahlstrom et al., 1972).

F-4-8   See the 4-8-F combination, p. 113.

F-8

1. A person with the **F-8** combination may have tendencies toward withdrawal (Marks, 1961).

2. Blacks in a rural, isolated area had this profile pattern (Gynther, Fowler, & Erdberg, 1971).

F-8-6-4-9 See the 8-6-4-9-F combination, p. 160.

F-8-9-6   See the 8-9-6-F combination, p. 162.

F-9

1. This combination may indicate manic behavior (Blazer, 1965b).

SUMMARY OF F SCALE INTERPRETATIONS*

T Score	Interpretations
50 or below	Scores in this range may indicate a normal person relatively free from stress.
50 thru 60	The majority of people score within this range.
60 thru 70	The person may be worried about an area of life, such as religion or health.
	The person may think somewhat differently than the general population.
	The person may be involved in an atypical political or social organization or in an unusual religious group.
70 thru 80	This person may be anxious and asking for help.
	A person with a score in this range may have had difficulty in reading or interpreting the test. (This is more likely in mental health clinics.)
	College students with identity problems may score in this range.
80 thru 90	At this level, before interpreting the MMPI, check that the person was not out of contact with reality, did not have a low reading level, or did not have reason to malinger purposefully.
	If the elevation is not because of any of these reasons, then the person's problems are such as to give him or her a long list of bizarre, peculiar, and atypical experiences.
	This may be a person who is anxious and asking for help.
90 thru 100	This may be a random marking of the test. It may or may not be deliberate.

F

If this is not a random marking of the test, then the person's problems may have produced a long list of bizarre, peculiar, and atypical experiences.

100 or above A score in this range may indicate confusion in marking items.

The confusion usually is not deliberate at this level.

This score may indicate that the person's deliberately trying to look bad.

It may reflect the severity of psychopathology of the person.

With low **L** and **K** (T = 45 and below), an **F** score in this range may indicate an all-true response set. See Figure 4, p. 28.

---

*Where T scores are listed in two categories (i.e., 50 or below and 50 thru 60) and a score is obtained that is listed for two categories, use whichever interpretation seems to be most appropriate for the individual.

K SCALE
(Correction Scale)

This scale measures defensiveness and guardedness. Therefore, it evaluates some of the same behavior as the L scale but much more subtly.

In order to evaluate the K scale properly, the specific population, college or mental health center, must be noted. In addition, the K scale interpretation must be modified for special groups of people within the population. In this introduction are discussed the usual interpretations for the two major populations with whom this book is concerned and, when appropriate, modifications are noted.

In a college population, a T score on this scale between 55 and 70 is typical. People scoring in this range are indicating that their lives are satisfactory, that they are basically competent, and that they can manage their lives. Such scores are usual for people coming for counseling about an academic major or for students taking the MMPI as part of some experiment. When T = 70 or above for the K scale, these people are indicating not only that they are competent people and can manage their own lives, but also that they are being a bit cautious about revealing themselves. Such scores are usually attained when a person is defensive, and/or when the test administrator does not fully explain the reason for the test, the use to which it will be put, or the confidentiality of the results.

When K is below 45 and the F scale is elevated above 60 T score points, the college student may be experiencing some stress. The K scale score usually elevates to the 55 through 65 range when the stress is alleviated.

When K is in the 45 through 55 range, and the F scale is below 60 score points, the college student may be feeling that life has been rough, that he or she has had fewer advantages than most people. Students whose scores are 45 or below indicate that several things are awry.

In a mental health setting, if the client has not had any college education and is having difficulties, he or she usually scores below 45 on the K scale. The severity of the problem is usually indicated by how low the K score is (the lower the score, the more severe the problem). Below a T of 35, the prognosis for successful therapy is poor. A score in this range does not indicate that the person will or should be hospitalized for his or her problem, but more that the person is unable to improve at this time. Scores between 35 and 45 typically reflect situational difficulties, such as marriage, family, or job problems.

Elevations over 55 are unusual in the mental health population. Typically such scores are attained by persons who blame others for their situation, e.g., the other mate in marriage counseling. A person in this range also may be bringing someone else in to be counseled, such as a parent who brings a child in with school difficulties. As the K goes above 60, defensiveness is usually present. When the person has a T score over 70, the prognosis for the person recognizing problems he or she may have is poor. Marks, Seeman, and Haller's (1974) "K+" profile should be studied for further information concerning this pattern (see point 5 under the marked elevations, p. 38).

College counseling and mental health centers personnel frequently evaluate persons for other agencies. In these instances, the above rules for interpretation of the K scale do not always hold since the person may have an ulterior motive for taking the test, rather than just taking it to tell how he or she is at the moment. Persons applying for jobs and students being screened for specific programs (doctoral admissions, for example) tend to have a T score of approximately 70. Conversely, persons applying for such things as disability pensions (where the person wishes to look bad) tend to have unusually low K scores and elevated F scores.

Persons under scrutiny by the courts tend to have either high or low K scores, depending upon their situations. If the person is seeking parole, a high K score may be obtained. If the person is seeking to avoid a sentence by appearing to be mentally ill, a low K score may result. Therefore, in these special instances the examiner must know the purpose of the examination and what the person expects to gain from it.

When the **L** scale (T = 60 or above), the **3** scale (T = 70 or above), and/or the **R** scale (T = 60 or above) also are elevated with the **K** scale (T = 65 or above), the diagnosis of defensiveness is reinforced. The person not only does not want to look bad to others (**L** and **K** elevations), he or she does not want to think bad of others (**3** scale elevation), and he or she also does not want to look or talk about certain areas of life (**R** scale elevation).

GENERAL INFORMATION

1. The **K** scale of 30 items was chosen as a correction factor to sharpen the discriminatory power of certain Clinical scales, specifically scales **1, 4, 7, 8,** and **9.**

2. The **K** scale was developed after the other Validity scales when it was noted that there was no correction for defensiveness on the test.

3. The **K** scale was developed to measure how much the examinee wished to "look good" on the test. The higher the **K** score the more the indication was that the person desired to look good and thus a portion of the **K** score was added to five Clinical scales (**1, 4, 7, 8,** and **9**) to correct for this attitude. The five Clinical scales were the only ones seemingly affected by this "looking good" attitude; therefore, the correction is applied only to them.

4. In spite of the **K** correction additions to Clinical scales, high scores on **K** are usually associated with *lower* profile elevations, whereas low scores on **K** are usually accompanied by *higher* profile elevations (Dahlstrom et al., 1972).

5. This is a subtle scale. The items are not as obvious as those on the **L** scale. The **K** scale is thus intended to detect defensiveness in psychologically sophisticated people.

6. Caldwell (1977) hypothesized that the **K** scale may measure a fear of emotional intensity and an avoidance of intimacy when

it goes over 65 T score points for non-college populations and above 70 T points for college populations.

7. Some authors (Adams, 1971; Dahlstrom et al., 1972; Heilbrun, 1961; Himelstein & Lubin, 1966) have suggested that **K** scores in the 60 thru 70 range do not always mean covering up more subtle atypical psychological characteristics, but may, at least in part, reflect a true assertion of psychological health, especially for females, for college students, and for people from higher socioeconomic levels. When the **K** scores go above a T of 70, however, the authors feel the scores do seem to reflect defensiveness for these groups.

   a. According to one study (Heilbrun, 1961), **K** corrections are defensible for male maladjusted college students, are somewhat less useful for adjusted male college students and maladjusted female students, and are a source of invalidity for adjusted female students.
   b. Because of the findings of this study the suggestion has been made that the **K** weights for college populations be revised as follows: scale **3**, men —**.7K**, women —**.5K**; scale **7**, men **1K**, women **.8K**; scale **8**, men and women **.7K** and eliminate the **K** weightings on scales **1, 4,** and **9** (Heilbrun, 1963).

8. Generally speaking, therapy prognosis tends to be poor with extremely low (T = 45 or below) or extremely high (T = 70 or above) **K** scale scores (Carson, 1969).

9. The higher values of **K** have not been used for discarding a profile as invalid as has been the case with higher values on the other Validity scales.

10. Test-retest reliabilities are fair to good (between .60 and .80) (Dahlstrom and Welsh, 1960).

11. A fairly high negative correlation occurs between the **L** and **K** scales and between the **O** and **K** scales (Karson and Pool, 1957; Laforge, 1962).

12. Under ideal self-instructions ("take this test trying to look as good as possible"), the **K** scale tends to become elevated to between 60 and 65 T score points (Gloye & Zimmerman, 1967;

K

Grayson & Olinger, 1957; Hiner et al., 1969; Parsons, Yourshaw, & Berstelmann, 1968).

13. Post therapy profiles tend to show an increase in **K** (Cottle, 1953).

AVERAGE SCORES
(T = 45 thru 55)

1. An average score on the **K** scale is an indication of a balance between self-disclosure and self-protection (Blazer, 1966; Dahlstrom et al., 1972).

2. Adults with elementary school education and lower middle-class socioeconomic status generally will score in this range (Dahlstrom et al., 1972).

3. Occasionally, people with higher socioeconomic status (including college students) will score in the range between 45 and 50. In such cases these people may be undergoing some stress and thus do not feel as good about their lives as others at their socioeconomic level usually do (Dahlstrom et al., 1972).

HIGH SCORES

Moderate Elevations (T = 55 thru 65)

1. Scores of moderate elevation are typical for people in the upper-middle class and lower-upper class, and for college students (Dahlstrom et al., 1972; Meehl & Hathaway, 1956).

2. These people tend to have good mental health. They are independent and are easily capable of dealing with their day-to-day problems. The generally favorable view they show of themselves on the **K** scale is correct and therefore appropriate (Dahlstrom et al., 1972).

Contrary to the conclusions of the response set studies, these people seemingly are not merely describing themselves favorably to achieve social acceptance. Their lives actually are under control and well managed.

3. If someone from the lower socioeconomic class has this elevation, it is more likely to reflect some defensiveness or a set
toward looking socially desirable.

4. Job applicants may appear in this elevation because they wish
to make a good impression (Drasgow & Barnette, 1957).

Marked Elevations (T = 65 or Above)

See also the all false and the all-0 response set profiles, pp. 18 and
40.

1. Occasionally, a college student or a person of high socioeconomic status will score in the lower part of this range (T
= 65 thru 70), in which case the elevation probably reflects that
they have good mental health and can handle life's problems.

2. Because women tend to judge themselves more harshly than do
men on a test such as the MMPI, a high K score by a woman
is likely to reflect psychological effectiveness rather than
defensiveness (Dahlstrom et al., 1972).

3. The usual reason for this elevation is that the person is im-
pelled to present a psychologically healthy appearance to others.

   Limits do exist to this defensiveness however so that it does not
   usually include the obvious items of the L scale. Thus, extremely
   high elevations on the K scale are not usually accompanied by
   high scores on the L scale (Dahlstrom et al., 1972).

4. A very high K score with accompanying Clinical scale elevations may indicate an unwillingness or inability to look at
problem areas. In fact, the person may not perceive self as
having a problem at all.

5. Marks, Seeman, and Haller (1974) found a K+ pattern (only
the K scale elevated above 70) in their university hospital and
clinic population. People with this pattern tended to be shy,
inhibited, and defensive. They also tended to be uninvolved in
activities. Marks et al., book should be consulted for further information concerning this pattern.

K

However, Gynther and Brilliant in another study (1968) did not find the behavior that Marks, Seeman, and Haller have found for the **K+** profile.

6. A high **K** score is associated with the low probability of delinquency, especially with females (Carson, 1969).

7. A high **K** score with low **L** and **F** scores may indicate an "all-0" (all normal) response set. See Figure 5, the all-0 profile, p. 40.

LOW SCORES

Low Range (T = 35 thru 45)

1. People may have scores in this range for one of two reasons.

   a. They may have problems which they are quite willing to admit. This interpretation is likely to be true if the **F** scale is elevated *above* 60 **T** score points. If they do have problems, they are often sarcastic and caustic concerning themselves and the world (Carson, 1972).
      1) These people tend not to feel good about themselves and often feel that they lack the skills to deal with their problems (Hovey & Lewis, 1967). If this is so, the **Es** scale usually is below 45 T score points.
   b. They believe life has been rough for them and that they have not had some of the advantages that others have had. This interpretation is likely to be true if the **F** scale is *below* 60 score points.
      1) This belief may be an accurate perception because people scoring in this range frequently have had a deprived family background and/or limited income (Dahlstrom et al., 1972).

Markedly Low Range (T = 35 or Below)

1. A person with a score in this range is too willing to say uncomplimentary things about self and tends to exaggerate his or her faults (Carson, 1972).

2. The person has answered items on the test so as to create the impression that he or she is undergoing a serious emotional problem (Dahlstrom et al., 1972).

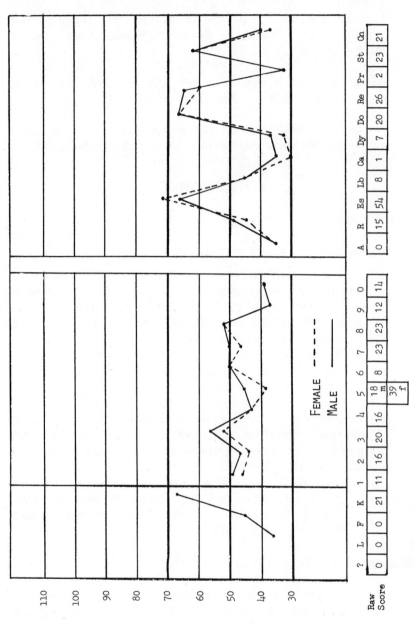

Figure 5. All-0 response set.

3. Scores below a T of 35 may arise from any of the following (Dahlstrom et al., 1972):

   a. Special pleading for help or attention.
   b. A general state of panic in which the person believes that his or her world or the control over his or her destiny is rapidly disintegrating.
   c. Deliberate malingering.
   d. The confusional state of an alcoholic on the verge of delirium tremens.

4. When the K score is in this range, the F scale and the Clinical scales usually are very high (Dahlstrom et al., 1972).

COMBINATIONS

The Validity scales, **?**, **L**, **F**, and **K**, in these combinations are at a T score of 60 or above, whereas the Clinical scales, **1** through **0**, are at at T score of 70 or above and are the highest Clinical scales on the profile.

K-?   See the **?-K** combination, p. 10.

K-?-L-F   See the **?-L-F-K** combination, p. 10.

K-L   See the **L-K** combination, p. 17,
              the **L-F-K** profiles, pp. 45.47.

K-L-F   See the **L-F-K** combination, p. 17,
              the **L-F-K** profiles, pp. 45-47.

K-L-3   See the **L-K-3** combination, p. 17.

K-F   See the **F-K** combination, p. 29.

K-1-3   See the **1-3-K** combination, p. 61.

K-3-F̄-8̄

1. Persons with this combination tend to be conventional persons who are joiners and overly concerned about being accepted and liked by others (Carson, 1969).

41   **K**

2. They have difficulty expressing and receiving anger, and they also have difficulty making decisions unpopular with their group (Carson, 1969).

3. They tend to be unrealistically optimistic, even when the facts indicate otherwise (Carson, 1969).

K-9

1. This combination indicates a person who is hypomanic but organized and efficient (Caldwell, 1974).

SUMMARY OF K SCALE INTERPRETATIONS*

T Score	Interpretations
35 or below	The client may have deep emotional difficulties and feel quite bad about them. He or she also may be deliberately malingering or pleading for help.
35 thru 45	People with this range of scores feel they are not as well off as most people. This appraisal may be accurate.
	People in this range may be having some situational difficulties. If they are, the **F** scale will be above 60.
45 thru 60	The majority of people score in this range.
69 thru 70	A person in therapy with this score tends to blame others for his or her problems or feels that it is the other person who needs counseling.
70 or above	The client may be defensive (as the T score increases, the client is more defensive), and does not wish to look at difficulties. The likelihood of the client recognizing the need for him or her to change is poor.

Relation to New Scales:

Es scale—If the **K** scale is below 45 T score points and the **Es** scale is also below 45 T score points, the person may be feeling bad about himself or herself as well as his or her life situation.

---

*Where T scores are listed in two categories (i.e., 35 or below and 35 thru 45) and a score is obtained that is listed for two categories, use whichever interpretation seems to be most appropriate for the individual.

— NOTES —

L-F-K SCALE PROFILES

In addition to looking at the Validity scales separately, the patterns produced by three of them (**L, F,** and **K**) also should be reviewed. The **?** scale is omitted from these patterns, because it is rarely high enough to be scored. Six validity patterns are presented in this section. The last two are less common than the others, but are still seen occasionally, usually in the mental health center setting.

1. The solid line pattern (Figure 6) is the one usually obtained with clients who admit emotional difficulties and request help. The **L** and **K** are typically below a T of 50 and the **F** is above a T of 60. The higher the **F** scale, dashed line, the more the person is saying he or she feels bad. When the **F** scale gets above 80 in this profile, possibly the client is exaggerating his or her symptoms, perhaps to be helped sooner. It is important in this profile that **L** and **K** are below 50 and that **F** is above 60.

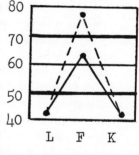

Figure 6

2. Figure 7 is a typical Validity scale profile for a job applicant, for those in counseling for vocational and/or educational help, and for those coming to counseling to help someone else. These interpretations hold true even when the **K** scale is above 70 and the **L** and **F** scales are lower than indicated as long as the **L** scale remains the lowest of the three scales.

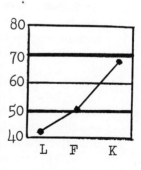

Figure 7

45

The Validity scale profile in Figure 7 is usually accompanied by Clinical scales below 70 except perhaps for scales **5** and **9**. For a profile with this Validity scale pattern, see the all-0 response set profile, p. 40.

3. People with the pattern shown in Figure 8 are presenting themselves in the best possible light. They feel very good about themselves and tend to deny common human foibles. They also tend to be simplistic and to see their world in extremes of good and bad. This profile is frequent for naive job applicants, public officer holders, and strict, moralistic clergy. Important considerations for the Figure 8 profile are that the **L** and **K** scales are above 60, and the **F** scale is the lowest point in the profile.

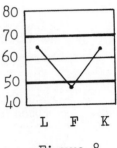

Figure 8

4. People with the profile shown in Figure 9 (solid line) tend to have long standing problems to which they have become adjusted to the extent that they feel good about themselves (elevated **K**) while still admitting to some bad feelings, usually about their situations (elevated **F**). As the **F** scale becomes elevated (dashed line), these people still feel rather secure about themselves, but they are more worried about their problems. Important considerations in the Figure 8 profile are that the **F** and **K** scales are 60 or above les and the **L** scale is 50 or below.

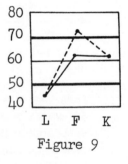

Figure 9

5. Figure 10 is an unusual profile, but still found frequently enough to be included in this section. The solid line is usually associated with a naive, unsophisticated person who is feeling bad. The person with this pattern is saying many of the same things as

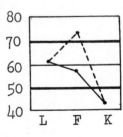

Figure 10

someone with the Figure 6 profile, but he or she has in addition a lack of sophistication. Even when the **F** scale is greatly elevated (dashed line), the person still shows the same behavior as long as the **L** scale is near 60 and the **K** scale is below 50.

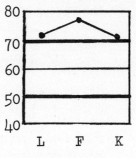

Figure 11

6. The total profile accompanying this Validity scale pattern (Figure 11) should be compared with the all-false response set profile, p. 18. The possibility is that the person with this validity pattern has answered the test from a response set of marking false to questions, rather than from his or her own feelings.

— NOTES —

F MINUS K INDEX
[Also called the Dissimulation Index by Gough (1956)]

The **F** minus **K** index was developed to detect faking bad and faking good profiles. The index number is obtained by subtracting the *raw score* of **K** from the *raw score* of **F**. If the resultant number is positive and above 9, the profile is called a "fake bad" profile. The person is trying to look worse than he or she really is. If the resultant number is negative, the profile is called a "fake good" profile. The person is trying to look better than he or she really is.

I do not use this index very much in my work with university and mental health clients. The "fake good" part of the index is usually grossly inaccurate for these populations, and the "fake bad" part can have another very dissimilar interpretation. In addition to the person scoring positively on this index because he or she is faking bad, a second interpretation can be made that the person really is feeling bad, and the index is accurately reflecting this fact.

I tend to suspect that the faking bad interpretation is the correct one when the client is seeking some disability compensation, is wanting to be judged insane by a court and thus escape some punishment, or if he or she is standing to gain by seeming to be extremely mentally ill.

GENERAL INFORMATION

1. This index is found by subtracting the *raw* score on the **K** scale from the *raw* score on the **F** scale. Positive scores are in the symptom-exaggeration direction ("fake bad"), and minus scores are in the defensive direction ("fake good"). However, the index is much more successful in detecting the former test-taking attitude than the latter.

F—K

2. The problem with detecting "fake good" profiles is that college students and people with good mental health tend to get elevated K scores and low F scores which, while accurately reflecting their psychological health, are incorrectly read as "faking good" by this index.

3. Because of these problems for the "fake good" direction of the index, the recommendation is that this index be used only for detecting "fake bad" profiles, and then only when the person is suspected of having something to gain by looking bad. If the person is not trying to look bad, then an F-K raw score difference of 9 or more usually is an indication of actually feeling bad.

4. Meehl (1951) has recommended that any profile with an F-K raw score difference of 9 or more should be considered a "fake bad" profile. Carson (1969), on the other hand, uses the raw score difference of 11 or more to detect looking bad.

chapter 3

CLINICAL SCALES

A history of the MMPI Clinical scales development and construction is available in the *MMPI Handbook: Vol. 1* by Dahlstrom, Welsh, and Dahlstrom (1972). Presently, the Clinical scale section of the MMPI profile is composed of ten scales, each with a number, abbreviation, and formal name. These scales are as follows:

1 Hs Hypochondriasis
2 D Depression
3 Hy Conversion Hysteria
4 Pd Psychopathic Deviate
5 Mf Masculinity-femininity
6 Pa Paranoia
7 Pt Psychasthenia
8 Sc Schizophrenia
9 Ma Hypomania
0 Si Social Introversion

In actual practice, the formal names and abbreviations are not usually used. The names are long and in many instances do not convey a clear picture of what is being measured by the scale. I prefer to use the numbers for the scales because they are neutral and the way the scales are usually reported in the research literature.

Most practitioners tend to view the Clinical scales as giving some indication of problem areas for a client. I feel such a viewpoint is incomplete because these scales also can, in some instances, indicate strengths and/or coping behaviors for the person.

For example, an elevation above 70 on scale **5** is fairly typical for college educated males in the arts (music, drama, literature, and art). An elevation on this scale shows aesthetic interests, and as such would be quite advantageous to an arts major. However, engineers with such an elevation on scale **5** may have a problem because their great interest in aesthetics may conflict with the demands from the engineering profession for "scientific rigor." Therefore, elevations on the Clinical scales must be evaluated in terms of the person's situation.

The term "elevation" as used with the Clinical scales usually indicates that a scale score is above 70 T score points. I have noted trends in behavior at lower T score levels. Consequently, I have devised two categories of elevations: Moderate Elevation refers to T scores of 60 thru 70, and Marked Elevation refers to T scores of 70 and above. This division of elevations into categories is a convenience and should not be taken as absolute. This is particularly true with T scores of 69 through 71. In these cases, the judgment of the tester must be used to determine if the Moderate or Marked Elevation interpretation is most appropriate.

I also have included information on Clinical scale low point scores of below 45 T score points. The information about the low end of the scales is scanty because little is written or researched about persons receiving such scores. Nevertheless, I do see some trends in these areas that can be useful.

Two other terms for some of the Clinical scales with which the reader should be familiar are the neurotic triad and the neurotic tetrad. The first term refers to scales **1**, **2**, and **3**, and the second term refers to scales **1**, **2**, **3**, and **7**. The use of these two terms can be misleading because the implication is that with these three or four scales one can diagnose neurotics. In fact, these scales do not do so with any degree of accuracy. Consequently, I prefer to use the terms triad and tetrad without the adjective "neurotic." In reality, I do not use the tetrad combinations at all because they have not been found to be very useful in diagnosis. However, the various combinations formed by the triad scales have been found to be very useful, and therefore, a section on them is included in this chapter after scale **3**.

SCALE 1
(Hs, Hypochondriasis Scale)

Scale 1 is a straightforward scale which measures the number of bodily complaints claimed by a person and whether these complaints are used to manipulate others. This scale does not distinguish actual from imagined physical difficulties.

When the T score of the scale is below 45, the person is generally seen as an alert, capable person who tends to deny bodily complaints. This T score is the normal level of the scale for persons in the medical profession and related areas (nurses, physical therapists, etc.). Others who also may receive a scale score at this level are the children of those in the medical profession, the children of hypochondriacs, and student nurses. These people have been around illness a lot and have seen others use it as a manipulative device. They do not wish to be classified with these manipulators, and therefore, they deny they have illnesses and tend not to seek medical help in the early stages of real somatic complaints.

Recently I have been seeing people with low scale 1 scores who do not fit the above categories. For these people, what seems to be the common reason for the low scores is that they mind illness and see it as a sign of some weakness. Frequently, joggers and health food enthusiasts score in this range.

Most people score in the 45 thru 60 range on this scale which indicates they have the usual number of physical complaints. T scores of 60 thru 70 are common for persons who are physically handicapped. Persons with this elevation who do not have such a physical disability may be suffering from a cold or flu and thus tend to be lethargic and feeling slightly "under the weather."

As the elevation on this scale increases, particularly when the scale goes above 75, people tend to use bodily complaints (either real or imagined) to avoid dealing with psychological difficulties and to manipulate those around them. When the manipulation does not work, particularly with physicians and counselors, clients may shop around until a physician or counselor is found who can be manipulated. Thus, the higher the elevation, the less likely the person is to stay in productive counseling.

Elevations above 70 on scale 1 are rare in college populations but are found frequently in mental health clinic populations. I have found about 10 percent of the people in my two mental health clinic populations scoring above 70 on this scale. This elevation is more likely to be on a woman's profile than a man's. However, when either one has an elevation on this scale, it usually indicates behavior of long standing.

GENERAL INFORMATION

1. The 33 items of this scale are fairly obvious questions having to do with bodily problems (Carson, 1972).

2. I believe this scale to be "characterological," that is, elevations on the scale tend to reflect long-term behavior.

3. Test-retest reliabilities are high, ranging between .80 and .90 (Dahlstrom and Welsh, 1960). Scale 1 is one of the most stable scales for clinic populations (Carkhuff et al., 1965).

4. When the person is actually physically ill and this scale is markedly elevated, the person is likely to be using the physical illness in a manipulative way to control others.

5. When no physical illness exists and this scale is elevated, the person tends to be using vague somatic complaints in a manipulative way to control others around him or her.

6. Although this scale may rise somewhat with physical disease, more likely scale 2, depression, would be affected by the illness rather than scale 1 (Carson, 1972).

1

7. One study found this scale to be related to functional (non-organic) menstrual disorders (Spero, 1968).

8. Blacks and/or people from lower socioeconomic backgrounds tend to have higher scores on this scale (McDonald & Gynther, 1963; Nelson, 1952; Perlman, 1950).

9. This scale is negatively correlated (—.60) with intelligence (Brower, 1947).

10. The suggestion has been made (Heilbrun, 1963) to eliminate the K scale weightings from scale 1 (as well as from scales 4 and 9) for college students, in order to detect maladjustment more accurately.

HIGH SCORES

Moderate Elevations (T = 60 thru 70)

1. Physically ill persons may score in this range.

2. Kunce and Anderson (1976) have hypothesized that when this scale is in the moderate range, [and there are no Clinical scales above 70 T score points except perhaps the 5 scale for men], it may measure a constructive concern for one's own and others' physical well-being.

Marked Elevations (T = 70 and Above)

1. People in this range tend to complain a great deal and to be whiny (Carson, 1969).

2. They tend to get rid of their hostilities by making others miserable (Carson, 1969).

3. People with scale 1 scores in this range may be very cynical and defeatist, especially towards those who are helping them (Carson, 1969).

4. The following adjectives frequently are used to describe these people: unambitious, stubborn, and egocentric (Carson, 1969).

5. In therapy, persons with high **1** scores tend to frustrate the therapist in any efforts toward psychological change. This elevation is associated with poor progress in psychotherapy.

6. People with scale **1** scores in this range tend to "shop" for physicians and may see one after another, or several at one time (Carson, 1969).

7. The higher the score on this scale:

   a. The more manipulative the client is with his or her physical complaints.
   b. The more unable he or she is to cope with life.
   c. The more he or she has the attitude "you must take care of me."
   d. The more the person uses his or her somatic complaints to get out of responsibility and to gratify dependency needs.
   e. The more immaturely he or she behaves.

8. This scale may measure dependency needs which are channeled into claims of physical illness (Carson, 1972).

   These people force others to take care of them, and thus, the dependency needs are met.

LOW SCORES
(T = 45 or Below)

1. People with these scores are described as alert, capable, and responsible (Carson, 1969; Hovey & Lewis, 1967).

2. These people tend to get things done, are effective, and are often admired by others (Carson, 1972).

3. They seem to be free from hampering inhibitions and undue concern about the adverse reactions of others (Dahlstrom et al., 1972).

4. These scores may indicate people who have been closely associated with others who have used illness in a manipulative way. Because they do not want to appear hypochondriacal them-

selves, they reject even admitting a normal amount of aches and pains.

5. These scores tend to be characteristic of female college students, who usually average around a T of 45 (Hampton, 1947).

6. However, low scores also may indicate persons who have considerable somatic concerns, but are unwilling to admit them (Good & Brantner, 1961).

COMBINATIONS

All scales in the combinations are at a T score of 70 or above and are listed in order from the highest to the lowest peaks. The scales in the combinations must be the highest Clinical scales on the profile

1-2
See also point 1a in the **1-2-3** Triad profile, p. 96.

1. People with this **1-2** combination tend to be irritable and depressed. They overemphasize minor problems (Hovey & Lewis, 1967).

2. Graham (1977) has found that people with this combination complain about pain and somatic discomfort, especially in the digestive tract. They tend to react to stress with physical symptoms and resist psychological explanations for their discomfort.

3. State hospital and mental health clinic inpatients with this pattern, **1-2/2-1**, were found to have multiple somatic complaints, insomnia, and physical problems. However, they seemed to be less disturbed than other state hospital patients. Older males tended to have histories of alcoholism. These findings may not apply to females (Gynther, Altman, Warbin, & Sletten, 1973).

   In another study (Gynther, Altman, & Sletten, 1973), this pattern was found to be similar to Gilberstadt and Duker's (1965) **1-2-3-4** code type, pp. 58-59.

4. Caldwell (1974) has hypothesized that this combination possibly indicated a phobic fear of death.

5. Male college counselees with these scores tend to have tension, insomnia, insecurity in social situations, worry, and introversion (Drake & Oetting, 1959).

6. Female college counselees with these scores (especially with a low 5 scale) tend to have headaches, depression, worry, anxiety, social insecurity, and indecisiveness, (Drake & Oetting, 1959).

1-2-3

See also the 1-2-3-$\overline{5}$ pattern, p. 59,
the point 1b in the 1-2-3 Triad pattern, p. 97.

1. A person with this pattern (called the 1-2-3 slope) usually is male, tends to be in declining health, and feels "over the hill." He usually had poor health in childhood. Also, he does not tend to take risks or to change jobs frequently. He may feel a profound sense of loss of body functioning (Caldwell, 1972).

2. Gilberstadt and Duker (1965) found this 1-2-3 pattern in a VA hospital male population. Men with this pattern usually reacted to stress and physiological symptoms. They tended to lack aggressiveness and sexual drive. Gilbertstadt and Duker's book should be consulted for further information concerning this profile.

3. Some persons with valid physical disabilities that result in declining health also have this pattern. However, in this instance not all three scales are above 70.

1-2-3-4

1. Gilberstadt and Duker (1965) found this 1-2-3-4 pattern in a VA hospital male population. Men with this pattern tended to be demanding and dependent. They developed somatic symptoms, especially ulcers and gastrointestinal disturbances. They tended toward alcoholism, which appeared to be associated with physiological hyperactivity of the gastrointestinal tract. Gilberstadt and Duker's book should be consulted for further information concerning this pattern.

2. Fowler and Athey (1971) also have found the same behavior as Gilberstadt and Duker for this code type: general psychological discomfort, depression, hostility, and heavy drinking.

3. Gynther (1974) reported Gilberstadt and Duker's (1965) description of persons with this pattern also is accurate for the populations he has studied.

4. This person may have a history of gastrointestinal difficulty. He or she may be prone to ulcers (Caldwell, 1974).

1-2-3-5̄ (5 scale T = 45 or Below)

See also point 1b in the 1-2-3 Triad profile, p. 97.

1. In women, this combination tends to be shown through masochistic behavior with self-depreciation, long-suffering sacrifice, and unnecessary assumption of burdens and responsibilities (Dahlstrom et al., 1972).

1-2-3-5̄-L (L scale T = 60 or Above)

1. This pattern may be found in women who are characterized by one of the following (Blazer, 1965a):

   a. Having marital difficulties.
   b. Feeling sexually frigid.
   c. Complaining about infidelity or drinking by their husbands.
   d. Having menopausal difficulties.
   e. Having hysterical attacks (fear, palpitation, sweating, insomnia, and abdominal pain).
   f. Complaining of fatigue.
   g. Feeling conscientious about their work.
   h. Being easily hurt by criticism or rebuff.

1-2-3-7

1. Gilberstadt and Duker (1965) found this 1-2-3-7 pattern in a VA hospital male population. Men with this pattern tended to have physical complaints that may or may not have been real. They usually were weak, fearful, and unable to take ordinary stresses and responsibilities. Gilberstadt and Duker's book should be consulted for further information concerning this profile.

1-2-7

1. College women with this scale combination tend to be homesick when at school (Meehl, 1951).

1-2-8

1. This profile is found in some college students who are considered radical (Meehl, 1951).

1-3

See also the **1-3-K** combination p. 61.
the **1-3-$\overline{2}$** combination, p. 62,
the **3-1** combination, p. 91,
the point 1a for the **1-3-2** Triad profile, p. 97.

1. A person with this combination tends to convert his or her psychological difficulties into physical problems.

2. Gastrointestinal problems are common (Carson, 1972).

3. In highly disturbed patients, severe eating problems may be present, such as anorexic vomiting (Drake & Oetting, 1959).

4. This combination is more frequent with women and older persons. Physical symptoms tend to increase in times of stress. People with this combination are very difficult to deal with in psychotherapy because they see their problems as physical in origin, and they expect definite answers to their problems from the therapist (Graham, 1977).

5. The high scale **3** seems to temper the pessimistic complaining attitudes shown by the high **1** scale (Carson, 1969).

6. Marks, Seeman, and Haller (1974) found this **1-3/3-1** pattern in a university hospital and outpatient clinic. This tended to be a female profile. A woman with this pattern usually had a somatic complaint. Her behavior could best be described as agitated, depressed, and confused, with periods of weakness, forgetfulness, and dizziness. Marks et al., (1974) could be consulted for further information concerning this pattern.

1

7. In one sample of psychiatric inpatients, people with a **1-3** pattern showed significantly more somatic concern than other patients (Lewandowski & Graham, 1972).

8. Gynther, Altman, and Sletten (1973) also have found that psychiatric inpatients with this pattern, **1-3/3-1**, have an unusual amount of bodily concern.

9. Thirty-nine percent of all MMPI **1-3/3-1** patterns in one study had organic diagnoses. Thirty-four percent of all patterns had psychological diagnoses. However, 66 percent of the psychological diagnoses were found in the group members who were under 40. In other words, the older people with **1-3/3-1** patterns in the study tended to have organic problems, whereas the younger people with this pattern had psychological problems (Schwartz, Osborne, & Krupp, 1972).

10. Elevations on these two scales cannot be used reliably to distinguish functional disorders from actual physical disorders (Lair & Trapp, 1962; Schwartz & Krupp, 1971).

1-3-K

See also the **1-3-2̄** pattern, point 4, p. 62.

1. With the **1-3-K** combination if the person has had surgery, the individual may have intractable post-operative pain (Caldwell, 1974).

1-3-2

See also the point 1c in the **1-3-2** Triad pattern, p. 98.

1. Gilberstadt and Duker (1965) found this **1-3-2** pattern in a VA hospital male population. Men with this pattern tended to be extroverted, sociable, and highly conforming. Under stress, they tended to develop psychosomatic illnesses. Gilberstadt and Duker's book should be consulted for further information concerning this profile.

1-3-2 (scale 2 T = 45 or Below)

See also the 1-3 pattern, p. 60.
and point 1b in the 1-3-2 Triad pattern, p. 98.

1. This person tends to talk a lot about his or her physical complaints, but does not seem to be either depressed or anxious about them (Hovey & Lewis, 1967).

2. This person tends to believe that he or she does not have any emotional problems (Hovey & Lewis, 1967).

3. A history of hysteric pain which suddenly goes away often is present (Caldwell, 1972).

4. When the K score is also high with this pattern, intractable post-operative pain may exist (Caldwell, 1972).

5. A high incidence of overeating and odd eating habits may be present (Caldwell, 1972).

1-3-7

1. Gilberstadt and Duker (1965) found this 1-3-7 pattern in a VA hospital male population. Men with this pattern tended to have severe anxiety attacks. They tended to be clinging people. Under stress they developed psychosomatic illnesses. Gilberstadt and Duker's book should be consulted for further information about this profile.

1-3-8

1. A person with this profile tends to have strange ideas and/ or bizarre sexual and religous beliefs. He or she often may be depressed and changeable (Caldwell, 1972).

2. Usually a family background of psychosis and/or childhood deprivation exist (Caldwell, 1972).

3. This type of person seems to need structure. He or she tends to do well in school when the school is structured. However, when this structure or a significant relationship is gone, bizarre symptoms may be seen (Caldwell, 1972).

1

4. Gilberstadt and Duker (1965) found this **1-3-8-(2)** pattern in a VA hospital male population. The **2** scale is elevated above 70, but it is not necessarily the next highest scale after the **8**. Men with this pattern tended to have confused thinking, suspiciousness, and jealousy. These researchers hypothesize that these men may have somatic illnesses to defend against their schizophrenic tendencies. Gilberstadt and Duker's book should be consulted for further information concerning this profile.

1-3-8-2   See the **1-3-8** pattern, point 4, above.

1-3-9

1. Gilberstadt and Duker (1965) found this **1-3-9** pattern in a VA hospital male population. Men with this pattern tended to have chronic organic illnesses, frequently with organic brain dysfunction. Temper outbursts were seen at times, and occasionally these people became combative and disruptive. Gilberstadt and Duker's book should be consulted for further information concerning this pattern.

1-4

1. This combination is not found frequently, but when present is more likely a male's profile rather than a female's. There may be severe hypochondriacal symptoms, especially headaches. People with this combination may be rebellious but not express this directly (Graham, 1977).

2. Gynther, Altman, and Sletten (1973) have found that psychiatric inpatients with this pattern, **1-4/4-1**, may have a drinking problem. These researchers found almost no females with this pattern.

1-7

1. With this pattern, chronic, mild anxiety often exists (Hovey & Lewis, 1967).

1-8

1. These people tend to be remote from people and to feel inadequate socially (Hovey & Lewis, 1967).

1

2. People with this combination tend to have feelings of hostility and aggression which they either inhibit altogether or show in a belligerent way. Psychiatric patients may complain about somatic symptoms that are so bad as to seem delusional (Graham, 1977).

1-9

See also the **9-1** combination, p. 171.

1. This person is usually quite tense and may be distressed occasionally (Hovey & Lewis, 1967).

2. He or she tends to be very anxious, tense, and restless. On the surface the person appears to be extroverted, verbal, and aggressive, but underneath he or she is usually a passive, dependent person. These people tend to be ambitious but lack definite goals (Graham, 1977).

3. This person tends to be one who has coronary attacks (Caldwell, 1972).

4. This pattern may indicate some brain dsyfunction, especially when MMPI item 274F is marked together with three of the following: 10F, 51F, 159F, or 192F (Hovey & Lewis, 1967).

2-1-3   See the **2-3-1** combination, point 2, p. 73.

2-1-3-7   See the **2-3-1-(7)** combination, p. 73.

2-3-1   See p. 73.

2-3-1-7   See p. 73.

2-7-3-1   See p. 77.

2-8-1-3   See p. 81.

3-1-2   See the **3-1-2** pattern in the Triad section, p. 99.

3-2-1   See p. 92.

8-1-2-3   See p. 157.

8-2-1-3   See the 2-8-1-3 pattern, p. 81.

8-4-7-1   See p. 158.

8-7-4-1   See p. 161.

SUMMARY OF 1 SCALE INTERPRETATIONS*

T Score	Interpretations
45 or below	With a score in this range, a person is denying bodily complaints. This is typical of people in the helping professions, children of these people, and people with hypochondriacal parents. People scoring in this range tend to be alert, capable, and responsible.
45 thru 60	The majority of people score in this range.
60 thru 70	This level is usual for persons with valid bodily complaints.
70 or above	With this score, the person tends to use bodily complaints to avoid emotional situations and also tends to use these complaints as a way of manipulating others. He or she may be whiny, complaining, and makes others miserable. As the scale is elevated, these people tend to be defeatist, to solicit help from others, and then to sabotage this help. They may "shop" for physicians and/or counselors.

*Where T scores are listed in two categories (i.e., 45 or below and 45 thru 60) and a score is obtained that is listed for two categories, use whichever interpretation seems to be most appropriate for the individual.

SCALE 2
(D, Depression Scale)

Two observations should be noted in evaluating scale 2. First of all, this is a mood scale. It measures the degree of pessimism and sadness the person feels at the time the MMPI was administered. Thus, a change in mood will lower or raise this scale. Second, scale 2 is rarely elevated by itself; usually at least one or two other scales also are elevated. These other scales can be helpful in determining how the depression is shown.

Most people are in the 45 to 60 T score range. When the T score is between 60 and 70, a mild dissatisfaction with life may exist, but either the dissatisfaction is not enough for the person to be really concerned or the dissatisfaction is of long standing and the person has learned to live with it. When the 2 scale is at 60 and the 9 scale at 45, possibly the person took the inventory at the bottom of a mood swing (for example, during a post-exam let-down), at the end of a long work day, or when he or she had a cold. In these situations the person's real pattern is usually an elevated scale 9 (T = 60 to 65) and a lowered scale 2 (T = 45 to 55).

As the elevation increases, the person's attitude changes from sadness (T = 70) to gloom (T = 80) to all pervasive pessimism about self and the world (T = 90 or above).

Low scale 2 scores (45 or below) indicate that the person is cheerful, optimistic, and easy going. However, these attitudes should be checked in terms of their appropriateness for the person's situation, particularly if a tragedy has occurred recently.

Scale 2 is one of the most frequent high points on a profile for clients in college counseling centers and mental health clinics. It usually indicates a reaction to problems that are pressing on the person. Very rarely is this elevation an indication of chronic depression.

GENERAL INFORMATION

1. This 60-item scale concerns poor self-concept, sadness, pessimism, and a lack of hope (Carson, 1969).

2. Scale **2** is the most frequent high point in psychiatric profiles (Meehl, 1946).

3. This scale measures people's present attitudes about themselves and their relationships with others (Carson, 1969).

4. Scale **2** is the best scale for measuring a person's present feelings of contentment and security (Carson, 1969).

5. This scale quickly reflects changes in a person's day-to-day feelings (Carson, 1969). Therefore, it tends to be a fairly changeable scale (Jurjevich, 1966; Latta, 1968).

   Scale **2** is less reliable in a test-retest situation than the other Clinical scales (Carkhuff et al., 1965; Dahlstrom & Welsh, 1960).

6. An accurate interpretation of scale **2** relies on the rest of the profile (Carson, 1969). Therefore, high point combinations should be considered carefully.

7. This scale tends to decrease in elevation on a retest, even without intervening therapy.

8. Women who have an elevated **2** scale tend to report depression significantly more often (2 to 1) than men who have an elevated **2** scale (Gravitz, 1968).

9. A slight trend toward high **2** scale scores occurs with increasing age (Canter, Day, Imboden, & Cluff, 1962).

10. There may be an extroversion factor in the MMPI marked by a moderate positive loading on scale **9**, a high negative loading on

2   68

scale **0**, and a moderate negative loading on scale **2** (Hundleby & Connor, 1968).

HIGH SCORES

Moderate Elevations (T = 60 thru 70)

1. A person with a score in this range may have a feeling that something is not right, but he or she does not always recognize this feeling as depression.

2. Kunce and Anderson (1976) have hypothesized that when this scale is in the moderate range [and there are no other Clinical scales above 70 T score points except perhaps the **5** scale for men], it may measure a penchant for sorting out what is right and wrong, what is good and bad.

3. College freshmen with this elevation tend to report more home-sickness than freshmen without elevations on this scale (Rose, 1947).

4. This range of T scores (60 thru 70) for scale **2** was found in three studies investigating non-therapy male homosexuals (Dean & Richardson, 1964; Manosevitz, 1970, & 1971).

5. With a scale **2** score approximately at a T of 60 and a **9** scale score on or near a T of 45, possibly the MMPI had been taken when the person had had a long hard work day, had a cold, or was at the bottom of a mood-swing. If this is true, the person's usual pattern is an elevated **9** scale (T = 60 thru 65) and a lowered **2** scale (T = 45 thru 55).

Marked Elevations (T = 70 or Above)

1. A person with a **2** scale score at the lower end of this range (T = 70 to 80) may be withdrawn but may not show the typically tearful depression associated with higher elevations.

2. A person with a **2** scale elevation above a T of 80 tends to be self-deprecating, withdrawn, and may be feeling guilty. If the

person is feeling guilty, the **Es** scale also will be below 45 T score points. The higher the **2** scale becomes, the more these symptoms are seen, together with an over-riding feeling of hopelessness.

3. This scale is rarely elevated by itself. When it is, situational depression is usually present, even though the person may not admit to such feelings. In addition, the counselor should check for suicidal ideation (Carson, 1969).

4. Other high scales should be checked to determine how the depression is being felt and/or shown; for example, a high **7** with the high **2** usually means the person is in an agitated, depressed state.

5. When the **2** scale is the only one above 70 and scale **9** is the low point of the profile, the depression is usually mild, but the person may complain of fatigue and loss of energy. These complaints tend to yield readily to supportive therapy (Guthrie, 1949).

6. With college counselees, this elevation may reflect situational problems rather than long term depression (Mello & Guthrie, 1958).

    a. When it does, Mello and Guthrie have found that these people tend to remain superficial in therapy and resist efforts to go deeper.
    b. When the situational pressure lessens, these clients usually discontinue treatment.

7. Male heroin addicts tend to score high on this scale (Gilbert & Lombardi, 1967).

LOW SCORES
(T = 45 or Below)

1. People with this level of scale **2** tend to be optimistic, gregarious, and alert (Carson, 1969).

2. These people seem to have a naturalness, buoyancy, and freedom of thought and action that leads to easy social relations, confidence in taking on tasks, and effectiveness in a variety of activities (Carkhuff et al., 1965).

3. The typical lack of inhibition of a person with a low scale **2** score may sometimes lead to negative reactions from others (Carkhuff et al., 1965).

4. These scores tend to be seen more often with younger people, because scale **2** tends to become elevated with age (Canter et al., 1962).

COMBINATIONS

All scales in the combinations are at a T score of 70 or above and are listed in order from the highest to the lowest peaks, unless otherwise noted. The scales in the combinations must be the highest Clinical scales on the profiles.

For all combinations involving scales **1, 2,** and/or **3,** also see the Triad profiles, pp. 96-100.

1-2-3   See p. 58.

1-2-3-4   See pp. 58-59.

1-2-3-5̄   See p. 59.

1-2-3-5̄-L   See p. 59.

1-2-3-7   See p. 59.

1-2-7   See p. 60.

1-2-8   See p. 60.

1-3-2   See p. 61.

1-3-2̄   See p. 62.

1-3-8-2   See the **1-3-8** combination, point 4, p. 63.

2-1   See the **1-2** combination, pp. 57-58,
also point 1b in the **2-1-3/2-3-1** Triad profile, p. 98.

2-1-3   See the **2-3-1** combination, point 2, p. 73,
also point 1a in Triad profile, p. 98.

2-1-3-7   See the **2-3-1-(7)** combination, p. 73.

2-3

See also point 1c in the **2-1-3/2-3-1** Triad profile, p. 99.

1. People with the **2-3** combination typically are seen as over-controlled. They may be unable to start things or to complete them once they are started (Guthrie, 1949). They lack interest and involvement in life (Graham, 1977).

2. They are insecure persons who keep things inside themselves and are unable to express their feelings (Dahlstrom et al., 1972).

   a. They lack interest or involvement in things and feel constantly fatigued, exhausted, nervous, and inadequate.
   b. They are frequently described as inadequate and immature.
   c. Their troubles are typically of long standing.
   d. Their response to treatment is poor.

3. This combination is much more common for women than for men. It indicates a lowered standard of efficiency for prolonged periods of time (Graham, 1977).

4. Lewandowski and Graham (1972) have found that patients with the **2-3** pattern have significantly less conceptual disorganization, unusual mannerisms and postures, suspiciousness, hallucinatory

behavior, and unusual thought content than patients with other patterns.

5. Gynther, Altman, and Sletten (1973) found that a group of psychiatric inpatients with the 2-3/3-2 pattern, showed depressed mood and decreased activity. A person with the 2-3 pattern also had feelings of helplessness and multiple somatic complaints.

    a. Men may complain of lack of recognition on their jobs or of not being promoted when they should be, but they are adequate on their jobs (Dahlstrom et al., 1972; Guthrie, 1949).

    b. Women frequently have family or marital maladjustments, but divorce is rare (Dahlstrom et al., 1972; Guthrie, 1949).

2-3-1

See also point 1a in the 2-1-3/2-3-1 Triad profile, p. 98.

1. People with this pattern tend to be smiling depressives. They smile while they cry, and they do not know why. They deny aggression and hostility, and usually are inhibited. This profile is frequent for people with deteriorating neurological diseases (Caldwell, 1972).

2. Marks, Seeman, and Haller (1974) found this 2-3-1/2-1-3 pattern in a university hospital and outpatient clinic. People with this pattern tended to show a combination of depression and somatic complaints. They saw themselves as physically sick. Marks' book should be consulted for further information concerning this profile.

2-3-1-(7)

1. In this pattern, the 7 scale is also elevated above 70, but is not necessarily the next highest scale. People with this pattern tend to be older than patients in general. They feel they cannot get things done and are pessimistic. Their somatic complaints are secondary to their depression (Caldwell, 1972).

2-4

See also the 4-2 combination, p. 107.

73

2

1. People with this pattern are impulsive and unable to delay gratification. They feel frustrated by their own lack of accomplishment and are resentful of demands placed on them by others (Graham, 1977).

2. They tend to have behavioral difficulties which have developed over time (Hovey & Lewis, 1967).

3. They may be remorseful after acting out but not seem sincere about this remorse (Graham, 1977).

4. They tend to run from people's expectations for them and from their own problems.

5. The person cannot take pressure in therapy, and if it is applied, he or she will leave. Prognosis for change is poor.

    a. He or she will change jobs or leave town but will not confront the therapist directly.
    b. If the person cannot run from therapy, he or she will tend to have a "spontaneous" recovery.
    c. He or she will be superficially deferent to the therapist.

6. If these scales are both highly elevated, there may be suicidal ideation and attempts. The attempts are usually to get other people to feel guilty (Graham, 1977.)

7. These people tend to be ulcer prone. They may manipulate others. The ultimate manipulation is to attempt to kill themselves and then to blame others (Caldwell, 1974).

8. Lewandowski and Graham (1972) found in one study that patients with this pattern were significantly more sociable than patients with other patterns.

9. Gynther, Altman, and Warbin (1972) and Gynther, Altman, and Sletten (1973) have found psychiatric patients with this pattern, 2-4/4-2, are apt to show less psychotic pathology and fewer defects in judgment and orientation than the typical state hospital inpatient. Both males and females are more likely to be diagnosed as alcoholic than patients with other MMPI patterns. *Females* are more likely to show depressive symptoms and

males are more likely to have had a job loss than the average patient. There may be a recent history of suicidal behavior.

10. People with this combination do not tend to be a homogeneous group. Other high points are important and should be examined.

11. The 2-4 is the third most frequent two point combination found in a sample of psychiatric patients (Gynther et. al., 1972).

2-4-7   See the 2-7-4 combination, point 3, p. 78.

2-4-8

1. Persons with this pattern have a high incidence of sexual difficulties (Caldwell, 1972).

2. This pattern is found frequently in people with suicidal ideation (Caldwell, 1972).

2-4-8-9

1. Women with this pattern may have many affairs with men, but typically do not enjoy them (Caldwell, 1972).

2-6

1. These people are touchy, take offense easily, and become tired and depressed quickly (Guthrie, 1949).

2. They tend to induce rejection by others (Hovey & Lewis, 1967).

3. This profile is of an agitated, depressed person who gets others involved in his or her problems (Caldwell, 1974).

4. Little change is likely in therapy over time and prognosis is poor (Guthrie, 1949).

2-7

See also the 7-2 combination, p. 147.
1. These people tend to be very anxious and depressed and have feelings of worthlessness. They also tend to be agitated and obsessed about their problems (Hovey & Lewis, 1967).

2. They usually anticipate problems before they occur and over-react to minor stress. Somatic problems are typically seen (Graham, 1977).

3. Marks, Seeman, and Haller (1974) found the 2-7 pattern in a university hospital and outpatient clinic. These people tended to be seen as depressed and anxious. They also tended to be per-fectionistic and compulsively meticulous. Because they felt they must live up to their own high expectations, they tended to be self-punishing and feel hopeless. Marks' book should be consulted for further information concerning this profile.

4. Gilberstadt and Duker (1965) found the 2-7-(3) pattern in a VA hospital, male population. The parentheses around the 3 are to indicate that the 3 scale elevation is above 70, but it is not necessarily the next highest scale in the profile. A man with this pattern was usually a chronically anxious, ambitious person. When he was unable to tolerate stress, he tended to become depressed, self-deprecating, inadequate, and clinging. Gilberstadt and Duker's book should be consulted for further information concerning this profile.

5. A person with this elevation usually has been an achiever in the past and with lower 2-7 elevations may be an achiever still. Generally, the person has been successful in his or her field. Then something goes wrong and the person reverts to child-like behavior and cannot do anything. This is especially true when scale 3 is also elevated (Caldwell, 1972).

6. In one study, patients with the 2-7 pattern were found to be feeling blue and depressed. They did not tend to get angry or annoyed easily, were less irritable, and socially were more com-petent than other patients in the study (Lewandowski & Graham, 1972).

7. Suicidal preoccupation may be present with these people (check MMPI item #339) (Simon & Hales, 1949).

    The possibility of suicide is greater when the person does not act depressed than when he or she appears deeply depressed (Good & Brantner, 1961).

8. Gynther, Altman, and Warbin (1973e) and Gynther, Altman and Sletten (1973) also found psychiatric patients with the **2-7/7-2** pattern to have suicidal thoughts and feelings of worthlessness. When a patient had the **2-7** pattern, he or she had a "loss of interest" as well. They were less evasive, unrealistic, angry, hostile, deluded, and antisocial than patients in general. These researchers found this code pattern to be quite similar to the **2-7-8** pattern, and questioned the need for a separate three-point code type.

9. This person is usually a good candidate for psychotherapy, because he or she is hurting so much. However, with extreme elevations, the agitation and worry may be so excessive that the person cannot sit still for therapy (Carson, 1969). Consequently, these people may need medication to quiet them so that they can participate in therapy.

10. These people tend to have test anxiety in college with obsessive thinking and rigidity connected with this anxiety (Oetting, 1966).

2-7-3

See also the **2-7** pattern, points 4 and 5, p. 76.

1. People with this pattern are likely to be easily led and dependent. They usually encourage others to come to their aid, particularly therapists (Carson, 1969).

2-7-3-1

1. These people may be socially dependent, but they are not typically a member of any group (Caldwell, 1972).

2. They tend to have much self pity and self blame (Caldwell, 1972).

2-7-4

See also the **2-7-4-5** pattern, p. 79.

1. This pattern tends to indicate a situational depression (Caldwell, 1972).

2. Gilberstadt and Duker (1965) found the **2-7-4-(3)** pattern in a VA hospital male population. The parentheses around the **3** are to indicate that the **3** scale is elevated above 70, but it is not necessarily the next highest scale after the **4** scale. A patient with this profile tended to be a hostile, passive-aggressive, anxious, immature person who also had feelings of inferiority. Chronic alcoholism also was found with this pattern. The alcoholism tended to be associated with the anxiety and tension. Gilberstadt and Duker's book should be consulted for further information concerning this profile.

3. Marks, Seeman, and Haller (1974) found this **2-7-4/2-4-7/4-7-2** pattern in a university hospital and outpatient clinic. People with this pattern tended to be depressed and have many worries. They were usually described as passive aggressive, generally tearful, full of fear, nervous, and irritable. Marks' book should be consulted for further details concerning this profile.

4. If a person with this combination is an alcoholic but is no longer drinking and his or her life situation gets better, the person may become depressed and revert back to alcohol (Caldwell, 1972).

5. A man with this profile may have been a mama's boy, and his mother always came to his rescue. He often marries a woman similar to his mother, and if the wife also tries to rescue her husband and is unsuccessful, she may become sick (Caldwell, 1972).

6. Women with this profile tend to be daddy's girls. They may have long affairs with married men. They may have problems because of poor relationships with others and want to be rescued (Caldwell, 1972).

7. Females with this combination and a low **5** scale tend to show the same behavior as men with the **2-7-5-(4)** pattern.

2-7-4-3 See the **2-7-4** pattern, point 2, p. 77.

2-7-(4)-$\overline{5}$

(**5** scale T = 45 or Below)

1. In this pattern, the 4 scale is elevated above 70, but it is not necessarily the next highest scale after 7. Females with this pattern tend to show the same behavior as men with the 2-7-5-(4) pattern.

2-7-5-(4)

1. In this pattern the 4 scale is elevated above 70, but it is not necessarily the next highest scale after 5. Males with this combination usually try to look weak and submissive (Carson, 1969).

   a. They are self-effacing and try not to show any strength.
   b. They seem to ask others to act superior to them and are usually most comfortable when others act this way toward them.

2. Males with this combination tend to be ambivalent and have a sense of failure (Caldwell, 1972).

2-7-8

See also the 2-7 pattern, point 8, p. 77.

1. Gilberstadt and Duker (1965) found this 2-7-8-(4-0-1-3-5-6) pattern in a VA hospital male population. Scales 4, 0, 1, 3, 5, and 6 are elevated above a T of 70, but they are not necessarily the next highest scales in the profile after 2, 7, and 8. A man with this pattern tended to be depressed, shy, quiet, withdrawn, and anxious. He usually felt inadequate in all areas of his life. He may have had bizarre thinking and flat affect. Gilberstadt and Duker's book should be consulted for further information concerning this pattern.

2. Marks, Seeman, and Haller (1974) found this 2-7-8/8-7-2 pattern in a university hospital and outpatient clinic. A person with this pattern was typically described as tense, anxious, and depressed with confused thinking and much self-doubt. Marks' book should be consulted for further information concerning this pattern.

3. For women with a low scale 5 (T = 45 or below), the deep anxieties, depression, study problems, and lack of skills with the opposite sex, seen in the 2-7-8 pattern are intensified (Drake & Oetting, 1959).

2-7-8-(0)

1. In this combination the **0** scale is elevated, but it is not necessarily the next highest scale after **0**. For people with this pattern there usually is chronic depression, introversion, and shyness (Caldwell, 1972).

2. Over a period of time, the psychomotor responses in these clients may slow up. The clients appear to have mood swings, but in reality they have been steadily slowing down with occasional bursts of energy (Caldwell, 1972).

3. This person may report waking early in the morning (Caldwell, 1972).

4. He or she usually is negative concerning his or her achievements (Caldwell, 1972).

5. A person with this profile is a problem in therapy. He or she tends to intellectualize endlessly (Caldwell, 1972).

6. A person with this profile may report incidents of teasing in early childhood. The person may feel that he or she is the inferior member in the family (Caldwell, 1972).

2-8

1. A person with this profile tends to be withdrawn because of feelings of worthlessness.

2. The individual is usually confused and may have difficulty concentrating (Hovey & Lewis, 1967).

3. He or she also tends to be agitated, tense, and inefficient. Such persons are likely to say they are physically ill and have such symptoms as dizziness, blackouts, nausea, and vomiting (Graham, 1977).

4. Usually a history of repeated hurts in childhood exists. The person now fears being hurt more and therefore runs from closeness (Caldwell, 1972).

5. Marks, Seeman, and Haller (1974) found the **2-8/8-2** pattern in a university hospital and outpatient clinic. People with this pattern were usually anxious, depressed, and tearful. They tended to keep people at a distance and were afraid of emotional involvement. They tended to fear loss of control and reported periods of dizziness and forgetfulness. Marks' book should be consulted for further information concerning this profile.

6. Gynther, Altman, and Sletten (1973) and Warbin, Altman, Gynther, and Sletten (1972) also found that psychiatric inpatients with this **2-8/8-2** pattern showed symptoms of depression. For this code type, different diagnostic implications are associated with the **2-8** and the **8-2** codes.

    a. With a **2-8** profile, somatic delusions may be present.
    b. For the **8-2** profile, one or more symptoms of schizophrenia, i.e., hallucinations or delusions of persecution, may be present.

7. However, Lewandowski and Graham (1972) have found that patients with this pattern in comparison to other patients tend to be more grandiose and less likely to be anxious or to say they feel blue or depressed.

8. If both scales are highly elevated, this combination may indicate serious pathology.

2-8-1-3

1. People with this profile tend to have somatic complaints, chronic tension, and dramatic tremors. They also may have intellectual confusion (Caldwell, 1972).

2. They may attempt to promote rescue by their therapists but will back off when the therapists try to help them. This type of person often sets the therapist up with the result that the therapist gets angry at him or her (Caldwell, 1972).

3. If these people are older than 40, they may complain of having thinking and recall problems. They may show organic deficits in testing, but they are not really as bad as the tests indicate. Their slowness causes the low scores on these tests (Caldwell, 1972).

2-9

See also the **9-2** combination, p. 171.

1. This person tends to be agitated (Hovey & Lewis, 1967).

2. He or she may show agitated depression with the depression sometimes masked by activity.

   The person with the **2-9** combination is different from the person with the **2-7** combination, pp. 75-77, in that less obsessive thinking and rigidity is seen, and more motor activity is evident.

3. Alternating periods of activity and fatigue may occur (Graham, 1977).

4. A feeling of pressure for the client without euphoria and grandiosity may be observed in people with high **2** and **9** scale scores. This pressure usually alternates with fatigue. The prognosis is good for these people (Caldwell, 1972).

5. Graham (1977) has hypothesized that this code may be found primarily for people who have feelings of inadequacy and worthlessness but are trying to deny them.

6. This person, when a child, may have had to be emotional to get attention (Caldwell, 1974).

7. Heavy drinking may be present for men with this pattern.

8. Persons with this pattern may have brain dysfunction if MMPI item 274F is checked together with three of the following items: 10F, 51F, 159F, and 192F (Hovey & Lewis, 1967).

9. Aggressive and antagonistic behavior is found in college counselees with this pattern (Drake, 1956).

10. Test anxiety is seen in college students with this pattern (Oetting, 1966).

2-0

See also the **0-2** combination, p. 180.

2

1. These people are socially insecure and withdrawn (Hovey & Lewis, 1967).

2. They tend to have insomnia (Hovey & Lewis, 1967).

3. With a low scale 1 score, women may feel physically inferior (Drake and Oetting, 1959).

3-1-2 See the **3-1-2** pattern in the Triad section, p. 99.

3-2-1 See p. 92.

4-2-7-8 See p. 107.

4-6-2 See p. 110.

4-7-2 See p. 111.

4-8-2 See p. 113.

4-8-9-2 See the **4-8-9** combination, point 4, p. 114.

6-4-2 See the **4-6-2** pattern, p. 110.

8-1-2-3 See p. 157.

8-2-4 See p. 157.

8-2-4-7 See the **8-2-4** combination, point 2, p. 157.

8-4-2 See the **8-2-4** pattern, point 1, p. 157.

8-6-7-2 See the **8-6** combination, point 6, p. 159.

8-7-2 See the **2-7-8** combination, point 2, p. 79.

SUMMARY OF 2 SCALE INTERPRETATIONS*

T Score	Interpretations
45 or below	This person is cheerful, optimistic, and outgoing. For all persons with this score, their attitude should be checked as to whether or not it is appropriate for their situations.
45 thru 60	The majority of people score in this range.
60 thru 70	With this range of scores, a mild dissatisfaction with life may be present, or a long-term situation exists with which the person has learned to live. The person with a 2 scale in this range may not be aware of the dissatisfaction until questioned about it.
70 thru 80	At this level, usually a general sadness either about life or the world exists. This sadness tends to be situationally specific or temporary in nature. If the person is feeling guilty or self-deprecating, the **Es** scale will be below 45 T score points.
80 thru 90	At this level, gloom is usually the theme. To the person, not much exists about which to feel good. If the person is feeling guilty or self-deprecating the **Es** scale will be below 45 T score points.
90 or above	An all-pervasive pessimism is present. Nothing is positive in the person's world. All is dark. If the person is feeling guilty of self-deprecating, the **Es** scale will be below 45 T score points.

*Where T scores are listed in two categories (i.e., 45 or below and 45 thru 60) and a score is obtained that is listed for two categories, use whichever interpretation seems to be most appropriate for the individual.

SCALE 3
(Hy, Conversion Hysteria Scale)

One way many people avoid facing difficulty and conflict is to deny such situations exist. Scale **3** measures the amount and type of such denial. This characteristic tends to be a way of life and may be so ingrained that the person is not even aware that such a defense mechanism is being utilized. These people are extremely difficult in therapy, because they may adamantly refuse to recognize obvious realities. For example, in two recent situations, women with elevations above 70 on this scale refused to recognize that they were divorced. One became angry when the newspaper notice of her divorce was shown to her, and she claimed the notice referred to someone else with the same name. The second verbally acknowledged her divorce, but went back home to her ex-husband every day where she did the cooking and housework, going to her own place only at bedtime.

Interpretation of scale **3** is a bit complicated and involves at least three parts. First, evaluate the position of scale **3** itself to determine what information it gives one about the client. A low scale **3** score (45 or below) indicates a person who tends to face reality head-on in a tough, realistic manner. He or she may be caustic and questioning and believe that people in general see others in a too trusting and optimistic way. Scores between 45 and 60 are where the majority of people score and are not interpreted. As the scale elevates from 60 to 70, the person tends to "think positively" and to prefer not to think about unpleasant things. Above a T of 70, the person is probably not able to see unpleasantness and "bad things" (except as qualified in the next paragraph). In addition, people with scale **3** scores above 70 are usually very social but quite shallow in their relationships. Women with an elevated **3** also tend to have a sensuous, flirtatious quality about them.

3

Second, the actual areas of denial can be determined by comparing the elevation of scale 3 with the elevations on the other Clinical scales. Generally, symptoms indicated by scales with scores above scale 3 are seen and acknowledged by the client, while those indicated by scales with elevations below scale 3 are denied or not seen. For example, if scale 3 is at a T of 80, scales 2 and 8 at a T of 90, and scales 4 and 7 at a T of 70, the person is usually aware of being depressed (scale 2) and confused (scale 8), but will probably deny or not see the fighting (scale 4) and agitation or anxiety (scale 7) shown by the two scales lower than scale 3.

Third, if the elevation on this scale is above 60, it should be compared with scales 1 and 2 (see Triad Profiles, pp. 96-100). These other two scales influence the interpretation of scale 3 and therefore also have to be considered.

Scale 3 is more typically elevated on women's profiles than it is on men's. The behavior measured by scale 3 is much more likely to be considered by our society to be "good" behavior for women than it is for men, because the person tends to be passive and agreeable even though not quite accurately seeing other people's behavior or her own.

In college populations, an elevated scale 3 (T = 70 or above) is rare, but elevations between 60 and 70 for women are seen more frequently. Elevations even in this modest range for men are unusual. In mental health clinic populations however women do show elevations above 70.

GENERAL INFORMATION

1. This scale consists of 60 questions which are divided into two different categories, one centering around bodily problems and one rejecting the possibility that the person is in any way maladjusted or has problems (Carson, 1969; Cuadra & Reed, 1954).

2. For most people who take the inventory, these categories tend to be mutually exclusive. However, for some people who have elevated scale 3 scores, the categories do fit together so that these people acknowledge many physical problems but deny that they are worried about them (Carson, 1969).

3. When scale **3** is moderately elevated (60 to 70), a denial of problems (a "Pollyanna" attitude) may be all that is seen. When scale **3** becomes markedly elevated (70 or above), however, physical complaints and denial become more prominent.

4. Women with an elevated scale **3** (70 or above) tend to have an underlying sensuality and sexuality which become more obvious and denied as the scale is elevated and their scale **5** scores become lower (45 or below).

   When high scale **3** people act out sexually and/or aggressively (which is rare) they often are unaware of what they are doing.

5. People with high scale **3** scores tend to have specific physical complaints such as headaches, as opposed to high scale **1** people who tend to have more generalized and vague physical complaints.

6. Caldwell (1974) has hypothesized that a profound fear of emotional pain may exist with these people. To be rejected by or to lose a loved one is painful, and these people have a high incidence of such loss of love in childhood.

7. A large sex difference exists in respect to the frequency of scale **3** peaks. For women, scale **3** elevations are common, but for men such peaks are unusual (Dahlstrom et al., 1972).

8. Test-retest reliabilities are low (Carkhuff, 1965):

   a. The low reliabilities may be a result of the many different kinds of items that make up the scale.
   b. The tendency to phrase items in the present tense and the use of ambiguous modifiers such as "often" also may reduce the test-retest reliability.

9. There is a significant negative correlation (—.65) between IQ and scale **3** elevation (Brower, 1947).

3

HIGH SCORES

Moderate Elevations (T = 60 thru 70)

1. People with moderate elevations on scale 3 tend to be optimists and to think positively about people.

2. Kunce and Anderson (1976) have hypothesized that when this scale is in the moderate range (and there are no other Clinical scales above 70 T score points except perhaps the 5 scale for men), it may measure being in touch with one's emotions and an ability to show these emotions readily.

Marked Elevations (T = 70 or Above)

1. People with elevations this high tend to have much denial, suggestibility, and functional physical complaints (Hovey & Lewis, 1967).

   College women with this scale elevation are described by their peers in rather uncomplimentary terms such as irritable and having many physical complaints. However, they see themselves as trustful, alert, friendly, and loyal (Black, 1953).

2. They tend to be naive and self-centered (Carson, 1969).

3. They also are likely to be exhibitionistic, extroverted in their relations with others, and superficial (Carson, 1969).

4. They tend to have a great lack of insight into their own and other's motivations and actions (Carson, 1969).

5. They may have anxiety attacks when they are under pressure, with the physical symptoms of anxiety quite prominent.

6. When a person has a high scale 3, the individual is not likely to be diagnosed as psychotic, even when other Clinical scales are high (Carson, 1969).

7. People with this elevation initially express enthusiasm about psychological treatment, because they have a strong need to be liked and accepted (Carson, 1969).

a. However, they cannot stand questioning of their way of looking at the world (Carson, 1969).
b. They may make inordinate demands of the counselor or therapist (Carson, 1969).
c. They tend to want concrete solutions from the therapist while they resist developing insight into their problems.

8. College counselees with a scale **3** this high tend to present problems rooted in an unhappy home situation (Mello & Guthrie, 1958).

a. The prominent pattern seen involves a father described as rejecting, to which women react with somatic complaints and men with rebellion or covert hostility.
b. Their specific worries are concerned with scholastic failure, difficulties with authority figures, and lack of acceptance by their social group.

9. The behavior seen in point 8b with college students also is seen in clinic populations with work failure substituting for scholastic failure.

10. With scale **0** low, male college counselees tend to show aggressiveness and generally extroverted behavior (Drake, 1956).

LOW SCORES
(T = 45 or Below)

1. People with these scores may be caustic, sarcastic, and socially isolated (Carson, 1972; Hovey & Lewis, 1967).

2. They tend to feel that life is hard and tough (Carson, 1972).

3. They may have narrow interests (Hathaway & Meehl, 1951).

COMBINATIONS

All scales in the combinations are at T scores of 70 or above and are listed in order from the highest to the lowest peaks. The scales in the combinations must be the highest ones on the profile. For all combinations using scales **1**, **2**, and **3**, see the Triad profiles, p.

1-2-3   See p. 58.

1-2-3-4   See pp. 58-59.

1-2-3-5̄   See p. 59.

1-2-3-5̄-L   See p. 59.

1-2-3-7   See p. 59.

1-3-K   See p. 61.

1-3-2   See p. 61.

1-3-2̄   See p. 62.

1-3-7   See p. 62.

1-3-8   See pp. 62-63

1-3-8-2   See the **1-3-8** combination, point 4, p. 63.

1-3-9   See p. 63.

2-1-3   See the **2-3-1** combination, point 2, p. 73.

2-1-3-7   See the **2-3-1-(7)** combination, p. 73.

2-3-1   See p. 73.

2-3-1-7   See p. 73.

2-7-3   See p. 77.

2-7-3-1   See p. 77.

2-7-4-3   See the **2-7-4** combination, point 2, p. 78.

2-8-1-3   See p. 81.

3

3-L-K   See the L-K-3 combination, p. 17.

3-K-F-8   See the K-3-F-8 combination, pp. 41-42.

3-1

See also the **1-3** combination, p. 60,
the **3-1-2** Triad profile, p. 99.

1. In contrast to the **1-3** combination, people with a **3-1** pattern tend to have symptoms that are relatively restricted and specific in location (Guthrie, 1949).

2. Because people with a high scale **3** tend to deny that things are going badly, the whining and complaining about physical problems typically seen in persons with high scale **1** scores is modified when the **3** scale is higher than the **1** scale (Carson, 1969).

3. Marks, Seeman, and Haller (1974) found this **3-1/1-3** pattern, in a university hospital and outpatient clinic. This profile tended to be of a female. A woman with this profile usually had a somatic complaint. Her behavior could best be described as agitated, depressed, and confused, with periods of weakness, forgetfulness, and dizziness. Marks' book should be consulted for further information concerning this profile.

3-1-K   See the **1-3-K** combination, p. 61.

3-1-2   See the **3-1-2** pattern in the Triad section, p. 99.

3-2

See also the **2-3** combination, p. 72,
the **3-2-1** Triad pattern, point 1a, p. 100.

1. Women with the **3-2** combination tend to have a history of marital difficulties, but no divorces (Guthrie, 1949).

   a. They frequently are sexually frigid and not interested in sexual activity with their husbands.
   b. They tend to complain about the infidelity and drinking of their husbands.
   c. They tend to be conscientious and easily hurt by criticism.

3

2. Men with this pattern tend to be ambitious and conscientious (Dahlstrom et al., 1972; Guthrie, 1949).

    a. They may have much anxiety and show the physical effects of prolonged tension and worry. One of the main areas of concern for these men is their work.

    b. They may have stomach problems which could result in ulcers.

3-2-1

See also the **3-2-1** Triad profile, point 1b, p. 100.

1. For a woman, this pattern tends to be a hysterectomy or gyne-cological complaint profile. Typically, she has had a life-long history of ill health. Women with this pattern rarely date and usually are sexually inhibited. If they do marry, they may be sexually frigid (Caldwell, 1972).

2. Women with this profile may be quite involved with their parents in a symbiotic fashion. Frequently, these women report that their mother has physical complaints about which the mother cannot complain (Caldwell, 1972).

3. Marks, Seeman, and Haller (1974) found this **3-2-1** pattern in a university hospital and outpatient clinic. The pattern usually was for a woman who was described as anxious, tense, depressed, and tearful with somatic complaints. These researchers also found a high probability of hysterectomy and gynecological complaints. Marks' book should be consulted for further information concerning this profile.

3-4

See also the **4-3** combination, p. 108.

1. Scale **4** shows the amount of aggressive or hostile feelings the person has, while scale **3** indicates the controls the person has available (Dahlstrom et al., 1972). In this **3-4** pattern, since scale **3** is higher than scale **4**, the aggressions and hostilities shown by the **4** scale would tend to be masked and only shown indirectly because of the denial and controls shown by the higher **3** scale.

3

2. These people tend to be very immature. They may satisfy their own aggressions and hostilities in an indirect manner by having friends who are acting out (Carson, 1969).

3-5

1. Ideational homosexuals (those who think about being homosexuals) tend to have a 3-5 pattern, whereas professed, acting homosexuals tend to have a 4-5 pattern (Dahlstrom et al., 1972; Singer, 1970).

3-6

1. This individual tends to deny his or her own hostilities, aggressions, and suspicions (Carson, 1969).

2. He or she may be hard to get along with because the underlying hostility and egocentricity of this person are likely to be apparent the closer you get (Carson, 1969).

3. A person with this pattern may tend to have deep and often unrecognized feelings of hostility toward family members (Dahlstrom et al., 1972; Hovey & Lewis, 1967; Guthrie, 1949). The awareness of these feelings is unusually rationalized away.

4. He or she may report moderate tension and anxiety, but these do not seem to be acute or incapacitating. The person may be mildly suspicious and resentful of others as well as self-centered (Graham, 1977).

3-7

1. Some chronic physical symptoms resulting from mental stress may be likely with these people (Hovey & Lewis, 1967).

2. Women with this combination together with a low scale 0, usually lack academic drive, are anxious, and have insomnia (Drake & Oetting, 1959).

3-8

1. These people complain of problems in thinking clearly (Hovey & Lewis, 1967).

2. Possibly they may have delusional thinking (Hovey & Lewis, 1967).

3. They may have much psychological turmoil and have difficulty making even minor decisions (Graham, 1977).

4. Marks, Seeman, and Haller (1974) found this **8-3/3-8** pattern in a university hospital and outpatient clinic. This profile tended to be of a woman who was having difficulties thinking and concentrating. She usually was seen by others as apathetic, immature, and dependent. Marks' book should be consulted for further information concerning this profile.

3-9

1. These people may be dramatic, superficially open, and highly visible in social situations (Hovey & Lewis, 1967).

2. They may have episodic attacks of acute distress (Dahlstrom et al., 1972; Guthrie, 1949; Hovey & Lewis, 1967).

3. The physical problems of this group usually are not severe and tend to be easily treated (Dahlstrom et al., 1972; Guthrie, 1949; Hovey & Lewis, 1967).

4-3-5̄ See p. 108.

8-1-2-3 See p. 157.

8-2-1-3 See the **2-8-1-3** combination, p. 81.

SUMMARY OF 3 SCALE INTERPRETATIONS*

T Score	Interpretations

45 or below   These people tend to be caustic and tough. They may believe that others are too optimistic about life.

45 thru 60   The majority of people score in this range.

60 thru 70   These people tend to look on the "bright side" of life, are optimistic, and prefer not to think about unpleasant things. This does not mean that they cannot consider reality if it is unpleasant, only that they prefer not to do so.

70 or above   Persons at this level tend to be naive, lack insight, and deny psychological difficulties. They also tend to be un-inhibited and visible in social situations (particularly with a low scale 2). There may be some irritability and somatic complaints (especially when scale 1 is also elevated). When people with this elevation have their way of thinking questioned, the questioning usually meets with denial and hostility. If they are in conseling, although they may claim they are interested in working and say they need therapy, they are in fact usually looking for simplistic, didactic answers which do not require them to evaluate their emotions realistically. If they are required to evaluate their emotions, they tend to terminate counseling prematurely. Women with this elevation tend to be sensual and flirtatious.

*Where T scores are listed in two categories (i.e., 45 or below and 45 thru 60) and a score is obtained that is listed for two categories, use whichever interpretation seems to be most appropriate for the individual.

3

THE TRIAD PROFILES

Traditionally, scales **1**, **2**, and **3** are called the "neurotic triad." However, we feel this choice of terms is unfortunate for many reasons, not the least of which is that these scales do not differentiate neurotics from other groups of people. Consequently, we prefer to call these scales "The Triad," which eliminates the negatively loaded and ambiguous adjective, "neurotic." Interpretations of some selected Triad patterns follow.

1-2-3   Figure 12

1. In this pattern, scale **1** must be higher than scale **2**, and scale **2** must be higher than scale **3**. This pattern is usually associated with males, and generally indicates a concern about physical problems. This concern is used frequently as a means of not facing emotional problems.

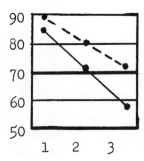

Figure 12

   a. At lower elevations (solid line) (scales **1** and **2** above 70 and scale **3** lower than 70), mental health clients tend to be irritable, to overevaluate minor dysfunctions, and to use physical complaints seemingly to avoid thinking about psychological problems. College counselees with such a profile are usually anxious, insecure in social situations, and have insomnia or headaches. (See also the **1-2** combination, pp. 57-58.)

b. An elevated **1-2-3** profile (dashed lines) (scales **1**, **2**, and **3** all above 70) is called a "declining health" profile. A person with this pattern is usually over age 35 and feels "over the hill" (see also the **1-2-3** combination, p. 58). This pattern is common in VA populations, male welfare and social security claimants, and long-term alcoholics. Females rarely have this elevated pattern; however, those who do and who also have a low **5** scale tend to be masochistic (see the **1-2-3-5̄** combination, p. 59).

1-3-2 Figure 13

1. This one of two patterns is known as the "conversion V" (see the **3-1-2** pattern, p. 99 for the other). For this pattern, scale **1** must be at least 5 T score points greater than scale **3**. The general meaning of the **1-3-2** pattern is that persons with it convert psychological stress and difficulties into physical complaints. The wider the T score spread between scale **2** and scales **1** and **3**, the more severe, long standing, and resistant to change are the physical complaints.

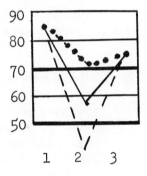

Figure 13

a. When scales **1** and **3** are above 70 and scale **2** is between 50 and 60 (solid line), people tend to be somewhat pessimistic and complaining. They also may have gastrointestinal complaints. With this pattern, there may or may not be valid physical complaints. The interpretation is that the real or imagined complaints are used to avoid facing up to emotional difficulty. (See also the **1-3** combination, p. 60.)

b. When scales **1** and **3** are above 70 and scale **2** is below 45 (dashed line), the interpretation of the pattern is similar to the one provided in the previous paragraph. The primary difference is that the person does not exhibit genuine concern about the physical difficulties. Also existing are more denials of emotional difficulties, histories or hysteric-like pain which suddenly abates, plus unusual eating patterns. (See also the **1-3-$\overline{2}$** profile, p. 62.)

c. When scales **1**, **3**, and **2** are all above 70 (dotted line), the person can be described as similar to the person discussed in paragraph "a," except that he or she is also depressed. (See the **1-3-2** combination, p. 61.)

2-1-3/2-3-1 Figure 14

1. These two patterns generally are considered to be interchangeable at the higher elevations (scales **1**, **2**, and **3** all above 70). However, at the lower levels each should be dealt with separately.

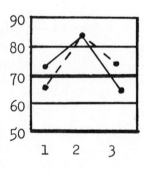

Figure 14

a. Persons with elevations above 70 on all three scales tend to be anxious and depressed with long-standing physical problems and gastrointestinal difficulties. (See the **2-3-1** combination, p. 73.)

b. When scales **1** and **2** are above 70 and scale **3** is below 70 (solid line), refer to the lower elevation interpretation of the **1-2-3** profile, point 1a, p. 96.

c. When scales **2** and **3** are above 70 and scale **1** is below 70 (dotted line), people usually are defined as over-controlled with bottled-up emotions. They frequently are fatigued, nervous, and filled with self-doubt, which prevents them from doing anything. Their difficulties are generally of long standing, and they frequently are described as inadequate and immature. (See also the **2-3** combination, pp. 72-73.)

3-1-2　Figure 15

1. This one of the two patterns known as the "conversion V" (the other is the **1-3-2** pattern, p. 97). Interpretation of this pattern is similar to the **1-3-2** pattern with some modifications. When the **3** scale is higher than the **1** scale, the person tends to be optimistic about his or her physical symptoms, instead of pessimistic about them as people with the **1-3-2** pattern are. These people play down their physical complaints, and they also deny that the physical complaints may have a psychological basis. Thus, they tend to be difficult in therapy. The physical complaints of this group in general are more specific and less global, in contrast to the **1-3-2** pattern. (See also the **3-1** combination, p. 91.)

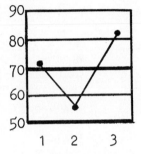

Figure 15

3-2-1　Figure 16

1. The **3-2-1** slope in general is associated with females and is commonly called the "hysterectomy profile." As its name implies, females with such a pattern usually present gynecological complaints.

1-2-3

a. At the lower levels (solid line) (scales **3** and **2** above 70 and scale **1** below 70) women may report marital difficulties such as frigidity, lack of sexual desire, and husbands with infidelity and drinking problems. (See the **3-2** combination, pp. 91-92.)

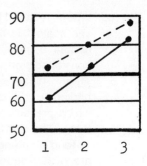

Figure 16

b. At the higher elevations (dashed line) with all three scales above 70, a history of female operations is quite common. These women may be frigid, have a life-long history of ill health, and may have symbiotic relationships. (See also the **3-2-1** combination, p. 92.)

Males rarely have this profile. However, when they do, the scores are usually at the lower levels. Such men usually have physical problems as the result of prolonged stress and worry.

SCALE 4
(Pd, Psychopathic Deviate Scale)

The key phrase for an elevation on this scale is "fighting something." The exact nature of the conflict and its appropriateness depends upon the target (parents, friends, spouse, society, or school), the amount of confusion connected with the fighting out (particularly as indicated by scale 8), and the context in which it occurs. Thus value judgments (for example, high **4** behavior is bad) are inappropriate to apply to elevations of this scale without some awareness of the person's situation. At the lower elevations of this scale, the fighting out may not be overt but rather a covert feeling that something or someone other than the client needs to be changed.

T scores of 60 to 70 are quite common in both the mental health clinic and college counseling center populations. This range is more typically seen in men than in women, but both may have elevations in this range. This range of scores is frequently seen with college students concerned with peaceful societal change, and frequently is found with persons in helping professions such as social work or psychology. Others with this elevation may be having situational stress such as marital problems and a gradual decline in this scale is observable as the problem is resolved.

As the elevation on this scale increases, the degree of fighting intensifies and becomes more noticeable. As the scale exceeds 70, clients may frequent places where trouble occurs, or hang around with people who get into trouble.

The permanence of such a fighting-out pattern appears to be correlated with age. An elevated **4** is common with adolescents, particularly those in difficulty with family, school, or the law. In most cases, the **4** scale elevation disappears as the person becomes older. However, if the **4** scale is still above 70 by the age of 40, it usually is indicative of long-standing antisocial behavior. Fighting out at this age may be shown by alcoholism or confidence rackets and bad check writing. Although this trait probably is unchangeable, vocational counseling may channel the antisocial behavior into more socially acceptable pursuits, by helping the person find a job where the behavior can be beneficial.

An interesting relationship exists between the **4** and **5** scales. When the **4** scale is elevated above 70 *and* the **5** scale is elevated above 60 for males or below 40 for females, then the fighting out shown by the **4** scale is tempered in such a way that the fighting tends to be more covert than overt.

Persons with a low scale **4** are usually described as conventional and concerned with correct social appearances. They are basically non-fighters and prefer a quiet, uneventful life. This non-fighting may have come about because of one of two reasons:

1. The person may have been born with a very easy-going nature.

2. He or she at one time might have been a fighter but because this behavior was so painful or nonproductive, the person switched to being a non-fighter.

As Carson (1972) has noted, these people may have a great capacity for tolerating a dull, boring life. One peculiarity noted by Meehl (1951) which I also have found in the mental health clinic and college counseling center populations is that persons with scale **4** scores in this range may be uninterested in sexual activity.

The **4** scale is frequently a high point for college student profiles and for people coming into mental health clinics who are in trouble with the law.

GENERAL INFORMATION

1. This scale consists of 50 items which concern social imperturbability and a lack of general social adjustment, such as family or authority problems, and social alienation (Carson, 1969).

4   102

2. The major features of a person with a high **4** scale may be as follows:

    a. An emotional shallowness toward others, especially sexually (Dahlstrom et al., 1972).

    b. A revolt against family and/or society (such as school, religion, or politics) (Carson, 1969).

    c. A continuous disregard for what is expected socially (Carkhuff et al., 1965; Dahlstrom et al., 1972).

    d. An inability to profit from experiences, both good and bad (Carkhuff et al., 1965; Dahlstrom et al., 1972).

3. Often the high **4** person goes undetected until he or she is in a situation demanding responsibility, loyalty, and an appreciation of social mores (Dahlstrom et al., 1972).

4. The older a person is with a high **4**, the less likely the scale will decline in elevation with time.

    a. At approximately age 40, an elevation on scale **4** most likely reflects long-standing antisocial behavior.

    b. At age 65 or above, this elevated score more likely reflects social alienation, apathy, absence of pleasure, and lack of involvement, rather than antisocial behavior (Good & Brantner, 1974).

5. The **4** scale is a frequent peak point for males and often appears in a variety of high point combinations. Other scales suppress (scale **5**) or activate (scale **9**) the behavior seen in scale **4**.

    a. When scales **1, 7,** or particularly **2** are high with scale **4**, the delinquency rate is reduced below the level expected for boys in general (Dahlstrom et al., 1972).

    b. When scales **3, 8,** and particularly **9** are high with scale **4**, the delinquency rate is greatly increased (Dahlstrom et al., 1972).

6. Scale **4** is correlated positively with scales **6** and **9** (Hathaway & McKinley, 1951; McKinley & Hathaway, 1944).

7. Test-retest reliability is fair (Carkhuff et al., 1965).

Scale **4** tends to be subject to maturational changes as well as shifts because of psychological treatment.

8. A high negative correlation (—.57) exists between intelligence and scale **4** (Brower, 1947).

9. High **4** scores tend to characterize Blacks more than whites (Hokanson & Calden, 1960; Mitler, Wertz, & Counts, 1961).

10. Separate college norms have been advocated, because college students average significantly higher than the original norming sample on scale **4** (Murray, Munley, & Gilbert, 1965).

Consequently, Heilbrun (1963) has suggested that the **K** scale corrections be dropped from this scale (as well as from scales **1** and **9**) for college populations.

HIGH SCORES

Moderate Elevations (T = 60 thru 70)

1. People in this range may be reacting to situational pressures which require them to act out against their own or others' morals; for example, getting a divorce. They may return to the normal range for the scale (T = 45 to 60) when the situational pressure is gone.

2. Kunce and Anderson (1976) have hypothesized that when this scale is in the moderate range [and there are no other Clinical scales above 70 T score points except perhaps the **5** scale for men], it may measure a readiness to assert oneself and to express one's physical energy and drive. People scoring in this range may adjust rapidly to new situations and show initiative and drive.

    Females seen in a college counseling center tend to have this moderate elevation (Clippinger, Martin, Michael, & Ingle, 1969).

4. Marks and Haller (1974) found that the mean score for this scale for their adolescent populations in counseling was a T of 68.

Marked Elevations (T = 70 or Above)

1. Many people at this elevation seem unable to plan ahead. They tend to disregard the consequences of their actions and not profit by them (Carson, 1969).

2. This elevation often indicates a resentment for rules and regulations.

   Depending upon other high peaks, the resentment and asocial feelings may be shown many different ways. See the combination section for further information.

3. People with **4** scale elevations of 70 or above tend to make good first impressions, but after longer acquaintance their unreliability and self-centeredness becomes apparent (Carson, 1969).

4. Gilberstadt and Duker (1965) found a high **4** pattern (a "spike **4**") in a VA hospital male population. A person with this pattern tended to be irresponsible, impulsive, egocentric, emotionally unstable, and also tended to have a low frustration tolerance. Gilberstadt and Duker's book should be consulted for further information concerning this profile.

5. Therapy seems to be less effective in changing a person with a marked elevated **4** scale than is age (Carson, 1969).

6. However, the higher the intelligence, the more likely a person with a high **4** scale can be channeled by therapy into constructive pursuits, such as finding a suitable job where the high **4** behavior can be used to advantage.

7. The following people tend to have an elevated **4** scale:

   a. Alcoholics.
   b. Drug users (Brill, Crumpton, & Grayson, 1971; Smart & Jones, 1970; Tack & Meyersburg, 1971).
   c. People in trouble with the law, juvenile delinquents (Stone & Rowley, 1963), and convicts.
   d. Adolescents labeled as "problems," but not identified as delinquents (Davies & Maliphant, 1971).
   e. Non-achievers in high school and college (Haun, 1965; Morgan, 1952).

4

8. A **4** scale in this range or higher with a low **2** scale (45 or below) may indicate little, if any, likelihood of significant personality change (Carson, 1969).

9. Female medical patients with this elevation may have recurrent marital difficulties and illegitimate pregnancies. Their medical symptoms tend to be mild in nature and over-shadowed by their behavioral problems (Mello & Guthrie, 1958).

10. In counseling centers, high **4** counselees may not show the classic amoral, asocial behavior, but the scale elevation may be an index of rebelliousness rather than an indication of acting out impulses (Mello & Guthrie, 1958).

LOW SCORES
(T = 45 or Below)

1. People with these scores tend to be very conventional and concerned with social status (Carson, 1969).

2. They may have a great capacity for a boring, routine life (Carson, 1972).

3. These scores tend to characterize older people (Canter et al., 1962; Swenson, 1961).

4. The low scores also may indicate people who have low sexual interest. This indication is particularly true when scale **4** is the low point of the profile (Meehl, 1951).

COMBINATIONS

All scales in the combinations are at a T score of 70 or above and are listed in order from the highest to the lowest peaks. The scales in the combinations must be the highest Clinical scales on the profile.

1-2-3-4 See pp. 58-59.

2-4-7 See the **4-7-2** pattern, p. 111.

2-4-8 See p. 75.

2-4-8-9 See p. 75.

2-7-4 See pp. 77-78.

2-7-4-3 See the **2-7-4** pattern, point 2, p. 78.

2-7-4-5 See pp. 78-79.

2-7-5-4 See p. 79.

4-1 See the **1-4** combination, p. 63.

4-2

See also the **2-4** combination, p. 73.

1. People with the **4-2** combination may seem to be depressed and feeling guilty, but they are not always very convincing or sincere in these feelings (Dahlstrom et al., 1972).

2. People with the **4-2** pattern say one thing, but their behavior is the opposite. For example, they may be self-condemning but act out continuously (Caldwell, 1972).

3. They tend to put their problems on other people so that other people will feel guilty (Caldwell, 1972).

4. Some heroin addicts have a **4-2** profile (Gilbert & Lombardi, 1967; Sutker, 1971).

5. The **4-2** combination was the two-point code with the highest frequency in a psychiatric population (Gynther, Altman, Warbin, & Sletten, 1972).

4-2-7-8

1. This profile was the mean profile found for a group of 45 male heroin addicts (Gilbert & Lombardi, 1967).

4-3

See also the 3-4 combination, p. 92,
the 4-3-5̄ combination, p. 108.

1. The elevation of scale **4** indicates the amount of aggressive or hostile feelings present, while the elevation of scale **3** indicates the repressive or suppressive controls available. Consequently, because scale **4** is higher than scale **3** in this combination, the controls seen in scale **3** are not always adequate to keep the aggressions seen in scale **4** within appropriate limits. Therefore, the person tends periodically to break out into violent behavior.

   a. A life-long pattern may exist of over-control, a sudden explosive episode, and then quiet again for about two years until the next episode. The pattern has been found in males and females (Davis, 1971; Davis & Sines, 1971; Persons & Marks, 1971).

   b. Caldwell (1972) saw the **4-3** person as a socially correct role player who periodically breaks out into antisocial behavior.

2. Gilberstadt and Duker (1965) found the **4-3** pattern in a VA hospital male population. A person with this pattern tended to be sensitive to rejection and had poorly controlled anger with temper outbursts. Suicide attempts and alcoholism occurred when this anger turned inward. Gilberstadt and Duker's book should be consulted for further information concerning this profile.

3. However, a recent study (Gynther, Altman & Warbin, 1973c) has failed to replicate the findings of antisocial and violent behavior for the **4-3** pattern.

4. The **4-3/3-4** pattern shows up in many studies of mothers with behaviorally disturbed children (Wolking, Quast, & Lawton, 1966).

4-3-5̄   (5 scale T = 45 or Below)

1. This pattern may be found for a woman who is hostile and aggressive. She represses anger, but she is unable to prevent her feelings from being acted out. Consequently, she resorts to overt masochistic behavior, which is intended to provoke rage in others. She can then pity herself for being mistreated (Carson, 1969).

4-5

See also the **5-4** combination, p. 126.

1. People with this pattern may be nonconforming but are not likely to act out in obviously delinquent ways. However, their low tolerance for frustration can lead to brief periods of problem behavior (Graham, 1977).

2. Professed male homosexuals tend to have a high **4-5**, whereas ideational homosexuals tend to have a high **3-5** combination (Dahlstrom et al., 1972).

3. However, when a man is not homosexual, an elevation on scale **5** may act as a suppressor of the acting out behavior that usually would be seen from the high scale **4**.

4-5-7-9

1. These elevations may indicate home conflict in male college counselees (Drake & Oetting, 1959).

4-5-9

1. For men with this pattern the high **5** score may be an indication that the **4-9** behavior is suppressed. Therefore, the person may not be acting out directly.

   When the **4-5-9** pattern is present in a male college student, the under-achievement which is typically seen with the **4-9** pattern, is not manifested. The **5** scale acts as a suppressor (Drake, 1962).

4-6

1. These people may be hostile, resentful, and suspicious (Hovey & Lewis, 1967).

2. People with this pattern tend to transfer blame for their problems onto others (Carson, 1969).

3. Seriously disruptive relationships may exist with the opposite sex, such as divorce (Dahlstrom et al., 1972; Guthrie, 1949).

4

4. These people tend to have poor work records (Dahlstrom et al., 1972; Guthrie, 1949).

5. Alcoholism or poor judgment may be associated with this pattern.

6. People with this pattern tend to convert everything into anger (Caldwell, 1974).

7. They may demand a great deal of attention for themselves but resent giving any to other people (Graham, 1977).

8. They tend to be poor risks for counseling (Carson, 1969).

9. Marks et al. (1974) found the **4-6/6-4** pattern in a university hospital and outpatient clinic. It tended to be found for females who were described as self-centered, hostile, tense, defensive, and irritable. They usually refused to admit their difficulties, and therefore did not deal with them. They frequently used rationalization as a primary defense mechanism. Marks' book should be consulted for further information concerning this pattern.

4-6-2

1. Marks, et al. (1974) found the **4-6-2/6-4-2** pattern in a university hospital and outpatient clinic. The pattern was primarily found for females. A woman with this pattern tended to be acting out, depressed, critical, and skeptical. Marks' book should be consulted for further information concerning this profile.

4-6-8

1. A person with a **4-6-8** pattern may be brought in for help by someone else. He or she usually has symptoms of seething anger. Prognosis is poor because the person tends to want his or her problems solved by having other people change (Caldwell, 1972).

2. This is an adverse pattern for most short-term therapy (Meehl, 1951).

3. Chronic runaway males tend to have these scales as their high points (Tsubouchi & Jenkins, 1969).

4-6-9

1. This pattern is found in people who suddenly are violent (Carson, 1969). This is especially true if scale **8** is elevated also.

4-7

1. People with this pattern tend to have repeated patterns of acting out and then being sorry for the acting out (Dahlstrom et al., 1972; Hovey & Lewis, 1967).

2. While they may be very remorseful about acting out, this remorse is not usually sufficient to prevent them from acting out again (Dahlstrom, et al., 1972).

3. These people may respond to therapeutic support, but they are unlikely to make long term changes in their personality (Graham, 1977).

4-7-2

1. Marks et al. (1974) found the **2-7-4/2-4-7/4-7-2** pattern in a university hospital and outpatient clinic. People with this pattern tended to be depressed and to have many worries. They were likely to be described as passive-aggressive, generally tearful, full of fear, nervous, and irritable. Marks' book should be consulted for further information concerning this profile.

4-8

See also the **8-4** combination, p. 158.

1. People with this pattern may be unpredictable, impulsive, and odd in appearance and behavior (Dahlstrom et al., 1972; Hovey & Lewis, 1967).

   One study (Lewandowski & Graham, 1972) has found that people with this pattern have more unusual thoughts than other psychiatric patients in their study.

2. People with this pattern tend to distrust others and have problems with close relationships (Caldwell, 1972).

3. These people tend to see the world as threatening, and they respond by either withdrawing or lashing out in anger. They may have serious concerns about their masculinity or femininity (Graham, 1977).

4. They tend to get into trouble because they have poor judgment as to when and how to fight out, rather than because they crave the excitement of trouble as people with the **4-9** pattern do.

5. Gynther, et al. (1973) found that psychiatric inpatients with the **4-8/8-4** pattern had a history of antisocial behavior such as promiscuity or deserting their families.

6. Delinquents typically have these two high points. The socialized delinquent (one who is in a gang) tends to have the **4-8/8-4** pattern; the runaway delinquent tends to have the **8-4-6** pattern; and the unsocialized aggressive delinquent tends to have the **8-4-7-9** pattern (Tsubouchi & Jenkins, 1969).

7. Emotionally disturbed adolescent males also may show this pattern (Rowley & Stone, 1962).

8. The **4** and **8** scales are two of the high points for LSD users. People who have "bad trips" with LSD tend to have high **8**'s, whereas those who do not have "bad trips" tend to have high **4**'s.

9. This pattern is found frequently in people with suicidal ideation (Caldwell, 1972).

10. The person with the high **4** and **8** scales and a low **9** scale may be the black sheep of the family and is constantly in trouble (Caldwell, 1972).

11. Fifty-eight percent of a group of females (N = 26) who each had three illegitimate children had these high points (Malmquist, Kiresuk, & Spano, 1967).

12. Caldwell (1972) found in one MMPI study of prostitutes and call girls that all of them had the **4-8** combination.

13. Crimes committed by persons with this profile often are senseless, poorly planned, and poorly executed. They may include

4 112

some of the more savage and vicious forms of sexual and homocidal assault (Pothast, 1956).

14. The **4-8** two point code was the second highest in frequency in a psychiatric population (Gynther, et al., 1972).

4-8-F

1. These elevations tend to be obtained by potential juvenile delinquents (Hathaway & Monachesi, 1958).

2. They also are found in emotionally disturbed adolescents (Rowley & Stone, 1962).

3. When these elevations occur with a low **2** scale, the person is usually an aggressive, punitive individual who likes to arouse anxiety and guilt in others (Carson, 1969).

   Such people may end up in jobs where their behavior is socially approved, e.g., law enforcer, school disciplinarian, or over-zealous clergyman.

4-8-2

1. Marks et al. (1974) found the **4-8-2/8-4-2/8-2-4** pattern in a university hospital and outpatient clinic. A person with this profile tended to be distrustful of others, keeping them at a distance. The person usually was described as depressed, tense, irritable, and hostile. Marks' book should be consulted for further information concerning this profile.

4-8-9

1. A person with a **4-8-9** profile may have a history of repeated aggressive situations where others get hurt. These people typically do not realize how they hurt others (Caldwell, 1972).

2. When a male has this profile, he may be violent but has charisma and vitality (Caldwell, 1972).

3. Highly aggressive males have the **4-8-9** scales as high points (Butcher, 1965).

4. When the **2** scale also is elevated (but not necessarily the next highest scale after the **4, 8,** and **9**), people talk about depression and tend to manipulate others so that they can get their own way (Caldwell, 1972).

4-8-9-2   See the 4-8-9 combination, point 4, above.

4-9

See also the **9-4** combination, pp. 171-172.

1. People with elevations over 70 on the **4** and **9** scales tend to be arousal seekers. They must maintain excitement and will stir things up to get it (Carson, 1969, 1972). In contrast to people with high **4-8** scales (when poor judgment may get the person into trouble), the high **4-9** person seems to be seeking the excitement of the trouble.

   The **9** scale activates and energizes the feelings shown by the **4** scale.

2. The person with an elevated **4-9** profile may be self-defeating.

3. A marked disregard for social standards and values may exist (Graham, 1977).

4. Lewandowski and Graham (1972) found that patients with an elevated **4-9** profile were younger at their first hospitalization than other patients. They also were irritable, angry, and easily annoyed. They became upset quickly if things did not suit them.

5. Gilberstadt and Duker (1965) found the **4-9** pattern in a VA hospital male population. A man with this pattern tended to be self-centered, moody, and irritable. He tended to be superficially friendly, but he had a low frustration tolerance. Gilberstadt and Duker's book should be consulted for further information concerning this profile.

6. Marks, et al. (1974) found the **4-9** pattern in a university hospital and outpatient clinic. A person with this pattern tended to be self-centered, under-controlled, insecure, irritable, and hostile. Marks' book should be consulted for further information concerning this profile.

7. Two recent studies (Gynther et al., 1973a; Gynther et al., 1973) also have found antisocial behavior such as excessive fighting and attempts to harm others for this pattern **4-9/9-4**. Men with this pattern also tended to have a history of alcoholic benders. This description may not apply to Blacks who have a **4-9** profile.

8. The **4-9** pattern tends to characterize the following people:

    a. Juvenile delinquents (Briggs, Wirt, & Johnson, 1961; Stone & Rowley, 1963).
        1) However, accompanying high scores on scales **2, 5, 7,** and **0** act as inhibitors of the delinquent behavior (Carkhuff, et al., 1965).
        2) This pattern may disappear with age.
    b. Convicts (Panton, 1958).
        1) Habitual criminals are higher on **4** and **9** than first offenders of the same age (Panton, 1962).
        2) With male adults, this tends to be a chronic fixed pattern.
    c. School and college under-achievers (Barger & Hall, 1964; Brown & Dubois, 1974; Yeomans & Lundin, 1957). This is especially true for males if the **5** scale is low, whereas high **5** acts as a suppressor to the under-achievement tendency of the **4-9** pattern (Barger & Hall, 1964; Drake, 1962; Drake & Oetting, 1959).
    d. Students in trouble for college misconduct (Nyman & LeMay, 1967).

9. College students with high points on these scales have lower grade point averages and higher dropout rates than would be expected according to their ability (Barger & Hall, 1964).

10. College counselees with these high points were rated difficult to deal with (aggressive and opinionated) by their counselors (Drake, 1954).

11. Smokers in college tend to have elevations ($T = 60$ or above) on scales **4** and **9** and a low scale **0** (Dvorak, 1967; Evans, Borgatta, & Bohrnstedt, 1967).

12. In one study 8 to 9 percent of the freshmen in one college had these high points (Fowler & Coyle, 1969).

6-4-2   See the **4-6-2** pattern, p. 110.

8-2-4   See p. 157.

8-2-4-7 See the **8-2-4** pattern, point 2, p. 157.

8-4-2   See the **4-8-2** pattern, p. 113.

8-4-6   See p. 158.

8-4-7-1 See p. 158.

8-4-7-9 See p. 159.

8-6-4-9-F See p. 160.

8-7-4-1 See p. 161.

9-8-4   See p. 173.

SUMMARY OF 4 SCALE INTERPRETATIONS*

T Score	Interpretations
45 or below	Persons with these scores tend to be conventional. They usually are able to tolerate much mediocrity and boredom. They may lack interest in heterosexual activity.
45 thru 60	The majority of people score in this range. People scoring at this level seldom show dissatisfaction with authority figures, and they tend to go along with society as it is presently constituted.
60 thru 70	With college educated persons, this level usually indicates concern about the social problems of the world. It is a common level for social workers, psychologists, and others in the helping professions. Other people with this elevation may have a situational crisis such as marital discord. In this latter instance, the elevation tends to go down after the problem is resolved.
70 or above	Persons at this level tend to be angry and fighting out. If the **5** scale is above or within 5 T score points of the **4** scale, this fighting out will be more covert than overt. People with scores at this level may be unable to profit from their experiences, both good and bad. These people may not be in actual trouble with authority figures, but instead may associate with persons who are. Adolescents usually outgrow this difficulty, but at age 40, such an elevation, if it is one of the highest scales, can be considered a long-standing trait and is probably very difficult to change. The key to success with these people is to try to channel the drive indicated by the high **4** into socially acceptable behavior.

Relation to New scales:

Do scale—if the 4 scales is above 70 T score points and the **Do** scale also is above 70 T score points, the person frequently will be seen as domineering.

---

*Where T scores are listed in two categories (i.e., 45 or below and 45 thru 60) and a score is obtained that is listed for two categories, use whichever interpretation seems to be most appropriate for the individual.

SCALE 5

(Mf, Masculinity-Femininity Scale)

Scale **5** is probably the most misunderstood of all the Clinical scales for three reasons. The first is the scale's name, "Masculinity-Femininity." The implication is that this scale can determine if one is more or less masculine or feminine. The problem in today's society is that the definitions of masculinity and femininity are changing rapidly, and the current one may not be very much like the original definitions used when this scale was constructed.

A second difficulty with the scale is the frequent assumption that it can detect males who are actual or latent homosexuals. Such an assumption is not warranted. Some males with homosexual preferences do receive elevations on this scale, but many false positives and false negatives exist. This scale just does not do an adequate job of identifying male homosexuality.

The third difficulty with this scale is purely mechanical. Actually two **5** scales exist, one for males and one for females, and each scale has its own interpretations.

How, then, does one read this scale? I have found it best to consider scale **5** as two scales and to interpret each separately.

Males

Scores between 45 and 55 on this scale indicate that the man is interested in traditional masculine activities. Between 50 and 55 seems to be the typical range for non-college educated males and for college educated males interested in majors such as engineering and agriculture. When this score goes lower than a T of 45, the man tends

5

to adopt the attitudes of the legendary he-man, particularly in the treatment of females (examples: "love them and leave them" and "a woman's place is in the home"). In fact, some of these men appear to score conquests by carving notches on the bedpost (particularly so if their **4** scale is elevated).

As the elevation on this scale increases to above 60, one of two types of behavior may be observed. One is an interest in aesthetics such as art, music, and literature. This interest tends to increase with education (a score in the 60 thru 70 range is the norm for college graduates). The second thing that can emerge is passivity. By passivity, we mean a preference for working through things in a covert and indirect manner, rather than in an overt and direct manner. The question of which of the two behaviors is indicated by the **5** scale score is best determined by consulting other scales (particularly the New scales **Dy** and **St**). High **Dy** (dependency) plus high **5** usually indicates some passivity. High **St** (status) plus high **5** usually is indicative of aesthetic or achievement interests. When both the **Dy** and **St** scales are elevated above 60 T score points, the relative heights of the two scales can indicate how much passivity and/or aesthetic or achievement interests are being shown by the **5** scale.

Above a T of 80, both an appreciation for aesthetics and passivity usually are present. With persons actively involved in the arts however the passivity may not be present until a T score of 85 is reached.

While the **5** scale is the most frequent high point on male college student profiles, with scale **9** a close second, for male non-college clients this is not a typical elevation. They rarely score high on this scale; in fact, their typical score is approximately 50.

Females

In the counseling center and mental health clinic populations, the usual maximum scale **5** score for women is 50; very rarely do I see scores above this level. Those few women I have seen who do score above 50 tend to be uninterested in being seen as feminine. They may or may not have masculine interests, but they definitely are not interested in appearing or behaving as other women do. They usually like to think of themselves as unique or different from women in general.

Scores between 35 and 50 are typical and indicate interest in traditional feminine pursuits. This does not mean that the woman has no interest in a career outside the home, but, instead, that she may prefer both a career and the traditional activities connected with being a woman. As the score on this scale goes below 35, a seductive, helpless, coyness usually begins to emerge. When the score of 30 is reached, the helplessness usually is very evident. The woman is not always actually helpless, but she probably uses this approach to get others to help her, particularly males.

GENERAL INFORMATION

1. The **5** scale of 60 items contains questions concerning aesthetic interests, vocational choices, and passivity (Carson, 1969).

2. The same scale is used for both sexes, but high raw scores are elevations for men and low points for women.

3. This scale is highly correlated with education and intelligence.

   However, Gulas (1973) has indicated that the **5** scale may be more correlated with IQ, educational aspiration, and/or socio-economic status than with years of education, *per se.*

4. Caldwell (1977) has hypothesized that the **5** scale may measure emotional caring on the feminine end of the scale (high **5** for men, low **5** for women) and practical survival self-caring on the masculine end of the scale (low **5** for men, high **5** for women).

5. The **5** scale frequently is elevated for men, but not for women.

6. This scale appears to be most useful as an indication of aesthetic interests (Cottle, 1953).

7. This scale correlates —.53 with the MF scale on the Strong Vo-cational Inventory Blank for males (Himelstein & Stoup, 1967).

8. In one study, twenty out of the sixty items on the **5** scale did not differentiate significantly between college men and women. Of the remaining forty, interest items are the most discriminating (specifically MMPI items #1, 77, 132, 223, 261, and 300) (Murray, 1963).

9. Test-retest reliabilities are good (Carkhuff et al., 1965; Dahlstrom & Welsh, 1960).

10. For males, high **5** tends to negate the overt acting out behavior indicated by elevations on certain scales such as **4**, **6**, and **9**. Passive-aggressive behavior may be seen instead.

11. A high **5** scale may indicate homosexuality for men. However, this cannot be assumed without evidence from other sources (Hathaway & McKinley, 1951).

    Male homosexuals are able to score in the typical range on this scale if they wish to, because obvious sex-oriented items can be avoided easily (Benton, 1945).

12. For college men, a strong tendency exists for scale **5** to increase over a period of time from entrance to graduation from college (Lough, 1947).

13. With females, if a large number of questions are left unanswered, the scale is elevated (Carkhuff et al., 1965).

HIGH SCORES

Moderate Elevations — Male (T = 60 thru 70)

1. High **5** tends to be more characteristic of college males than of college females (Clark, 1953, 1954).

2. This elevation is characteristic of males having a wide range of interests, especially aesthetic ones (Hathaway & Meehl, 1951).

3. Kunce and Anderson (1976) have hypothesized that when this scale is in the moderate range, it may measure role-flexibility. A person who is role-flexible can enjoy a wide range of interests and may be perceived as interesting, colorful, complex, inner-directed, insightful, tolerant, and possibly dramatic.

4. This elevation tends to characterize the following male populations (Carkhuff et al., 1965):

a. College students in general (Canter et al., 1962).
b. College students excelling in academics (Barger & Hall, 1964; Yeomans & Lundin, 1957).
c. Non-athletes (Booth, 1958).
d. Music students (Nance, 1949).
e. Art students (Spiaggia, 1950).
f. Actors (Chyatte, 1949; Meehl, 1951).
g. Seminary students (Bier, 1948; Vaughn, 1965).
h. Architects (MacKinnon, 1962).
i. Teachers (Nance, 1949).

5. A high **5** scale is more characteristic of male arts and science majors than of male engineers (Butcher, Ball, & Ray, 1964; Simono, 1968).

6. The **5** scale tends to be one of the two most frequent high points for male college students. The other frequent high point is scale **9**.

Gulas (1973) found that the two most frequently elevated scales (two-point code groups) in a study of 609 college males were (from most frequent to least frequent) **3-5/5-3**, **5-9/9-5**, **2-5/5-2**, **5-7/7-5**, **5-8/8-5**, and **5-6/6-5**. These two-point patterns were *not* necessarily above a T score of 70.

Moderate Elevations — Female (T = 50 thru 55)

1. Women with this elevation on the **5** scale may enjoy sports and/ or outdoor activities.

2. They also tend to be not interested in being considered feminine.

3. They may prefer mechanical, computational, and scientific pursuits, and tend not to prefer literary pursuits (Carkhuff et al., 1965).

4. Scale **5** moderate elevations are frequent for females who drop out of school (Barger & Hall, 1964).

5. This elevation may be shown by girls in their late teens and by women from atypical cultural backgrounds (Carson, 1969).

Marked Elevations — Male (T = 70 or Above)

1. As elevations increase, the likelihood that passive behavior will be seen in men increases.

2. This elevation is characteristic of college males having a wide range of interests, especially aesthetic ones (Hathaway & Meehl, 1951).

3. Scores in this range for blue collar men tend to indicate passivity rather than aesthetic interests.

4. Male homosexuals tend to show marked elevations on the **5** scale (Manosevits, 1971). However, since this is an obvious scale, males with same-sex preferences can produce scores in the typical ranges by avoiding these obvious sex-oriented items.

5. A high score suggests that the man does not identify with the culturally prescribed role for his sex (Carson, 1969).

Marked Elevations — Female (T = 55 or Above)

1. As the elevation increases, the likelihood that aggressive behavior will be seen in women increases (Carson, 1969).

2. A high score suggests that the woman does not identify with the culturally prescribed role for her sex (Carson, 1969).

3. Women with this elevation may become anxious if they are expected to adopt a feminine sexual role (Carson, 1969).

LOW SCORES

Male (T = 50 or Below)

1. Low scores suggest strong identification with the prescribed masculine role (Carson, 1969).

2. Males with scores in this range may be described as easy going, adventurous, and "coarse" (Carson, 1969).

3. Some males with low **5** scores may appear to be compulsive and inflexible about their masculinity (Carson, 1969).

Female (T = 35 or Below)

1. Low scores suggest strong identification with the prescribed feminine role (Carson, 1969).

2. Females with very low **5** scale scores may be passive, sub-missive, yielding, and demure, at times living caricatures of the feminine stereotype (Carson, 1969).

   These women may be unusually constricted, self-pitying, and fault-finding.

3. White females tend to have lower scores than Black females (Butcher et al., 1964).

COMBINATIONS

All scales in the combinations are at a T score of 70 or above and are listed in order from the highest to the lowest peaks. The scales in the combinations must be the highest Clinical scales in the profile.

1-2-3-5̅   See p. 59.

1-2-3-5̅-L See p. 59.

2-7-4-5̅   See pp. 78-79.

2-7-5-4   See p. 79.

4-3-5̅   See p. 108.

4-5   See p. 109.

4-5-7-9   See p. 109.

4-5-9   See p. 109.

5-?

1. An elevation on the **5** scale for females can result from the omission of items (elevated **?** scale), because a low raw score on scale **5** produces elevations on the women's profile.

5-3

See also the **5-4** combination, below,
the **3-5** combination, p. 93.

1. If men have homosexual impulses and scales **5** and **3** are high, they tend not to have acted upon their sexual impulses but only may be thinking about them (Singer, 1970).

5-4

See also the **5-3** combination, p. 126.
the **4-5** combination, p. 109.

1. If men have homosexual impulses and scales **5** and **4** are high, they tend to be overt homosexuals (Singer, 1970).

2. Males with this combination may have a passive-aggressive personality (Good & Brantner, 1961).

   This combination may be associated with male sexual delinquents of the more passive type.

3. The **5-4** combination is a common configuration for men who are nonconformists. They seem to delight in defying social conventions in their behavior and dress (Carson, 1969).

   Many male homosexuals who have this combination are proud of their unconventionality and tend to flaunt it.

4. Women who are rebelling against their female role tend to have this combination (Carson, 1969).

   Their behavior becomes more atypical with increasing elevation of the **4** scale (Carson, 1969).

5-4 (5 Scale T = 45 or Below)

1. Men with this combination tend to be flamboyantly masculine. In teenagers, this is often manifested in delinquent behavior (Carson, 1969).

2. Women with this combination may be hostile and angry, but they are unable to express these feelings directly. Therefore, they may provoke others to get angry at them. Then they can pity themselves, because they have been mistreated (Carson, 1969).

3. Women with this pattern may be passive-aggressive (Good & Brantner, 1974).

5-8-9

1. When the **5-8-9** pattern is present, the lack of academic motivation seen for males with the high **8-9/9-8** profile is not manifested. The **5** scale acts as a suppressor (Drake & Oetting, 1959).

5-9

1. Male college counselees with the **5-9** pattern present problems concerning conflicts with their mothers, especially when scale **0** is low (Drake, 1956).

5-0

1. Male college counselees with the **5-0** pattern tend to show introverted behavior (Drake, 1956).

SUMMARY OF 5 SCALE INTERPRETATIONS
FOR FEMALES*

T Score	Interpretations

35 or below A woman scoring in this range may appear to be coy, seductive, and helpless (the southern belle syndrome). The behavior may be a manipulative device, or the woman may be truly helpless.

35 thru 50 The majority of women score in this range. A woman with a **5** scale in this range usually is interested in traditional feminine and domestic activities. However, she also can be interested in a career that is feminine in nature (teaching, being in a helping profession).

50 or above A woman scoring in this range may see herself as being unique and not like a typical woman.

Relation to New scales:

Dy scale and **St** scale—if the **5** scale is below 45 T score points, the relative heights of the **Dy** and **St** scales above 60 T score points can indicate how much passivity **(Dy)** and/or aesthetic-achievement interests **(St)** are present.

*Where T scores are listed in two categories (i.e., 35 or below and 35 thru 50) and a score is obtained that is listed for two categories, use whichever interpretation seems to be most appropriate for the individual.

SUMMARY OF 5 SCALE INTERPRETATIONS
FOR MALES*

T Score	Interpretations

45 or below A man scoring in this range may be pre-occupied with being tough and virile (the he-man syndrome).

45 thru 55 A man scoring in this range usually is interested in traditional masculine pursuits such as sports, hunting, outdoor life. Between 50 and 55 is the typical range of this scale for non-college males, engineers, and men studying agriculture.

55 thru 80 This level is typical for males with more than one year of college, particularly in the humanities and fine arts. This person usually has an interest in aesthetics. There also may be some passivity. This latter is more likely as the 5 scale gets closer to 80. For non-college educated males, a score above 70 on the 5 scale usually indicates passivity with a possible interest in aesthetics.

80 or above At this level, the person is most likely passive and also interested in aesthetics.

Relation to New scales:

Dy scale and St scale—if the 5 scale is elevated above 60 T score points, the relative heights of the Dy and St scales above 60 T score points can indicate how much passivity (Dy) and/or aesthetic-achievement interests (St) are present.

*Where T scores are listed in two categories (i.e., 45 or below and 45 thru 55) and a score is obtained that is listed for two categories, use whichever interpretation seems to be most appropriate for the individual.

5

SCALE 6
(Pa, Paranoia Scale)

Scale **6** measures three things. One, at the lower elevations (60 thru 70), the scale usually shows interpersonal sensitivity, usually of the kind, "What are you thinking and feeling, and how can that affect me?" Second, When the **6** scale gets above 70, suspiciousness is usually added to the sensitivity. The motives of others are assumed to be malevolent, and therefore the client feels a need to watch out for others and what they can and will do to him or her. Very rarely is this scale elevated above 70 without the sensitivity and/or suspiciousness being seen. Thus, these people typically are difficult persons with whom to work, because the suspiciousness and sensitivity towards others can include the counselor. I have had this suspiciousness and sensitivity take the form of questioning my credentials, checking whether the client will be fairly treated, and doubting the good intentions of others. In transactional analysis terms, this person exemplifies the "I'm O.K., you're not O.K." stance.

The third element in scale **6** is much like a subtle spice and flavors the whole scale. This pervasive element is self-righteousness. A person with an elevation on this scale tends to have the feeling of "I've done all this for you, and now look what you have done to me in return." Occasionally this statement actually is expressed, but more commonly this attitude is implied strongly.

This scale is rarely elevated by itself; usually other scales also are elevated. In addition, this scale rarely is the highest peak on my profiles but most likely the second or third highest point. The person may come for therapy because of some situational stress. Once this stress is alleviated successfully, the person typically will leave counseling with the paranoid behavior gone.

Scale **6** rarely goes below 40, but when it does two interpretations are possible. The first is that the person really is a high **6**, sensitive and suspicious. Because the scale has somewhat obvious items, he or she has avoided marking these items in the scored direction; and instead has answered them in the typical way to such an extent that he or she has overcompensated and shows unusually low on this scale. These people are fairly easy to spot in therapy, because the sensitivity/suspiciousness is not always easy to hide in this kind of intimate relationship.

The second interpretation for a low **6** scale is that the person is answering honestly, he or she tends to be a gullible type of person who is taken in occasionally by some others, because he or she is not sensitive enough to perceive what others really are like.

GENERAL INFORMATION

1. The 40 items of scale **6** reflect suspiciousness, interpersonal sensitivity, and self-righteousness.

2. This scale is made up of obvious items. Thus, the paranoid person, who is typically interpersonally sensitive and suspicious, can mark the answers so as to show only what he or she wants you to see on this scale.

   Therefore, a suspicious person can score low on scale **6**. In this instance, the person is too cautious, avoids obvious material, and overcompensates beyond normal limits.

3. This scale rarely produces false positives. People with elevations are suspicious and sensitive and readily show these characteristics (Carson, 1972).

4. Scale **6** has a tendency to be positively correlated with scales **4** and **9** (Hathaway & McKinley, 1951; McKinley & Hathaway, 1944).

5. This scale does not tend to change under "fake good" instructions ("try to look as good as you can on this test") (Latta, 1968).

6. Test-retest reliabilities are fair (Carkhuff et al., 1965).

Scale **6** is sensitive to changes in suspiciousness.

HIGH SCORES

Moderate Elevations (T = 60 thru 70)

1. This elevation tends to characterize sensitive people (Carkhuff et al., 1965; Cottle, 1953).

2. Kunce and Anderson (1976) ·have hypothesized that when this scale is in the moderate range [and there are no other Clinical scales, above 70 T score points except perhaps the **5** scale for men], it may measure inquisitiveness and investigative behavior.

3. College women clients with an elevation in this range tend to be sensitive specifically to physical defects in themselves (Loper, 1976).

Marked Elevations (T = 70 or Above)

1. This elevation tends to characterize suspicious people.

    a. They feel that what is said or done around them is aimed specifically at them.
    b. They often interpret criticism of their ideas as criticism of themselves. This may be seen even when the T score is as low as 55.

2. A person with a **6** scale score of 70 or above usually is more verbal about suspiciousness and feelings of injustice than someone with a moderate elevation on this scale.

3. People with this elevation tend to be highly suspicious and usually feel that they are not getting what they deserve (Carson, 1969).

4. The most minor rejection is remembered.

5. This elevation tends to characterize people who make mistakes costly to others (Carson, 1969). This seems to be an unconscious passive-aggressive way of coping with perceived injustice.

6. A relationship is difficult to establish in therapy with these people because their marked suspiciousness and sensitivity includes the therapist as well as others.

In treatment, high scorers tend to be argumentative and rigid (Carson, 1969).

LOW SCORES
(T = 45 or Below)

1. A score of 45 or below on scale **6** may indicate a lack of personal sensitivity to others (Drake & Oetting, 1959).

2. Low scores on this scale also characterize people who are cheerful, conventional, and trusting.

3. A suspicious person can score low on scale **6**. In this instance, the person is too cautious, avoids the obvious paranoid questions, and over-compensates beyond normal limits.

The person resists revealing self in any way, because he or she feels a calamity will follow such a revelation (Carson, 1969).

4. These scores characterize college students who have problems related to underachievement or non-achievement. The necessity to deny hostility may drain off excess energy, thus reducing the student's effectiveness (Anderson, 1956; Morgan, 1952).

In addition, difficulty with parents often exists. This difficulty may be related to repressed or denied hostility.

COMBINATIONS

All scales in the combinations are at a T score of 70 or above and are listed in order from the highest to the lowest peaks. These scales in the combinations must be the highest Clinical scales on the profile.

4-6   See pp. 109-110.

4-6-2   See the **6-4-2** pattern below.

4-6-8   See p. 110.

4-6-9   See p. 111.

6-2   See the **2-6** combination, p. 75.

6-3   See the **3-6** combination, p. 93.

6-4

See also the **4-6** combination, pp. 109-110.

1. Marks et al. (1974) found the **4-6-2/6-4-2** pattern in a university hospital and outpatient clinic. It was primarily a female pattern. females who were described as self-centered, hostile, tense, defensive, and irritable. They usually handled their difficulties by refusing to admit them, and frequently they used rationalization as a primary defense mechanism. Marks' book should be consulted for further information concerning this profile.

6-4-2

1. Marks et al. (1974) found the **4-6-2/6-4-2** pattern in a university hospital and outpatient clinic. It was primarily a female pattern. A woman with this pattern tended to be acting out, depressed, critical, and skeptical. Marks' book should be consulted for further information concerning this profile.

6-7

1. Counselors rated men with this pattern plus no elevation on scale **5** as non-responsive and had difficulty relating to them (Drake, 1954).

6-7-8

1. This pattern may indicate a poor prognosis for vocational success (Harmon & Wiener, 1945).

6-7-8-9

1. This pattern may suggest behavioral difficulties, especially among college freshmen women (Osborne, Sander, & Young, 1956).

   These women tend to approach problems with animation, are sensitive, and feel that they are unduly controlled, limited, and mistreated.

2. This pattern may indicate poor prognosis for vocational success (Harmon & Wiener, 1945).

6-8

See also the **8-6** combination, p. 159.

1. These people could have marginal psychological adjustment (Hovey & Lewis, 1967).

2. These people tend to have intense feelings of inferiority and insecurity. They are suspicious and distrustful of others and avoid deep emotional ties (Graham, 1977).

3. Relationships with others tend to be unstable and characterized by resentment (Dahlstrom & Welsh, 1960).

4. They may present a wide variety of complaints which shift from one time to the next (Dahlstrom & Welsh, 1960).

5. They tend to be drawn towards fads and quacks (Dahlstrom et al., 1972; Guthrie, 1949; Hovey & Lewis, 1967).

6. If these people can get verbally angry with the therapist, they tend to get better rapidly (Caldwell, 1974).

7. One study (Lewandowski & Graham, 1972) has found that patients with the **6-8** pattern have spent more time in a neuropsychiatric hospital than other patients. They tended to be unfriendly with others; to have less social interests; to be more emotionally withdrawn, conceptually disorganized, and suspicious; and to have more hallucinatory behavior and unusual thought content.

8. Another study reported in two references (Altman, Gynther, Warbin, & Sletten, 1972; Gynther et al., 1973) has found patients in a mental hospital with this **6-8/8-6** pattern often seem unfriendly and angry for no apparent reason. They also have thought disorders, hallucinations, delusions, hostility, and lack of insight. Poor judgment was typical. Of those patients labeled psychotic, schizophrenia was the most frequent diagnosis, especially paranoid schizophrenia. For the **6-8** profile, the delusions are apt to be delusions of grandeur. For the **8-6** profile, the effect is apt to be blunted.

9. Marks et al. (1974) found the **8-6/6-8** pattern in a university hospital and outpatient clinic. They found this pattern primarily for females who were having unconventional, delusional thoughts. These women were also suspicious. Marks' book should be consulted for further information concerning this profile.

10. Black psychiatric patients show this configuration significantly more than white psychiatric patients matched on age, sex, hospital status, socioeconomic status, and duration of illness (Costello & Tiffany, 1972).

6-8-9

1. This pattern may indicate a poor prognosis for vocational success (Harmon & Wiener, 1945).

2. It typifies male Blacks from a rural, isolated background (Gynther et al., 1971).

6-9

1. These people tend to be angry, rational, and insistent about why they do things. They tend to give much moral justification for whatever they do (Caldwell, 1972).

2. They have difficulty with criticism, therefore they use projection frequently as a defense mechanism (Caldwell, 1972).

3. These people tend to be tense and over-react to possible danger (Hovey & Lewis, 1967).

4. They are vulnerable to threat and feel anxious and tense much of the time. They may alternate between overcontrol and emotional outbursts (Graham, 1977).

5. Marks et al. (1974) found the **9-6/6-9** pattern in a university hospital and outpatient clinic. It was found primarily for females who were agitated, tense, excitable, suspicious, and hostile. Marks' book should be consulted for further information concerning this profile.

6. In another study reported in two references, Gynther et al. (1973d) and Gynther (1973) found patients with this code type, **6-9/9-6**, to be excited, hostile, loud and grandiose, with little likelihood of having depressive symptoms.

6-0

1. With women counselees, this pattern is indicative of feelings of inferiority in regard to some physical feature and of great shyness (Drake & Oetting, 1959).

8-4-6 See p. 158.

8-6 See p. 159.

8-6-4-9-F See p. 160.

8-6-7-2 See the **8-6** combination, point 6, p. 159.

8-9-6-F See p. 162.

SUMMARY OF 6 SCALE INTERPRETATIONS*

T Score	Interpretations

45 or below	A person may score in this range for two reasons. First, the person may be gullible and taken in by other people because he or she is not suspicious enough of other people. Second, the person may have a low score on this scale because he or she is really very sensitive and suspicious but has been able to guess which questions would reveal this and has answered them in the opposite way, thus showing low on the scale.
45 thru 60	The majority of people score in this range.
60 thru 70	People who score in this range tend to be interpersonally sensitive to what others think of them.
70 or above	In addition to the sensitivity observed at the 60 thru 70 level, suspiciousness is usually present when this scale goes above 70. The client may assume that other people are after him or her. Righteous indignation also is usually present.

*Where T scores are listed in two categories (i.e., 45 or below and 45 thru 60) and a score is obtained that is listed for two categories, use whichever interpretation seems to be most appropriate for the individual.

— NOTES —

SCALE 7
(Pt, Psychasthenia Scale)

Scale **7** measures anxiety, usually anxiety of a long-term nature. The scale may go up during times of situational stress (state anxiety), but tends mainly to measure a type of living which includes worrying a great deal (trait anxiety). The state anxiety component in the MMPI is most likely measured by scale **A** of the New scales, while the trait anxiety is most likely measured by scale **7**. See the **A** scale general information section (pp. 187-189) for further comments about the relationship between the two scales.

Scale **7** is one of the most frequent high points on profiles of clients in college counseling centers and mental health clinics. It usually is elevated with scale **2** and/or scale **8**. A special relationship exists between scales **7** and **8**. When they are both elevated, special note is to be made as to which scale is the higher. When scale **7** is higher than scale **8**, especially by ten points or more, the person usually has a better prognosis than when scale **8** is higher because the person is still fighting his or her problem and is highly anxious about it. When the **8** scale is higher, mental confusion keeps the person from focusing on solutions to his or her problems, and therefore therapy usually is not very productive.

At the lower elevations of scale **7** (T = 60 thru 70 and no other Clinical scales elevated above 70 T score points except perhaps the **5** scale for men), a person generally is punctual in meeting important assignments and deadlines and does not feel anxious. However, when a fear (actual or imagined) exists of not meeting an obligation, an anxious agitation emerges until the obligation is fulfilled. People with scale **7** at this level usually feel they cannot put off until tomorrow what they should do today without some dire consequences happening. As a result of their compulsivity, these people tend to make higher grades and faster promotions than others do. Of additional interest is the fact that people with an elevation of 60 thru 70 on the 7 scale tend to be great intellectualizers.

Under pressure or over-obligation, where deadlines or tasks cannot be met, scale 7 may begin to elevate for people who originally scored in the lower elevations of scale 7. When T = 70, the anxiety usually is evident to others but not necessarily to the person. A fear of failure or of making the wrong decisions may appear also.

As the elevation of scale 7 increases, particularly beyond a T of 80, an element of omnipotence begins to emerge in that the person tends to adopt the attitude that he or she must not fail for fear of hurting others. Also, as this elevation increases, anxiety causes a loss of productivity further raising fears of failure and thereby raising more anxiety, *ad infinitum*.

Persons with a low scale 7 (T = 45 or below) generally are secure with themselves and quite stable. These people are reported to be persistent and success-oriented by other authors. However, my experience has been that they do not appear to take deadlines and work obligations as seriously as others because they are less anxious about them; and therefore, these persons may give the impression of not caring about what others want to have done. This attitude may make employers uneasy. I hypothesize that some people with low 7 scale scores were at one time in the 70+ T score range, but the anxiety was so bothersome that they decided to become nonworriers and over compensated into the low range of the scale.

One anomaly frequently seen is the person who obviously is anxious but who has no elevation on scale 7. Most likely in this case, scale A will be elevated instead of scale 7. The reason for this is that the person is not characterologically anxious (which the 7 scale measures) but presently is upset from a situational difficulty and is showing state anxiety which is being measured by the A scale.

GENERAL INFORMATION

1. Scale 7 consists of 48 items having to do with anxiety and dread, low self-confidence, undue sensitivity, and moodiness (Carson, 1969; Dahlstrom et al., 1972).

2. This scale shows general characterological anxiety. Variations in the anxiety depend upon what other scale is elevated along with **7**.

   a. For example, when scale **2** is elevated with scale **7**, depression and indecisiveness are associated with the worries and anxieties.
   b. When scale **8** is the second member of the high pair, confusion and disorganized thinking appear with the anxiety.

3. Scale **7** may be indicating high level intellectualizing as a defense rather than compulsivity (Caldwell, 1972).

4. Scales **7** and **8** are highly correlated (+ .78) (Lough & Green, 1950), but diagnosis and prognosis depend upon their relative heights.

   a. When scale **7** is higher than scale **8**, regardless of the height of scale **8**, the person is still trying to fight his or her problem and is using defenses somewhat effectively (Carson, 1969).
   b. When both scales are elevated above 75 and scale **8** is higher, the problem is likely to be more severe because the person is not fighting the problem as much as when the scale **7** is higher (Carson, 1969).

5. Test-retest reliabilities are high, indicating this scale does not fluctuate drastically over time (Dahlstrom & Welsh, 1960).

6. Under a "fake good" set ("try to look as healthy as possible on this test"), scale **7** was one of the scales to change the most. Scores tended to decrease in elevation (Latta, 1968).

HIGH SCORES

Moderate Elevations (T = 60 thru 70)

1. Kunce and Anderson (1976) have hypothesized that when this scale is in the moderate range [and there are no other Clinical scales above 70 T score points except perhaps the **5** scale for men], scale **7** may measure the ability to organize and to be punctual, decisive, and methodical.

2. This elevation tends to characterize students who are less satisfied with their college majors (Norman & Redlow, 1952).

3. Both over and under achievers tend to have scale 7 at this level (Jensen, 1958; McKenzie, 1964).

   a. Overachievers have scales 4 and 7 high.
   b. Underachievers have scales 2, 5 (male), and 7 high.

4. This elevation tends to characterize art students (Spiaggia, 1950).

Marked Elevations (T = 70 or Above)

1. Single peaks on scale 7 are not particularly frequent; elevations for this scale tend to occur with elevations in other scales (Dahlstrom et al., 1972).

2. People with an elevation in this range on the 7 scale tend to be worried, tense, indecisive, and unable to concentrate (Carson, 1969).

3. They tend to have a low threshold for anxiety and characteristically over-react with anxiety to any new situation.

4. They tend not to change much. The basic personality pattern is difficult to change, but insight and relief from general stress may lead to improved adjustment (Hathaway & McKinley, 1951). It is my experience that even with counseling the elevation usually remains in the 60 thru 70 range.

5. Individuals having marked elevations on this scale almost always exhibit extreme obsessionalism. That is, they go over the same thoughts again and again.

   However, some compulsive people have no elevation on this scale, presumably because their compulsivity is working for them and wards off any feelings of insecurity and concern about their own worth (Carson, 1969).

6. The following groups tend to score high on this scale:

   a. Male mental health clients (Apostal, 1971). (Women mental health clients tend to be in the 60 to 70 range.)

7   144

b. Amphetamine users (Ellinwood, 1967).

c. Homosexuals (Manosevitz, 1970).

d. College students who later receive personal adjustment counseling (Cooke & Kiesler, 1967).

7. College counselees with this elevation tend to be characterized by obsessive-compulsive ruminations and introspection (Dahlstrom et al., 1972; Mello & Guthrie, 1958).

a. The problems with which these students are concerned are usually poor study habits and poor interpersonal relationships.

b. They also are very concerned about religion and morals.

c. These counselees tend to remain, in therapy over an extended period of time.

d. They tend to become more dependent upon the therapist the longer they see him or her, particularly when they are starting to make changes.

e. They tend to improve slowly.

LOW SCORES
(T = 45 or Below)

1. This person tends to be secure, comfortable, and stable (Carson, 1972).

2. Low scores tend to characterize relatively well adjusted and intellectually above average males who are described as success-oriented, persistent, efficient, and capable (Dahlstrom et al., 1972; Gough et al., 1955).

3. In some cases, a person with a low 7 scale score may once have been a worrier (7>70 T score points) but decided this style of life was too painful and so became even less anxious than people in general.

COMBINATIONS

All scales in the combinations are at a T score of 70 or above and are listed in order from the highest to the lowest peaks. The scales in the combinations must be the highest Clinical scales on the profile.

1-2-3-7   See p. 59.

1-2-7   See p. 60.

1-3-7   See p. 62.

2-1-3-7   See the **2-3-1-(7)** combination, p. 73.

2-3-1-7   See p. 73.

2-4-7   See the **4-7-2** pattern, p. 111.

2-7-3   See p. 77.

2-7-3-1   See p. 77.

2-7-4   See pp. 77-78.

2-7-4-3   See the **2-7-4** pattern, point 2, p. 78.

2-7-4-5̄   See pp. 78-79.

2-7-5-4   See p. 79.

2-7-8   See p. 79.

2-7-8-0   See p. 80.

4-2-7-8   See p. 107.

4-5-7-9   See p. 109.

4-7-2   See p. 111.

6-7-8   See p. 135.

6-7-8-9   See p. 136.

7-1   See the **1-7** combination, p. 63.

7-2

See also the 2-7 combination, p. 75.

1. With the **7-2** profile less depression but more anxiety and agitation is present than with the **2-7** profile (Guthrie, 1949).

7-3   See the 3-7 combination, p. 93.

7-4   See the 4-7 combination, p. 111.

7-8

See also the 8-7 combination, p. 160.

1. People with the **7-8** combination tend to be introverted with worrying, irritability, nervousness, and apathy present.

2. These people are in a great deal of turmoil and are not hesitant to admit to problems. They have feelings of insecurity, inadequacy, and inferiority; and they tend to be indecisive. They may feel inadequate in the traditional sex role (Graham, 1977).

3. If scale **7** is 10 T score points higher than scale **8**, the tendency is to see anxiety and indecisiveness as the predominant features. If scale **8** is higher than scale **7**, the tendency is to see mental confusion as the predominant feature.

4. Long-term counseling is usually necessary.

5. Gynther et al. (1973) have found that psychiatric inpatients with this pattern, **7-8/8-7**, may have bizarre speech. Depersonalization also was present at times.

6. Gilberstadt and Duker (1965) found this **7-8-(2-1-3-4)** pattern in a VA hospital male population. Scales **1**, **2**, **3**, and **4** are elevated above 70 but are not necessarily the next highest scales after **7** and **8**. A man with this profile tended to be shy, fearful, feel inadequate, and have difficulty concentrating. Gilberstadt and Duker's book should be consulted for further information concerning this profile.

7-9

1. A person with a 7-9 combination tends to present many unconnected thoughts and talks compulsively about them.

2. These people may alternate between grandiosity and self-condemnation (Hovey & Lewis, 1967).

7-0

1. Social problems are found in college students with the 7 and 0 scales as the two highest points in a profile (Drake & Oetting, 1959).

   a. These students tend to be non-verbal and lack confidence and social skills.
   b. College counselors rate these clients as "shy."
   c. They also are tense, confused, worry a great deal, and suffer from insomnia.

8-2-4-7   See the **8-2-4** combination, point 2, p. 157.

8-4-7-1   See p. 158.

8-4-7-9   See p. 159.

8-6-7-2   See the **8-6** combination, point 6, p. 159.

8-7-2   See p. 161.

8-7-4-1   See p. 161.

8-7-0   See p. 161.

SUMMARY OF 7 SCALE INTERPRETATIONS*

T Score	Interpretations

45 or below These people are non-worriers and may be secure with themselves and quite stable emotionally. They may appear to be somewhat lazy and non-task oriented.

45 thru 60 The majority of people score in this range.

60 thru 70 If no Clinical scales are above 70 T score points, except perhaps scale 5 for men, people in this range generally are punctual in fulfilling obligations or worry if they are not punctual. They usually prefer to get things done ahead of time. They tend to be seen as conscientious workers. They usually do not see themselves as anxious.

70 or above At this level, some agitation may develop. The person tends to become more overly anxious and fidgety. A fear of failure may become prominent. As this scale elevates, the person may become less productive because of his or her worrying.

*Where T scores are listed in two categories (i.e., 45 or below and 45 thru 60) and a score is obtained that is listed for two categories, use whichever interpretation seems to be most appropriate for the individual.

— NOTES —

SCALE 8
(Sc, Schizophrenia Scale)

Scale **8** measures mental confusion; the higher the elevation, the more confused the person is. At the lower elevations (60 thru 70), scale **8** may mean different thinking of one kind or another, especially in college counseling clients. We have found avant-garde or highly creative people sometimes scoring in this range. They tend to think differently than people usually do, and thus they have a moderately elevated **8** scale; however, they do not think so differently that they are out of touch with people.

When scale **8** is between 70 and 80, usually difficulties appear in the client's logic so that it does not hold together well over a period of time. The counselor may find that the client seemingly makes sense for short periods of time during the counseling session but does not when the total session is analyzed.

With a T above 80, the client may start using terms in an idiosyncratic manner. The person can deteriorate to a point where the meaning of words is not the same for him or her as for the rest of the world. This results in much confused communication between the client and other persons. Besides confused communication, this scale also may reflect confusion in perceiving people and situations. As a consequence, the person with a scale **8** elevated above a T of 80 usually has poor judgment and may get into difficulty because of it.

Elevations on the **8** scale may be the result of a chronic disorientation or a temporary disorientation. The prognosis obviously is better when the elevation is because of a temporary disorientation, usually the result of situational pressures. Since the person has not been confused in the past, usually with some therapy and a lessening of the stress, the person returns to a non-confused state. On the other hand, chronic disorientation is much harder to change. The person who has had it for a long period of time must learn an entirely new way of thinking in order to get rid of the confusion.

Elevations on scale **8** above 100 usually are due to situational stress rather than chronic disorientation. I have found that people with identity crises ("Who am I, what am I?") frequently score in this range. I also have found that warm, supportive, somewhat directive counseling is the best approach to use until the confusion ends. The client usually cannot take nondirective counseling very well because it is too ambiguous. As a matter of fact, for most clients with scale **8** elevations above 70, I have found the more directive and less ambiguous types of therapy to be the most helpful. They provide some direction out of the confusion the person is experiencing.

Persons with low scale **8** scores (45 or below) tend to see themselves as pragmatic realists with little interest in contemplation, theory, and/or philosophy. These people may have difficulty letting their minds imagine possibilities. They also tend to have difficulty with persons who are unable to perceive life as they do.

When this scale is elevated with scale **0** (social introversion), the problems with the confusion shown in the **8** scale elevation tend to become greater because of the person's isolation from others. These two scales frequently are elevated together, because the confusion the person is feeling tends to foster withdrawal from others, which increases the confusion because of a lack of contact with others, which leads to more isolation, and so forth.

GENERAL INFORMATION

1. Scale **8** consists of 78 items dealing with social alienation, peculiar perceptions, complaints of family alienation, and difficulties in concentration and impulse control (Carson, 1969; Dahlstrom et al., 1972).

2. This scale indicates a person's distortion of the world. He or she perceives things differently from others, and often reacts to things in unusual ways.

3. The higher the score is on the **8** scale, the more shared verbal symbolism is lost and the odder and more disorganized thinking becomes.

A low **0** scale appears to have some controlling effect on this disorganized thinking.

4. The score may be elevated by anxiety, homosexual panic, identity crisis, or sudden personal dislocation such as divorce or culture shock.

5. Test-retest reliabilities are high. This scale tends to remain stable over time, except when people receive psychological help or when the elevations are due to situations identified in point 4 (Dahlstrom & Welsh, 1960).

6. Scales **7** and **8** are highly correlated (+.78) (Lough & Green, 1950), but diagnosis and prognosis depend upon their relative heights.

   a. When scale **7** is higher than scale **8** regardless of the height of scale **8**, the person is still trying to fight his or her problems and is using defenses somewhat effectively (Carson, 1969).
   b. When both scales are elevated above 75 and scale **8** is higher, the problem is likely to be more severe because the person is not fighting the problem as much as when the **7** scale is higher (Carson, 1969).

7. Blacks tend to have the **8** scale elevated (Costello & Tiffany, 1972; Gynther et al., 1971; Hokanson & Calden, 1960).

8. Art students tend to have higher scale **8** scores than do non-art students (Spiaggia, 1950).

HIGH SCORES

Moderate Elevations (T = 60 thru 70)

1. Kunce and Anderson (1976) have hypothesized that when this scale is in the moderate range [and there are no other Clinical scales above 70 T score points except perhaps the **5** scale for men], it may measure the ability to think divergently and act creatively.

2. Some college students with this elevation may be highly creative or avant-garde.

3. This elevation may characterize relatively well adjusted college males who have internal conflicts and are at odds with themselves (Gough et al., 1955).

4. Academic nonachievers are significantly higher than academic achievers on this scale (Jensen, 1958).

5. Students on probation tend to get elevations on scale **8** (Carkhuff et al., 1965; Kahn & Singer, 1949).

6. A moderate elevation on scale **8** tends to indicate a poor prognosis for business administration majors (Kahn & Singer, 1949).

7. Soft drug users tend to have an elevated scale **8** (McAree, Steffenhagen, Zheuttin, 1969).

8. Homosexuals tend to score higher on this scale than heterosexuals (Manosevitz, 1970).

Marked Elevations (T = 70 or Above)

1. People with a T score above 70 on the **8** scale tend to feel alienated and remote from their general social environment (Carson, 1969).

2. They may have questions about their identity (Carson, 1969).

3. In the lower part of this range, people may appear to be in contact with reality, but others usually have difficulty following their logic (Carson, 1969).

4. They may feel they are lacking something which is fundamental to relating successfully to others (Carson, 1969).

5. Patients who are clinically diagnosed as schizophrenic usually get T scores in the 80 thru 90 range (Carson, 1969). Above this T score range, people do not seem to be psychotic, but rather severely neurotic or under acute stress.

8

6. Adolescents frequently score in this 70 or above range. If they are intelligent, the high **8** score may indicate creative thinking. If they have low intelligence, the high **8** score may indicate poor school performance (Good & Brantner, 1974).

7. These elevations may indicate people who are confused, vague in goals, lacking in knowledge or information, and/or lacking in academic motivation.

8. College counselees with scale **8** peaks present problems with peer relationships and people's acceptance of them. Sexual pre-occupation is frequent along with sexual confusion and bizarre fantasies (Mello & Guthrie, 1958).

   a. They tend to persist in treatment even though their response to treatment is quite variable.
   b. They do not have the psychotic features seen in older people with high **8** scales.

9. High school counselors should be aware that a male high school student with a high **8** scale could be a future dropout, even if bright (Hathaway, Reynolds, Monachesi, 1969).

10. Terminators in youth counseling had significantly higher scale **8** scores than continuers in counseling (Horton & Kriauciunas, 1970).

11. Amphetamine users have high scale **8** scores (Ellinwood, 1967).

LOW SCORES
(T = 45 or Below)

1. People with a score of 45 or below on the **8** scale may appear unimaginative, rigid, non-creative, or restrained (Hovey & Lewis, 1967).

2. A score in this range tends to typify mechanical engineering students (Blum, 1947).

COMBINATIONS

All scales in the combinations are at a T score of 70 or above and are listed in order from the highest to the lowest peaks. The scales in the combinations must be the highest Clinical scales on the profile.

1-2-8   See p. 60.

1-3-8   See pp. 62-63.

1-3-8-2   See the **1-3-8** pattern, point 4, p. 63.

2-4-8   See p. 75.

2-4-8-9   See p. 75.

2-7-8   See p. 79.

2-7-8-0   See p. 80.

2-8-1-3   See p. 81.

4-2-7-8   See p. 107.

4-6-8   See p. 110.

4-8-F   See p. 113.

4-8-2   See the **8-2-4** combination, p. 157.

4-8-9   See pp. 113-114.

4-8-9-2   See the **4-8-9** combination, point 4, p. 114.

5-8-9   See p. 127.

6-7-8   See p. 135.

6-7-8-9   See p. 136.

6-8-9   See p. 137.

8-F   See the F-8 combination, p. 30.

8-1   See the 1-8 combination, pp. 63-64.

8-1-2-3

1. Gilberstadt and Duker (1965) found the **8-1-2-3-(7-4-6-0)** pattern in a VA hospital male population. Scales **7, 4, 6,** and **0** are elevated above 70, but they are not necessarily the next highest scales after scales **8, 1, 2,** and **3**. A man with this profile typically was inadequate in all areas of his life. He usually had confused thinking and flat affect. Gilberstadt and Duker's book should be consulted for further information concerning this profile.

8-2

See also the **2-8** combination, pp. 80-81, especially point 6.

1. Marks et al. (1974) found this **2-8/8-2** pattern in a university hospital and outpatient clinic. People with this pattern were usually anxious, depressed, and tearful. They tended to keep people at a distance and were afraid of emotional involvement. They tended to fear loss of control and reported periods of dizziness or forgetfulness. Marks' book should be consulted for further information concerning this profile.

8-2-1-3   See the **2-8-1-3** combination, p. 81.

8-2-4

1. Marks et al. (1974) found this **4-8-2/8-4-2/8-2-4** pattern in a university hospital and outpatient clinic. A person with this profile tended to be distrustful of others, keeping them at a distance. He or she usually was described as depressed, tense, irritable, and hostile. Marks' book should be consulted for further information concerning this profile.

2. Gilberstadt and Duker (1965) also found an **8-2-4-(7)** pattern in a VA hospital male population. Scale **7** is elevated, but it is not necessarily the next highest scale after **8, 2,** and **4**. They found that a person with this profile was immature and had confused and hostile thinking. He tended to be irritable, tense, and restless. Gilberstadt and Duker's book should be consulted for further information concerning this pattern.

8-2-4-7   See the **8-2-4** combination, point 2, p. 157.

8-3

See also the **3-8** combination, pp. 93-94.

1. Marks et al. (1974) found the **8-3/3-8** pattern in a university and outpatient clinic. The pattern usually was for a woman who was having difficulties thinking and concentrating. She usually was seen by others as apathetic, immature, and dependent. Marks' book should be consulted for further information concerning this profile.

8-4

See also the **4-8** combination, pp. 111-113.

1. These people tend to be high school dropouts (Hathaway et al., 1969).

2. This profile is the most frequent one for LSD users who have had bad trips. LSD users who have not had bad trips tend to have the **4-8** combination (Ungerleider, Fisher, Fuller, Caldwell, 1968).

   This is the fourth most frequent two-point combination in a group of LSD users (9% LSD users as compared with 2% non-LSD users) (Smart & Jones, 1970).

8-4-2   See the **8-2-4** combination, point 1, p. 157.

8-4-6

1. In a group of juvenile delinquents, this profile characterized runaway delinquents as compared to unsocialized aggressive delinquents (**8-4-7-9** pattern) and socialized delinquents (**4-8/8-4** pattern) (Tsubouchi & Jenkins, 1969).

8-4-7-1

1. This is the mean profile found in a group of amphetamine users who became psychotic (Ellinwood, 1967).

8-4-7-9

1. In a group of juvenile delinquents, this profile characterized aggressive delinquents as compared to socialized delinquents (4-8/8-4 pattern) and runaway delinquents (8-4-6 pattern) (Tsubouchi & Jenkins, 1969).

8-6

See also the 6-8 combination, pp. 136-137.

1. A person with this pattern is usually in a panic and has diffused thinking. The person tends to break down when supports are gone (Caldwell, 1972).

2. Often these people do not marry, but if they do marry, they tend to show poor judgment in mate selection (Caldwell, 1972).

3. Women often have a little girl quality about them and look younger than they really are (Caldwell, 1972).

4. In a psychiatric hospital, this may be the profile of an assaultive person (Caldwell, 1972).

5. Marks et al. (1974) found this 8-6/6-8 pattern in a university hospital and outpatient clinic. They found this pattern primarily for females who were having unconventional, delusional thoughts. These women also were suspicious. Marks' book should be consulted for further information concerning this profile.

6. Gilberstadt and Duker (1965) found the 8-6-(7-2) pattern in a VA hospital male population. Scales 7 and 2 are elevated but are not necessarily the next highest scales after scales 8 and 6. A man with this pattern tended to have thinking disturbances, such as confusion and poor concentration. He tended to be shy and withdrawn. Gilberstadt and Duker's book should be consulted for further information concerning this profile.

7. This pattern tends to characterize Blacks (Costello & Tiffany, 1972).

8-6-4-9-F

1. In a Mexican prison, thirty women were found with this profile pattern. All were convicted of homocide, nine of them were self-made widows (Palau, 1972).

8-6-7-2   See the **8-6** combination, point 6, p. 159.

8-7

See also the **7-8** combination, p. 147.

1. Panic plus withdrawal may be present for a person with the **8-7** pattern (Caldwell, 1972).

2. The **8-7** pattern may indicate long-standing feelings of inadequacy, inferiority, and insecurity (Halbower, 1955). Very frequently the person feels himself/herself to be the inferior member of the family (Caldwell, 1972).

3. These people tend to be passive-dependent (Halbower, 1955).

4. Prognosis for therapy is poor, because these people do not form stable, mature, or warm relationships easily. They usually do not integrate what they learn or profit from their own experiences (Halbower, 1955).

5. This profile indicates more serious problems than a **7-8** profile does. There may have been previous mental hospitalization and/or therapy.

6. With a high **F** scale and an **8-7** pattern, the person may feel unreal (Caldwell, 1972).

7. With a high **0** scale and an **8-7** pattern, social withdrawal may exist (Caldwell, 1972).

8. With a low **0** scale and an **8-7** pattern, inappropriate behavior may exist (Caldwell, 1972).

8-7-2

1. Marks et al. (1974) found this **2-7-8/8-7-2** pattern in a university hospital and outpatient clinic. A person with this pattern typically was described as tense, anxious, and depressed with confused thinking and much self-doubt. Marks' book should be consulted for further information concerning this pattern.

8-7-4-1

1. This profile was found in a group of amphetamine users who did not become psychotic (Ellinwood, 1967).

8-7-0

See also the **8-7** combination, point 7, p. 160.

1. Inappropriate behavior is seen with this pattern.

8-9

See also the **9-8** combination, p. 172.

1. This is usually a serious pattern, indicating some severe psychological disturbances (Carson, 1969).

2. The person may be confused, disoriented, overly verbal, and under tremendous pressure (Caldwell, 1972).

3. People with this pattern are hyperactive and emotionally labile. They may have a high need to achieve but perform poorly. They tend to be uncomfortable in heterosexual relationships and poor sexual adjustment is common (Graham, 1977).

4. Psychiatric patients with the **8-9/9-8** pattern are more likely to have hostile-paranoid excitement than patients in general. They also have frequent ratings for flight of ideas, loud voice, labile mood, and unrealistic hostility. Onset of this behavior frequently is rapid however there may have been behavior problems in school. For the **8-9** profile increased speech and activity typically are found. With the **9-8** profile, the patient may not know why he or she is hospitalized (Altman et al., 1973).

5. These people's problems may center around lack of achievement or impending failure (Caldwell, 1972).

6. This pattern may indicate an identity crisis in which the person does not know who or what he or she is (Caldwell, 1972).

   a. Onset of the crisis is usually sudden.
   b. The crisis does not usually last long when the person receives counseling.

7. Other scales usually are elevated with this pattern.

8. Therapy is difficult with these people, because they have a hard time settling down to anything long enough to deal with it (Carson, 1969).

9. Marks et al. (1974) found this **8-9/9-8** pattern in a university hospital and outpatient clinic. They found the pattern usually for females who were characterized by delusional thinking, rumination, anxiety, and agitation. Marks' book should be consulted for further information concerning this profile.

10. Gilberstadt and Duker (1965) found this **8-9** pattern in a VA hospital male population. A person with this profile tended to be hyperactive and to have confused thinking. He also tended to be tense and suspicious. Gilberstadt and Duker's book should be consulted for further information concerning this profile.

11. This is a common profile for adolescents on drugs (Caldwell, 1972).

12. Lack of academic motivation is found with this profile, especially if scale **0** is low (Drake, 1962; Drake & Oetting, 1957).

8-9-6-F

1. This pattern was found in a group of rural, isolated, Black males (Gynther, Fowler & Erdberg, 1971).

8-0

See also the **0-8** combination, p. 180.

1. College counselees with this pattern tend to be nervous and non-

8

verbal as well as introverted. They tend to be poor communicators in counseling sessions (Drake & Oetting, 1959).

9-8-4   See p. 173.

SUMMARY OF 8 SCALE INTERPRETATIONS*

T Score	Interpretations

45 or below These people tend to see themselves as realists and usually are not interested in contemplation, theory, or philosophy. They may be unimaginative.

45 thru 60 The majority of people score in this range.

60 thru 70 Persons with scores in this range may think somewhat differently than other people. These may be avant-garde or highly creative people.

70 thru 80 At this level, difficulties in logical thinking may develop. To follow the person's train of thought over a period of time may be difficult.

80 thru 100 People may start using language in unusual ways at this level. Communication usually becomes quite confused. The person also may have trouble perceiving people and situations accurately and thus may have poor judgment.

100 or above People at this level usually are suffering from some kind of identity crisis, not knowing who or what they are. This elevation is usually the result of situational stress.

*Where T scores are listed in two categories (i.e., 45 or below and 45 thru 60) and a score is obtained that is listed for two categories, use whichever interpretation seems to be most appropriate for the individual.

SCALE 9
(Ma, Hypomania Scale)

Scale **9** measures psychic energy. That is, the higher the elevation, the more a person is actively thinking, and the more he or she feels compelled to act. Another element which seems to occur with an elevation on this scale is an increase in diversity and multiplicity of thoughts. As with some of the other scales, elevations must be interpreted in light of the population involved.

In college populations, particularly with graduate school students, elevations of 60 thru 70 are typical and indicate mental activity, probably with accompanying physical energy. As the scale increases to over 70, a concomitant increase in psychic energy often presents difficulties. The person may begin to "spin his wheels," become over involved and over committed, and get fewer things done. A good phrase for a person with a score over 80 is "running around like a chicken with its head cut off."

Scale **9** is one of the most common elevations on the MMPI, especially with college populations. This scale and scale **5** for men are the most frequent peaks on college profiles.

Low scale **9** scores with a college population are unusual, especially with graduate students. When this occurs, several interpretations might be made.

1. If these people are succeeding in college with little difficulty and scale **2** is not elevated, they may be directing all their available energy into academic pursuits. In other words, they are succeeding in college even with low energy because they have directed what energy they have into academic activities.

2. If these people are succeeding in college with little difficulty and scale 2 is near 60, they could have been tired when they took the inventory, or they could be at the bottom of a mood swing (such as a post-exam letdown). In this instance, these people's usual scale scores are a 9 scale near 60 and a 2 scale near 45.

3. If these people are not succeeding in college, they probably have limited energy available which they are either channeling into a single non-academic pursuit such as a job, emotional concerns, or social activities, or they are dissipating their limited energy into too many areas.

The typical level on scale 9 for non-college educated people is near 50, which is adequate for usual occupational and recreational pursuits. As the scale increases to 60, a need for activity is manifested. If this need for activity is not fulfilled (particularly on the job), an agitation may set in with a mild dissatisfaction about life in general. Where opportunities for the release of this energy occur, no difficulty usually is noted. As the elevation increases over 70, usually not enough opportunity exists to release all of the energy. As a result, fantasy may become a part of the person's life, while the activity also increases (usually not directed too wisely). If people with scale 9 scores over 70 also have scale 2 scores below 45, they may report becoming depressed if they cannot be highly active.

A low scale 9 score (40 or below) in a non-college population usually evidences itself in lethargy. The person tends to feel chronically tired, has difficulty getting out of bed, and may have poor job performance.

For both college and non-college populations, an elevation on the 9 scale tends to energize the behavior or problems seen in elevations on the other Clinical scales. For example, if scale 4 also is elevated with scale 9, the fighting out of scale 4 usually is accentuated and tends to become overt behavior rather than covert thinking about fighting out.

GENERAL INFORMATION

1. The 49 items on this scale measure self-centeredness, grandiosity, and irritability (Carson, 1969).

9

2. This is a psychic energy scale. When other scales are elevated, they tell the direction in which the energy will be expended. For example, a high 4-9 combination may mean the person is overtly fighting someone or something, whereas a high 2-9 combination may mean the person is an agitated depressive.

3. Up to a T score of 70, the person is probably active, energetic, and exuberant.

4. Above a T of 70, the person may be overactive, have maladaptive hyperactivity, be irritable, and/or have insufficient restraints on his or her behavior.

5. High scores on scale 9 probably do not indicate classic textbook hypomanics, because classic hypomanics will not sit still long enough to take the MMPI (Carson, 1972).

6. Scale 9 is positively related to scales 4 and 6 (Hathaway & McKinley, 1951; McKinley & Hathaway, 1944).

7. Test-retest reliabilities are rather low (Dahlstrom & Welsh, 1960).

8. Education is positively correlated with scale 9.

9. The suggestion has been made by Heilbrun (1963) that the K scale weightings be eliminated from scale 9 for college students (as well as from scales 1 and 4) in order to detect more accurately maladjustment.

10. In a study of college students, the 9 scale was positively correlated (.35) with other directedness rather than innerdirectedness as had been hypothesized (Rapfogel & Armentrout, 1972).

11. Blacks tend to have higher scores on scale 9 than whites (Costello & Tiffany, 1972; Gynther et al., 1971; Hokanson & Calden, 1960; McDonald & Gynther, 1963; Mitler et al., 1961).

12. An extroversion factor in the MMPI marked by a moderate positive loading on scale 9, a high negative loading on scale 0, and a moderate negative loading on scale 2 may exist (Hundleby & Connor, 1968).

HIGH SCORES

Moderate Elevations (T = 60 thru 70)

1. A person with a moderate elevation tends to be gregarious (Carson, 1969).

2. Kunce and Anderson (1976) have hypothesized that when this scale is in the moderate range [and there are no other Clinical scales above 70 T score points except perhaps the 5 scale for men], it may measure zestfulness and enthusiasm.

3. The following groups of people tend to have moderate elevations:

    a. Terminators in youth counseling (as opposed to continuers) (Horton & Kriauciumas, 1970).
    b. College smokers (Evans et al., 1967).
    c. Art students (Spiaggia, 1950).
    d. High school dropouts (Hathaway et al., 1969).

4. If the person with a **9** scale at this level is on a boring job (such as an assembly line), he or she may fantasize a lot.

5. Scale **9** tends to be one of the two most frequent high points for college students. The other is scale **5** for college males.

6. A moderate elevation on the **9** scale (T = 60 thru 70) usually is desirable for college students, particularly graduate students, indicating energy enough to carry projects through.

7. Under ideal self-instruction ("take this test trying to look as good as possible"), scale **9** tends to be the high point on the MMPI clinical profile and to be at a moderate elevation (Gloye & Zimmerman, 1967; Grayson & Olinger, 1957; Hiner et al., 1969; Lanyon, 1967).

Marked Elevations (T = 70 or Above)

1. As scale **9** goes up, people tend to become increasingly involved in activities but less efficient in what they are doing. They may start "spinning their wheels."

2. Three features characterize a high scorer on this scale—over-activity, emotional excitement, and flight of ideas.

3. The mood of the person with a marked elevation on this scale may be good-humored euphoria, but on occasion he or she can become irritable with outbursts of temper (Dahlstrom et al., 1972).

4. The following groups of people tend to have marked elevations on scale **9**:

   a. Juvenile delinquents (in conjunction with a high **4** scale) (Stone & Rowley, 1963).
   b. Highly aggressive boys (not necessarily labeled as delinquent) (Butcher, 1965).
   c. College underachievers (Drake, 1962; Drake & Oetting, 1959; Jensen, 1958; Yeomans & Lundlin, 1957).
   d. College dropouts (Barger & Hall, 1964).
   e. College counselees who are considered by their counselors to be aggressive or opinionated (Drake, 1954).

5. Gilberstadt and Duker (1965) found this pattern, a spike **9**, in a VA hospital male population. The men with only scale **9** elevated were hyperactive and talkative people who were involved in many projects. They may have had previous attacks of depression. Gilberstadt and Duker's book should be consulted for further information concerning this profile.

6. When scale **9** is the peak score in college counselees, other traits the person has are expressed in a more energetic fashion than when the **9** scale is low (Drake, 1956).

7. A high **9** and low **0** (45 or below) combination is called the "socializer" pattern, whereas a high **0** and low **9** combination is called the "nonsocializer" pattern (Good & Brantner, 1974).

LOW SCORES
(T = 45 or Below)

1. People with low scale **9** scores tend to have low energy and a low activity level. They are difficult to motivate and may be apathetic.

2. When this scale is near a T of 45, it may indicate that the person is tired or temporarily ill (for example, has a cold).

3. At the lowest levels of this scale, people may be depressed, even if scale 2 is not elevated (Carson, 1969).

4. Male college counseless with scale 9 at a low level are perceived as dependent and wanting reassurance. Women counseless are perceived as shy (Drake & Oetting, 1959).

COMBINATIONS

All scales in these combinations are at a T score of 70 or above and are listed in order from the highest to the lowest peaks. The scales in the combinations must be the highest Clinical scales on the profile.

1-3-9   See p. 63.

2-4-8-9   See p. 75.

4-5-7-9   See p. 109.

4-5-9   See p. 109.

4-6-9   See p. 111.

4-8-9   See pp. 113-114.

4-8-9-2   See the **4-8-9** combination, point 4, p. 114.

5-8-9   See p. 127.

6-7-8-9   See p. 136.

6-8-9   See p. 137.

8-4-7-9   See p. 159.

8-6-4-9-F See p. 160.

8-9-6-F   See p. 162.

9

9-F   See the F-9 combination, p. 30.

9-K   See the K-9 combination, p. 42.

9-1

See also the 1-9 combination, p. 64.

1. Patients with the 9-1 combination who were seen by a physician were all in acute distress. They seldom were hypomanic; but they were tense, restless, and ambitious. They were frustrated by their failure to reach their high levels of aspiration. Physical complaints for men centered around the gastrointestinal tract and headaches (Guthrie, 1949).

9-2

See also the 2-9 combination, p. 82.

1. The 9-2 combination tends to typify people for whom activity is no longer effective in keeping off their depression. These people may be seen as agitated depressives (Dahlstrom et al., 1972).

2. Activity may alternate with fatigue (Caldwell, 1972).

3. These people may set it up so they will fail when they feel they cannot succeed (Caldwell, 1972).

4. This combination may be an indication of organic brain damage (Dahlstrom et al., 1972; Hathaway & Meehl, 1951; Hovey & Lewis, 1967).

9-3   See the 3-9 combination, p. 94.

9-4

See also the 4-9 combination, pp. 114-115.

1. Patients seen by a physician with the 9-4 pattern showed the general effects of tension and fatigue. These effects followed periods of great overactivity (Guthrie, 1949).

171   *9*

a. These patients showed poor family adjustment and had problems centering around their sexual adjustments.

b. They did not stay in treatment long; therefore, they could only be treated superficially.

2. The **9-4** combination is the most common one found in entering college freshmen (9 percent of the men's profiles and 8 percent of the women's) (Fowler & Coyle, 1969).

9-5 See the 5-9 combination, p. 127.

9-6

See also the **6-9** combination, pp. 137-138.

1. Marks, et al. (1974) found the **9-6/6-9** pattern in a university hospital and outpatient clinic. The profile primarily was found in females who were agitated, tense, excitable, suspicious, and hostile. Marks' book should be consulted for further information concerning this profile.

9-7 See the 7-9 combination, p. 148.

9-8

See also the **8-9** combination, p. 161.

1. The **9-8** pattern is more likely found in mental hospital populations than in non-hospitalized populations. It indicates more serious problems than the **9-4** combination (Dahlstrom et al., 1972; Guthrie, 1949; Hathaway & Meehl, 1951).

The **F** scale elevation tends to vary with the severity of these people's condition. The higher the **F** scale with the **9-8** pattern the more serious the condition tends to be (Guthrie, 1949).

2. Marks et al. (1974) found the **8-9/9-8** pattern in a university hospital and outpatient clinic. The pattern occurred mostly with women characterized by delusional thinking, ruminations, anxiety, and agitation. Marks' book should be consulted for further information concerning this profile.

3. This is the most frequent pattern found with LSD users (21 percent of the cases). The second most frequent pattern (17 percent) is **9-4** (Smart & Jones, 1970).

9-8-4

1. This pattern is found frequently in LSD users (Smart & Jones, 1970).

9-0

1. In college counselees, when the **9-0** pattern occurred the behavior shown by the **0** scale seemed to dominate in that the people were socially shy and withdrawn (Drake & Oetting, 1959).

SUMMARY OF 9 SCALE INTERPRETATIONS*

T Score	Interpretations

45 or below   Persons may have scores in this range of scale **9** for two reasons. One, they may have been tired when they took the test; or two, they may have a limited amount of energy.

45 thru 60   This range of scores is typical and indicates an average amount of energy. College students tend to score in the upper range of these scores from 55 to 60.

60 thru 70   Persons with these scores tend to be quite active and have many projects which they usually complete. This range is typical for graduate students.

70 or above   People in this range seem to have an excess of energy. They may take on more projects than they can complete. They may fantasize a lot if they cannot keep busy. With a low **2** scale, people may report that if they cannot keep busy they tend to become depressed.

*Where T scores are listed in two categories (i.e., 45 or below and 45 thru 60) and a score is obtained that is listed for two categories, use whichever interpretation seems to be most appropriate for the individual.

SCALE 0
(Si or Sie, Social Introversion Scale)

Scale **0** measures a person's preference for being alone (high **0**) or being with others (low **0**). The difficulty in working with this scale is in avoiding the value judgments implied in the scale's title (social introversion). I have found it best not to use the scale name when interpreting the MMPI to clients because the tendency in our culture is to feel that extroversion is good, whereas introversion is bad. This is not true, of course. Each type of social adjustment has its advantages and disadvantages, depending upon the context in which it is operating.

Persons with scale **0** elevated to between 60 and 70 prefer to be by themselves or with a few select friends. This fact usually does not mean that they cannot interact with others; it only means that this is not their preference. One advantage of this preference in college is that people with it are able to isolate themselves from others so that assignments, studying, and reading can be done. One disadvantage of **0** scores between 60 and 70 for college students is that people with these scores tend not to be socially adept. Because they prefer to be by themselves, they tend not to be at ease with people and may not know current music or slang. One procedure I have found helpful in working with people having scale **0** in this range is to have them join one activity of their choice, so they can keep social ties, while not overwhelming them with people. The **0** scale may elevate to between 60 and 70 as a person becomes older.

A real difficulty with an elevated scale **0** in conjunction with an elevated scale **8** is that these two scales tend to accentuate each other. As people become confused (high **8**), they also tend to isolate themselves. And, as they become more isolated, they tend to become more confused because they lack contact with others.

Persons with scale 0 scores above 70 tend to be people who are withdrawing from others, not because of an inherently introverted nature, but because they either have been hurt in some way or the problems indicated by other Clinical scale elevations are overwhelming them and consequently they are isolating themselves. In these situations, the 0 scale accentuates the problems seen in the other clinical elevations because the person withdraws from people who might be helpful. People with 0 scale scores above 70 usually do not enter counseling because of their aversion to being with others. If they do become clients, it is because their problems are overwhelming them.

People with low scale 0 scores (45 or below) prefer to be with people as opposed to being alone. They tend to be socially adept and involved with people. An advantage of the low 0 score for these people is that they remain in touch with the world when there is psychological difficulty. This level of the 0 scale particularly is helpful when people have an elevated scale 8 and are confused. The primary disadvantage for persons with this level of the 0 scale is that they may have difficulty being alone. Thus, in college, they usually would rather play bridge or go to a party than study by themselves. These people also tend to have difficulty in occupations where they are not involved with people.

I find most college students (non-clients) scoring in the low range on the 0 scale, with the average for this group being near 45.

An interesting use of the 0 scale is to note its location for each of the persons in marital counseling. Good and Brantner (1974) have suggested that the behavior shown on the 0 scale can be an important factor in marital conflict if the couple are 20 or more T scores apart on the 0 scale. When the 0 scale scores are that much apart, one of the couple is more of a socializer than the other; and this may be one cause of their marital difficulty.

GENERAL INFORMATION

1. Scale 0 consists of 70 items concerning uneasiness in social situations, insecurities, worries, and lack of social participation (Dahlstrom et al., 1972).

0

2. The higher the scale, the more the person prefers being by himself or herself; the lower the scale the more the person seeks social contacts.

3. This scale assesses the tendency to withdraw from social contact with others, i.e., introversion. It has a high negative (—.61) correlation with the extroversion scale on the Maudsley Personality Inventory (Hundleby & Connor, 1968).

4. Few people see themselves as introverts. Of those who do, more men than women label themselves as introverts (Lieberman & Walters, 1971).

5. The normal range for this scale is 30 thru 70 T score points (Carson, 1972); however, college students are in the 40 through 45 range.

6. As a high point, scale **0** is most frequently paired with scales **2**, **7**, and **8**.

7. Under ideal-self instructions ("take this test trying to look as good as possible"), the **0** scale score becomes lower (Parsons et al., 1968).

8. Education is negatively correlated with this scale (Thumin, 1969).

9. There may be an extroversion factor in the MMPI marked by a moderate positive loading on scale **9**, a high negative loading on scale **0**, and a moderate negative loading on scale **2** (Hundleby & Connor, 1968).

10. Reliability studies show stability over time for this scale (Dahlstrom et al., 1972).

HIGH SCORES

Moderate Elevations (T = 60 thru 70)

1. A moderate elevation on this scale indicates that an individual feels more comfortable alone or in a small group whose members are well known (Cottle, 1953).

2. Kunce and Anderson (1976) have hypothesized that when this scale is in the moderate range [and there are no other Clinical scales above 70 T score points except perhaps the **5** scale for men], it may measure personal autonomy, self-direction, and perhaps self-actualization.

3. It indicates less participation in activities (Gough, 1949a).

   Girls who participated in fewer than four activities in college scored in the 60 thru 70 range (Drake & Thiede, 1948).

4. College people with this elevation tend to be more introverted than the typical college student, because the median score for college students is near a T of 45.

5. This elevation tends to typify engineers (Blum, 1947).

Marked Elevations (T = 70 or Above)

1. People with marked elevations tend to be withdrawn and anxious around people (Carson, 1969). They also are shy and socially insecure.

2. Other scales when combined with scale **0** often give an indication of the type and seriousness of the social adjustment problems.

   An elevation on this scale tends to suppress the acting out behavior typically seen with high **4** and **9** scale elevations; however, it may enhance the ruminating behavior seen with high **2** and **7** scales, and especially may enhance the ruminating behavior seen with the high **8** scale.

3. A high **0** and low **9** scale combination is called the "non-socializer" pattern, while the high **9** and low **0** combination is called the "socializer" pattern (Good & Brantner, 1974).

LOW SCORES
(T = 45 or Below)

1. Low scores indicate socially extroverted persons who are poised

and confident in social and group situations (Carkhuff et al., 1965; Drasgow & Barnette, 1957).

2. Caldwell (1977) has hypothesized that a low score on this scale may show a liking to be in front of people or a certain amount of exhibitionism.

3. Scores of 45 or below seem to be indicative of an adequate social adjustment even when other Clinical scales are high, particularly scales **2**, **7**, and **8**, which usually are associated with serious problems (Graham, Schroeder, & Lilly, 1971).

4. With women, low scale **0** scores seem to be associated with good social adjustment including parental relationships. With men however the social adjustment does not necessarily mean freedom from parental conflicts (Drake & Oetting, 1959).

5. This elevation seems to be related to social aggressiveness, in some men (Drake & Oetting, 1959).

6. These scores tend to be typical of college students.

   Gulas (1974) found the **0** scale to be the most frequent (39%) low point for a group of college males, N = 609.

7. Low scale **0** scores typify college students who underachieve because of their tendency to be involved in many social activities (Cottle, 1953).

8. Low scores tend to characterize girls who participate in four or more activities in college (Drake & Thiede, 1948).

9. Below a T of 30, persons may show a certain flightiness and superficiality in their relationships. These individuals have well-developed social techniques and many social contacts, but they do not tend to establish relationships of real intimacy.

COMBINATIONS

All scales in these combinations are at a T score of 70 or above and are listed in order from the highest to the lowest peaks. These scales in the combinations must be the highest Clinical scales on the profile.

0

2-7-8-0 See p. 80.

8-7-0 See p. 161.

0-2

See also the **2-0** combination, p. 82.

1. In college counseless, men with a **0-2** combination typically appear unhappy and tense, worry a great deal, and lack effective social skills, particularly with members of the opposite sex (Drake & Oetting, 1959).

2. College women also show the same presenting picture as college men, with the addition of depression, lack of self-confidence, and (when scale **1** is the low point) feelings of physical inferiority (Drake & Oetting, 1959).

0-5 See the **5-0** combination, p. 127.

0-6 See the **6-0** combination, p. 138.

0-7 See the **7-0** combination, p. 148.

0-8

See also the **8-0** combination, p. 162.

1. Counselees with a high **0-8** combination tend to be shy and to have problems communicating with the counselor (Drake & Oetting, 1959).

2. Women counselees with a high **0-8** combination may vacillate between conflicts with mother and conflicts with father (Drake & Oetting, 1959).

3. Women counselees tend to be nonrelaters and have serious problems, especially when scale **5** is the low point of the pattern (Drake & Oetting, 1959).

0-9 See the **9-0** combination, p. 173.

0

SUMMARY OF 0 SCALE INTERPRETATIONS*

T Score	Interpretations
45 or below	A person with a score in this range prefers to be with others and not by himself or herself. The typical range for college students for this scale is between 40 and 45.
45 thru 60	The majority of people score in this range.
60 thru 70	At this level, the person prefers to be alone or with one or two good friends.
70 or above	A score in this range may indicate that the person's problems are causing active withdrawal from others.

*Where T scores are listed in two categories (i.e., 45 or below and 45 thru 60) and a score is obtained that is listed for two categories, use whichever interpretation seems to be most appropriate for the individual.

0

— NOTES —

chapter 4

NEW SCALES

Jane Duckworth and Wayne Anderson

The MMPI originally was developed to include only the Validity and Clinical scales. However, over a period of time, more than 550 experimental scales have been constructed by researchers. Of the more than 550 experimental scales, 11 have been selected by most computer services to be scored as part of their regular profile printouts. These scales, called the New scales, are as follows:

A First Factor or Conscious Anxiety
R Second Factor or Conscious Repression
Es Ego Strength
Lb Low Back Pain
Ca Caudality
Dy Dependency
Do Dominance
Re Social Responsibility
Pr Prejudice
St Social Status
Cn Control

We find these New scales to be tremendously helpful in interpreting the MMPI; however, little information about them has appeared in the research literature. Consequently, this chapter is based primarily upon our own work in various counseling and clinical settings (four university counseling centers, a community mental health center, a psychiatric clinic, and a drug treatment center). The items which comprise each of these New scales are listed in Appendices A and B. If scoring keys for the New scales are desired,

Psychological Assessment Resources, P.O. Box 98, Odessa, FL 33556 has keys for them.

In contrast to the Clinical scales, elevations on the New scales do not necessarily have negative connotations. In some instances, they have positive interpretations. To interpret most accurately these New scales, each one must be dealt with individually, then in combination with other scales, and finally in light of the context in which it occurs. This last factor especially is important. For example, an elevation on scale **A** (which indicates conscious anxiety) may or may not have negative implications. Such an elevation is appropriate if the person is awaiting sentencing for a crime or if his or her mate has just died. Such an elevation may have a negative connotation if the person does not have an outside reason for worry, but instead has much free-floating anxiety. Conversely, a low scale **A** may be positive if the person is well balanced psychologically and is taking the MMPI as part of an experiment; but such a score generally would not be considered appropriate for a person in difficulty with the law. In general, then, these New scales are most accurately interpreted when all the factors noted above are taken into consideration.

We use some of these New scales in combination with each other such as scales **A** and **R**, **Dy** and **Do**, **Re** and **Pr**, and **Es**, **Do**, and **St**. These combinations will be dealth with specifically in the various scale sections.

We are now beginning to work on developing profile configurations for the New scales. The first profile configurations were easy to develop. These were extensions of the traditional all-true, all-false, all-X, all-0 and random response set profiles found in the *MMPI Handbook* (Dahlstrom et al., 1972). These profiles including both the Clinical and New scales are found in the Validity scale section.

We believe we also have isolated two additional profiles for the New scales, one indicating good mental health and the other indicating poor mental health. Good mental health seems to be indicated primarily by elevations (T = 55 or above) on **Es**, **Do**, and **St**, and low scores (T = 50 or below) on **R** and (T = 45 or below) on **A**, **Dy** and **Pr**. The poor mental health profile is indicated primarily by low scores (T = 45 or below) on **Es** and **Do**, and high scores (T = 55 or above) on **A**, **R**, **Dy**, and **Pr**.

As a final note, the New scales not always are considered moderately elevated at 60 or markedly elevated at 70 as are the Clinical scales. What is called high for each scale differs from these conventional classifications. Each scale section must be consulted to find out what is considered elevated for that scale.

We are hoping that our presentations in this chapter will encourage others to start using these New scales in their work, particularly with non-hospitalized populations. We feel much more research needs to be done with them before a truly comprehensive understanding of them can be achieved.

Since the previous paragraphs were written in 1975, we have been expanding our knowledge concerning the New scales. The material on each scale has been revised and enlarged in this second edition to reflect our latest thinking about them.

Appendix C has been added to this edition to show the intercorrelations among the Validity, Clinical, and New scales for two groups of non-psychiatric subjects. The figures reported in the light type are scale intercorrelations for over 5,000 medical patients at the Mayo Clinic (Swenson, Pearson, & Osborne, 1973). Psychiatric patients were excluded from this sample.

The second set of figures, reported in bold type, are intercorrelations for 847 profiles from people in the Muncie, Indiana, area. Many of these profiles came from students in graduate level courses in Counseling Psychology at Ball State University and their friends who took the test to help these students fulfill requirements for a testing course. As far as could be determined, none of the people in this sample was being counseled for psychological problems.

Pertinent intercorrelations for each of the New scales is reported in the chapters on the individual scales. Our hope is that these correlations will help clarify the relationships between the various New scales and the more familiar Validity and Clinical scales.

The research and analysis we have done concerning the New scales during the past four years have further convinced us that these scales are of great use for MMPI interpretations, especially with mentally healthy people.

— NOTES —

A SCALE
(First Factor or Conscious Anxiety Scale)

The **A** scale seems to measure the amount of overt anxiety present when the test was taken. Scores on this scale frequently are elevated on profiles of clients seeking help for personal problems in college counseling centers and in mental health agencies. The higher the **A** score, the more anxiety the person is reporting. A low scale score (T = 45 or below) indicates relative freedom from conscious anxiety. The **A** scale correlates highly with measures of anxiety for medical patients, (.90 with scale **7**, .85 with the **Ca** scale Appendix C) (Swenson et al., 1973).

An individual with a high **A** score is likely to have the following characteristics:

1. self-doubt,

2. difficulty in concentrating,

3. a tendency to worry and brood,

4. lack of energy, and

5. a negative outlook on life generally.

The high **A** scale score with high Clinical scale scores is an indication that the person is hurting enough to be a good therapy risk, unless the situation that provoked the high **A** has changed dramatically since the test taking, thereby lessening the pressure on the client. Clients with low **A** scale scores (45 or below), but with

187

A

many problems indicated on the Clinical scales, are usually poor therapy risks because they are not highly anxious about their problems and/or have learned to live with them even though these problems have not been solved.

People with high **A** scores and high Clinicals may be good therapy risks. First, high **A** scorers tend to be very ready to admit to having psychological problems, and therefore, the Clinical scales may be elevated because of this tendency and not because of having serious problems. Second, because high **A** scorers have much self-doubt, they may be more aware of a need to change their behavior and may be willing to work at doing so. Third, high **A** scorers may be cautious about showing unusual feeling and behavior. Such individuals do not want to be viewed as abnormal, and they may be in less trouble because of their cautious behavior.

In summation, a client who is highly anxious (high Scale **A**) and who generally feels maladjusted (high Clinical scales) is more likely to seek help and work on changing than a client whose answers on the test indicate pathology (high Clinicals) but who does not seem to be overtly anxious about his or her psychological adjustment (low **A** scale).

Scale **A** seems to represent short-term, situational anxiety, whereas scale **7** (the other anxiety scale on the MMPI) seems to represent long-term characterological anxiety, a way of dealing with life by ruminating and worrying a great deal. This rumination and worrying may go on all or most of the time, even when a specific situation about which to worry is not present. High scale **7** people, in general then, tend to be chronic worriers, even when the worry is not immediately necessary.

Scale **A** usually shows anxiety in response to a particular situation and may be high when scale **7** is in the typical range (45 thru 60). A person with this combination (high **A** scale, average **7** scale) is usually worrying about a specific problem but does not have the chronic worrying shown by a high scale **7**. We have found that a typical reason for a person having this combination is because he or she is anxious about taking the test but is not an anxious person in general.

In some cases, the **7** scale may be elevated without the **A** scale being above 60. In this instance, the person tends to be a chronic

A

188

worrier, but at the time of taking the test he or she was not overtly worried about a specific situation.

An examination of the items that make up the **A** scale in comparison with those which make up the **7** scale is useful in pointing out some of the differences between the two scales. One group of items on both scales has to do with self-doubt. The **7** scale self-doubt items seem to involve the total person more than those on the **A** scale. For example, "I certainly feel useless at times," is an item on scale **7**. The self-doubt of the individual with a high **A** scale score is more in regard to interactions with people such as, "I feel unable to tell anyone all about myself."

A second group of items that sets the **A** scale apart from the **7** scale are ones that have to do with phobias which are on the **7** scale but not on the **A** scale. A third set of items indicates that a high **7** scale individual is likely to have fits of excitement and anxiety whereas the high **A** scale individual is more likely to report the presence of steady anxiety.

Despite these differences, scales **7** and **A** have much overlap and usually are seen as elevated together rather than one elevated and the other not. When these two scales are elevated, the anxiety is both chronic and situational.

Scales **A** and **R** have a unique relationship to each other. In addition to looking at them separately, they also should be looked at together and interpreted in light of each other. We would suggest that you look at the **A** and **R** combinations, pp. 201-202, in your work with the **A** scale as well as the individual **A** scale interpretations.

GENERAL INFORMATION

1. The 39 items of the **A** scale reflect general, conscious emotional upset by asking questions concerning thinking and thought processes, negative emotional tone, lack of energy, pessimism, and personal sensitivity.

2. Welsh (1956) factor analyzed the MMPI items, and from this analysis he derived the **A** scale as a measure of one of the two main MMPI factors. (Scale **R** measures the other factor.) This first factor has high positive loadings on scales **7** (.90) and **8** (.79)

and a high negative loading on scale **K** (—.71) (Swenson et al., 1973).

3. The **A** scale is strongly related to indices of overt anxiety and seems to measure tension, nervousness, and distress.

4. The **A** scale measures general conscious anxiety of a situational nature, as contrasted to scale **7**, which measures a more characterological, long-term anxiety.

5. Welsh's **A** scale (1956) appears to be the most satisfactory single measure of conscious anxiety on the MMPI for most purposes.

6. High and low scores can be "good" or "bad," appropriate or inappropriate, helpful or a hindrance, depending upon the specific situation of the person.

   For example, if a person is facing a situational trauma and he or she is not very anxious about it (low to average **A** score), this lack of anxiety could be a hindrance to working through the trauma.

7. In addition to interpreting the **A** scale alone, in certain instances shown in the **A** and **R** combination table, pp. 201-202, the **A** scale should be considered in relationship to the **R** scale.

8. In one test-retest study, over a period of 11 days, the **A** scale was unstable (Jurjevich, 1966). This fact implies that the scale is quite mobile, hopefully in response to differing levels of anxiety.

9. Items of the **A** scale tend to be of uniformly low social desirability (Wiggins & Rumrill, 1959).

10. Under ideal-self instructions ("Take this test trying to look as good as possible") the one scale with the largest shift was the **A** scale; it became significantly lower (Parsons et al., 1968).

11. An excellent reference for the **A** scale is "Factor Dimensions **A** and **R**" by Welsh in *Basic Readings on the MMPI In Psychology and Medicine* (Welsh & Dahlstrom, 1956).

HIGH SCORES
(T = 60 or Above)

See also the **A** and **R** combinations, pp. 201-202.

1. High **A** scores indicate that the person is overtly anxious. The higher the score, the more anxious the person is.

2. Men with high **A** scores have been described as lacking confidence in their own abilities and unable to make decisions without hesitation, vacillation, or delay (Block & Bailey, 1955).

   a. They tend to be suggestible and respond more to evaluations made of them by others than they do their own self-evaluations. They may not act on others' evaluations however but just worrry about them.
   b. These men tend to lack social poise and are upset easily in social situations.
   c. They usually are pessimistic about their own professional future and advancement.

3. Gough (Welsh & Dahlstrom, 1956) reported people with high **A** scores have slow personal tempo and are pessimistic, hesitant, and inhibited.

4. Sheriff and Boomer (1954) found high **A** scorers showed more self-doubt in examination situations.

LOW SCORES
(T = 45 or Below)

See also the **A** and **R** combinations, pp. 201-202

1. Clients with low scores tend not to be consciously anxious.

2. This non-anxiety may be "good" (when nothing exists about which to be anxious) or "bad" (when the Clinical scales indicate problems exist which should concern the person).

3. Men with low **A** scores are described as more active and vigorous than men with high **A** scores. Men with low **A** scores

also may be considered ostentatious and exhibitionistic (Block & Bailey, 1955).

a. They seem to prefer action to contemplation.
b. In general, they are fluent and persuasive and take the initiative in social relationships.
c. They tend to be competitive, emphasizing success and productive achievements as a way of gaining status, power, or recognition.

COMBINATIONS

A-R

1. Nine combinations of **A** and **R** are discussed by Welsh (1965) and are found in the 1972 Dahlstrom, Welsh and Dahlstrom *MMPI Handbook*. These interpretations have not been very accurate for our populations, except for the high **A** and high **R** interpretation, which follows:

   High **A** (55 or above) and high **R** (55 or above): Depression often is encountered with accompanying tenseness and nervousness as well as complaints of anxiety, insomnia, and undue sensitivity. Generalized neurasthenic features of fatigue, chronic tiredness, or exhaustion may be seen. These subjects are perceived as rigid by others and are chronic worriers. They suffer from feelings of inadequacy and a brooding preoccupation with their personal difficulties (Welsh, 1965).

2. For a summary of selected **A** and **R** scale combinations, see the chart on pp. 201-202.

SUMMARY OF A SCALE INTERPRETATIONS*

T Score	Interpretations
45 or below	This person is not consciously anxious. He or she is possibly active, verbally fluent, and achievement oriented.
45 thru 60	This person has minimal (T = 45-50) to mild (T = 50-60) conscious anxiety. The majority of people score below 50 T score points.
60 or above	This person has a high level of conscious anxiety, which may cause debilitation as the scale is elevated. The person may lack poise, be easily upset, pessimistic, and not trusting of himself or herself. Such a person tends to be influenced by others' evaluations of him or her, although he or she may not always act overtly on these evaluations.

*Where T scores are listed in two categories (i.e., 45 or below and 45 thru 60) and a score is obtained that is listed for two categories, use whichever interpretation seems to be most appropriate for the individual.

— NOTES —

R SCALE
(Second Factor or Conscious Repression Scale)

We feel the **R** scale is a conscious repression scale (or suppression scale to be more accurate). A person with a high score on this scale seems to be saying, "Some areas of my life are none of your business." It is impossible to tell what areas are off limits until the client is asked. For example, in one recent situation, a client with a high **R**, but with an otherwise average profile, stated that he did not want to talk about his recent departure from the ministry of his church. He felt fairly comfortable about his decision, as was indicated by the MMPI profile in general, but was still not ready to talk with others about his change in vocation.

While the high **A** scale seems to have some relationship to seeking help at a university counseling center, the **R** scale does not. Clients coming for help with personal problems tend to score above 55 T score points on the **A** scale whereas they average around 50 for the **R** scale. Normal college students tend to score below 45 T score points on the **A** scale whereas they average around 50 for the **R** scale (Anderson & Duckworth, 1969). Thus, the **R** scale seems to average around 50 T score points regardless of personal adjustment.

Another unusual feature of the **R** scale is that it does not correlate above .50 with any of the other scales on the MMPI. (See Appendix C). This is in spite of the fact that it is supposed to be a scale that accounts for the second largest amount of variance in the MMPI. [The **A** scale measures the largest amount (Welsh, 1956).]

The items in the scale are quite varied. A high score on the **R** scale suggests that the person

1. has health concerns,

2. denies feelings of anger,

3. is socially introverted,

4. denies being stimulated by people,

5. is not aggressive and lacks social dominance, and

6. does not enjoy manual activities.

As has been mentioned previously, the **R** scale is not frequently elevated in clients seeking help at a college counseling center. Some clinical impressions however based on a sample of 32 MMPI's from a college counseling center population are as follows.

1. When the **R** scale is elevated 60 T score points or higher and the **A** scale is 5 T score points or more lower than the **R** scale, the client is likely to be seen as shy and guarded in his or her behavior or in his or her reactions to the interviewer. In some cases, these clients may even be resistive to being in therapy or to having a psychological evaluation. In spite of the client's resistance to this particular situation, a history of dependency is likely. Physical complaints are common and are of an unshakable nature. No comments in the case notes of these people indicate that they have any level of insight into their problems. People working with them find them quite unresponsive to psychological explanations for their problems.

2. On the other hand, when the **R** scale is elevated above 60 T score points and the **A** scale is at least 5 T score points or more *higher*, a much more pathological picture of the clients is represented. The person not only is shy and guarded, but also he or she is typically complaining of being isolated, depressed, and having suicidal thoughts. In a disproportionate number of these cases, some attempt at suicide has been made, although some of these attempts will have been of the attention-getting kind. These people complain of difficulty in concentrating and have periods of confusion. Usually also a negative family history is present, but this could be the result of a phenomenon which Chance (1957) reported in her investigation of individuals who had pleasant memories as opposed to those who had unpleasant memories. Those individuals with pleasant memories had **R** scores higher than their **A** scores. Those with unpleasant memories had **A** scores higher than their **R** scores.

R

3. When both the **R** and the **A** scales are above 60 T score points and approximately equal to one another (within 5 score points), the person tends to be shy and guarded with feelings of isolation, depression, and some history of dependency upon others for support.

This analysis of college student profiles would suggest that the interpretation of an elevated **R** scale is highly dependent upon its relationship with the **A** scale. A summation of the relationship between these two scales is found on pp. 201-202.

The low **R** score indicates a lack of conscious repression and perhaps a willingness to be open and self-disclosing to others. The **R** scale, as a conscious repression scale, contrasts with the **3** scale, which we see as an unconscious repression scale. In general, when a person has an **R** scale score above 55, scale **3** also is elevated. One scale may be elevated however without the other one being so. In the previous example of the ex-minister's non-willingness to talk about his departure from his church, the **R** scale was elevated (above 60) whereas the **3** scale was not. He recognized the problem area (average level **3** scale) but did not want to talk about it (high **R**). We have seen many situations where the opposite also was true: the clients used unconscious repression and denial a great deal (scale **3** high), but they were not consciously saying some areas were off limits (**R** scale average or below). These people are willing to talk about their problems if they recognize them, which they may not (high **3**).

Scale **R** also has points in common with the **K** and **Cn** scales. An elevated **K** scale indicates that the person feels everything is all right with him or her. A person with this scale elevation may not be able to look at things that are not going well. An elevated **Cn** scale indicates that the person controls to whom his or her behavior is shown. Some profiles have all four of these points (**K, 3, R,** and **Cn**) above 65. When this pattern occurs, these people may be saying in many ways and on many scales that they tend to restrict themselves to talking about some subjects (**R**) that usually are positive (**K** and **3**), and that they will not expose themselves or their behavior to all people (**Cn**). The overall impression is that of a highly constricted person.

GENERAL INFORMATION

1. The **R** scale consists of 40 items measuring health and physical symptoms; emotionality, violence, and activity; reactions to other people in social situations; social dominance, feelings of personal adequacy and personal appearance; and personal and vocational interests.

2. From his factor analyses of the MMPI, Welsh (1956) developed the **R** scale as a measure of the second factor in the MMPI. (The first factor is measured by scale **A**.)

3. This scale appears to measure the use of denial and rationalization as coping behaviors and a lack of effective self-insight.

4. The **R** scale measures conscious repression and denial, as contrasted with scale **3**, which tends to measure unconscious denial.

5. High or low scores can be "good" or "bad," appropriate or inappropriate, helpful or a hindrance, depending upon the specific situation of the person.

    For example, if a person has lost a loved one, a high **R** score may indicate a situation that is therapeutic for a while, thus helping the person to keep going in daily life without collapsing.

6. Scale **R** items are more heterogeneous and neutral in social desirability value as compared to scale **A** items, which are homogeneous and of low social desirability (Wiggins & Rumrill, 1959).

7. Because all the items on the **R** scale are keyed false, one study has proposed that the **R** scale seems to be a measure of acquiescence, with low **R** scores indicating more acquiescence than high **R** scores (Edwards & Abbott, 1969).

8. In addition to interpreting the **R** scale alone, in certain instances shown in the **A** and **R** combination table, pp. 201-202, the **R** scale should be considered in relationship to the **A** scale.

9. An excellent reference for the **R** scale is "Factor Dimensions **A** and **R**" by Welsh in *Basic Readings on the MMPI in Psychology and Medicine* (Welsh & Dahlstrom, 1956).

R   198

HIGH SCORES
(T = 60 or Above)

See also the **A** and **R** combinations, pp. 201-202.

1. Clients scoring high on **R** seem to be saying that some areas of their lives exist which they do not want to talk about with others.

2. Graham (1977) reported that high **R** scale scorers may be plodders and unimaginative people.

3. In one study, high **R** males were seen as people who readily made concessions and sidestepped trouble or disagreeable situations rather than face unpleasantness of any sort (Block & Bailey, 1955).

   a. They appeared highly civilized, formal, and conventional.
   b. They seemed clear-thinking, but they were rated slow, painstaking, and thorough.

LOW SCORES
(T = 45 or Below)

See also the **A** and **R** combinations, pp. 201-202.

1. People with low **R** scores are not trying to repress consciously any topics covered on the MMPI.

2. They probably are willing to discuss with someone problem areas covered by the MMPI insofar as they recognize these problems.

3. Their willingness to discuss these areas with a counselor may depend upon whether they see the counselor as one in whom they can confide and whether they feel the subject matter is appropriate to their counseling goals.

COMBINATIONS

A-R

1. For a summary of selected **A** and **R** scale combinations, see the summary on pp. 201-202 and also p. 192.

SUMMARY OF R SCALE INTERPRETATIONS*

T Score	Interpretations

45 or below   A person with a score in this range is not consciously repressing feelings or attitudes. Probably the person is willing to discuss recognized problems that are perceived as relating to his or her counseling goals. This person usually is outgoing, emotional, and spontaneous in life style.

45 thru 60   This person has minimal (T = 45-50) to mild (T = 50-60) conscious repression of feelings. The person may feel reluctant to discuss some topics with the counselor.

60 or above   A person with a score in this range has a strong need to consciously repress feelings. The higher the T score, the greater the need to repress. This person usually prefers to avoid unpleasant topics and situations. He or she may be seen as formal, logical, and cautious.

*Where T scores are listed in two categories (i.e., 45 or below and 45 thru 60) and a score is obtained that is listed for two categories, use whichever interpretation seems to be most appropriate for the individual.

SUMMARY OF A AND R COMBINATION
INTERPRETATIONS

If the A Scale Score Is	If the R Scale Score Is	Interpretations
45 or below	45 or below	This person is neither consciously anxious nor consciously repressing feelings. Three types of persons are in this category: 1. Persons taking the MMPI as part of an experiment or class assignment. 2. Persons seeking counseling for vocational guidance. 3. Clients who are unconcerned and readily admit their behavior, such as alcoholics, hoboes, sociopathic persons, and so forth. These people may have a poor prognosis for change in therapy.
60 or above	45 or below	This person appears to be both anxious and open. This score combination usually is helpful for the counseling situation; the anxiety serves as motivation to work on problems, and the openness allows flexibility in both depth and breadth of subject areas. This combination is more common for people voluntarily seeking counseling for problems.
45 or below	60 or above	This person is not consciously anxious, but he or she is consciously repressing information. This person is difficult to work with in therapy, because he or she is limiting the areas of discussion and is not sufficiently anxious to work on his or her problems. This combination is common for two groups of people:

1. Persons seeking vocational counseling. The person feels that exploring certain areas of his or her life is not relevant to the task.
2. Job applicants who hold back certain data from the prospective employer and who wish to present themselves in a good light.

60 or above	60 or above	This person is both consciously anxious and consciously repressing feelings; however, if the R scale is higher than the A scale, the person could be denying he or she is anxious. This combination frequently occurs with an elevated 3 scale. This person is very difficult to work with in therapy. The prognosis for successful therapy is indicated by the relative heights of the two scales. If the A scale is 5 or more T score points higher than R, the person may overcome his or her repressive tendencies because of the greater anxiety. If the R scale is 5 or more T score points higher than A, the person might terminate counseling rather than look at his or her problems realistically.

For an additional interpretation of this combination, see Welsh's (1965) interpretation on p. 192.

A·R

Es SCALE
(Ego—Strength Scale)

The ego-strength scale seems to be one of the best indicators of psychological health on the MMPI. The higher the **Es** scale, the more likely the person is to be able to bounce back from problems without becoming debilitated by them. The lower the **Es** scale, the more likely the person is to have difficulty coping with his or her problems. This scale, then, seems to be a measure of ego-resiliency.

The lower the **Es** scale, the more worthless the person usually feels. When the score is below a T of 30, the person may be having some problems connected with employment. He or she may be unable to hold a job at this time because of feelings of worthlessness.

Besides measuring ego-resiliency, the **Es** scale may occasionally measure how much a person *feels* he or she can recover from problems. Obviously, determining whether or not this second interpretation rather than the first one is true for a client is important in order to treat him or her most adequately.

For example, if the low **Es** score is the result of poor ability to bounce back from problems or the possession of inadequate coping behaviors, the therapist probably would need to work on developing the person's ability to cope with problem situations. If the low **Es** score is the result of the person's feeling he or she cannot cope with problems, when in reality he or she can, then a therapist would most likely need to work with the person's self concept instead of the person's actual ability to cope.

In a few cases, a high **Es** score is also the result of feelings and not ability. These feelings are not usually the best thing for a client to have when they do not match up to reality. These people may not be meeting their problems very well, but they feel that they are and therefore have a high **Es** score. As long as these feelings of adequacy persist, these clients do not do anything to try to learn better ways of coping with their problems and therefore progress in therapy is stymied.

Despite the two previous examples, we have found most commonly that a person's feelings about his or her ability to cope with problems and the actual ability are the same.

The **Es** scale originally was developed by Barron (1953) to predict neurotic peoples' responses to psychotherapy, but there was early recognition that it was a useful scale for assessing a person's adaptability and personal resourcefulness in a variety of situations.

Barron's (1969) work on creative individuals has shown that highly creative people have **Es** scale scores in the high 50's. These people were assessed as thinking and associating to ideas in unusual ways, having nonconventional thought processes, and being interesting, arresting persons. Some negative characteristics were found because high scoring people often tended to be rebellious and nonconforming, self-dramatizing, and histrionic.

Some other characteristics also may exist with an elevated **Es** scale which usually would not be interpreted as positive. In another study, Barron (1956) found that high scorers sometimes had higher than average aggression and hostility. Further investigation showed that this was related to how pathological their early childhood was. Those who had the most difficulty as children were the most likely to be hostile as adults. That is, a high score on **Es** may show poor control over hostility along with general ego strength if the individual has had childhood experiences characterized by friction in the home, poor relations with his parents, or a mother lacking in emotional warmth. Low scores on the **Es** scale did not always present a consistent picture in the way people handled hostility; but, in general, they were submissive, rigid, and unadaptive.

Crumpton, Cantor, and Batiste (1960) did a factor analysis of the ego strength scale. The five most important factors would suggest that a reconsideration of the label might be needed. Factors 1, 4, and 5 seem to be related to absence of symptoms or denial of symptoms. Factor 1 was associated with the absence of physical symptomatology and phobic behavior. Factor 4 was the absence of symptoms related to anxiety, rumination, and distractibility; and factor 5 seemed to be the denial of weakness or a sissified attitude in the face of distress. Factor 2 was related to moderate religious interests, such as attending church but the avoidance of more fundamentalist beliefs or behaviors. Factor 30 was correlated with rebelliousness.

The authors feel on the basis of this factor analysis that what is being measured is the absence of specific ego weaknesses and not the presence of ego strength.

Dahlstrom and Welsh (1956) seem to feel, on the other hand, that ego strength is probably the best measure of personality control that we have on the test and it probably should be used in this vein.

GENERAL INFORMATION

1. The **Es** scale of 68 items measures physiological stability and good health, a strong sense of reality, feelings of personal adequacy and vitality, and spontaneity and intelligence (Barron, 1953).

2. Barron (1953) developed the **Es** scale to differentiate those individuals who showed a greater degree of improvement after psychotherapy from individuals with similar problems who did not improve.

   Some studies (Fowler, Teel, & Coyle, 1967; Getter & Sundland, 1962) have found that the **Es** scores are unrelated to changes in treatment progress. These studies used change after hospitalization to measure the **Es** predictability however instead of the change after psychotherapy that Barron (1953) used.

3. The **Es** scale seems to be a measure of ego-resiliency; that is, the ability to recover from environmental pressures and problems.

4. Crumpton, et al., (1960) have suggested in one study that what is measured by the **Es** scale is the absence of specific ego weaknesses and not the presence of ego strength.

5. While the **Es** score originally was developed as an index or prognosis in therapy, it also can be used as a criterion of improve-

ment in therapy. That is, people in therapy originally may have low **Es** scores, but with psychological improvement the **Es** scores tend to rise.

6. Abnormally low **Es** scores may result from a large number of unanswered items (see the **?** scale score) giving the impression erroneously of greater "ego weakness" than may be present (Dahlstrom et al., 1972).

7. The **Es** scale has high negative correlations with scales **2** (—.51), **0** (—.51), **A** (—.68), **Ca** (—.61), **Dy** (—.64), and **Pr** (—.53) for a group of normal people (Appendix C, p.   ). It has high positive correlations with **Do** (.60) and **St** (.54) for the same group.

8. The odd-even reliability of the scale in a clinic population was .76. Test-retest reliability over a three-month period was .72 (Barron, 1953).

9. Arnold (1970) has found that marital conflict is more likely to occur if the ego-strength scores for the couple are below 50 or if a difference of more than 15 points between the two T scores exists.

10. A shortened form (50 items) of the **Es** scale has been proposed (Canter, 1965). It was found essentially equivalent to the longer form (68 items) in a separate study (Gravitz, 1970a).

11. Women tend to score lower than men on **Es**. This difference may be because of sex related items (MMPI #140, 153, 174, 187, 261, 488, 510, 548). When these items were removed in one study (Holmes, 1967), male and female differences on **Es** were cancelled out, but the predictive effect of **Es** in regard to psychotherapy was not affected.

12. The **Es** scale is positively related to intelligence and to education (Tamkin & Klett, 1957).

13. Some studies (Tamkin & Klett, 1957) have found no correlation between age and **Es** score, but others (Getter & Sundland, 1962) have found that older people tend to have lower **Es** scores.

14. The **Es** score for college students averages between 55 and 65 (Anderson & Duckworth, 1969).

Es

15. In a study of vocational interests and personality, Crites (1960) found that individuals with higher **Es** tend to have more highly developed interest patterns on the SVIB (Strong Vocational Interest Blank).

16. Barron's original article proposing this scale is in the *Basic Readings on the MMPI in Psychology and Medicine* (Welsh & Dahlstrom, 1956).

HIGH SCORES
(T = 55 or Above)

1. High scores usually indicate an ability to deal with environmental pressures.

2. Occasionally, high scores are indications that people feel they can deal adequately with pressures when they really cannot.

Dahlstrom et al. (1975) have suggested that when a person has a high **Es** score and is having problems shown by Clinical scale elevations above 70 but is denying them, the high **Es** score may *not* be indicating a favorable response to treatment. If the person has a high **Es** score *and* admits to having difficulties however the **Es** score probably indicates a favorable response to treatment.

3. A person with a high score generally can profit from psychotherapy.

4. The high score indicates that the person may be able to work within the cultural, social, and personal limits of his or her society.

5. A high score may indicate that a person can deal effectively with others, gain their acceptance, and create favorable impressions on them.

6. High scores tend to be typical of college students. The usual score for such students is near 60 (Anderson & Duckworth, 1969).

LOW SCORES
(T = 45 or Below)

1. Low scores may indicate less self-restraint and environmental mastery than average scores do.

2. Occasionally, low scores are indications that people feel they cannot deal adequately with problems when they really can.

3. Low scores may occur when the person is feeling he or she needs help in therapy (the "cry for help" syndrome). A person who feels this way typically has a high **F** score as well as the low **Es** score.

4. Extraordinarily low scores (T = 30 or below) usually indicate real or imagined poor work records and an inability to cope with everyday occurrences.

COMBINATIONS

Es — Do — St (T = 55 or Above)

1. This combination tends to be typical of college students.

Es — Do — St (T = 45 or Below) plus Dy (T = 55 or Above)

1. These people feel they are not worth much and do not expect much out of life. They also feel they must rely on others to make decisions for them.

SUMMARY OF Es SCALE INTERPRETATIONS*

T Score	Interpretations

30 or below A person with this score tends to have a very poor self-concept and usually feels helpless to act in bettering his or her situation. This person often frustrates the counselor by having good intentions but not acting on them. The person usually has a poor work record. Prognosis for successful employment at this time is poor.

30 thru 45 This person tends to have a poor self-concept, is unable to face challenges at this time, and usually is devastated by even minor setbacks. The person needs ego building before he or she is able to deal with problems.

45 thru 60 This person usually has enough ego strength to deal with life's stresses and minor setbacks. For a college student, an **Es** score in the lower part of this range (45 thru 50) may indicate that he or she is in a transient state (going either up or down in ego strength).

60 or above This person is or feels that he or she is resilient and able to recover from most setbacks. If a client has emotional difficulties indicated by elevated Clinical scales and recognizes this, he or she usually will make a good response to treatment. If he or she has emotional problems and does not recognize this, the client may not have a favorable response to treatment. The person usually is able to tolerate confrontation in counseling regardless of his or her response to therapy. This level is typical for college students. Usually, scales **9, Do,** and **St** also are elevated.

*Where T scores are listed in two categories (i.e., 30 or below and 30 thru 45) and a score is obtained that is listed for two categories, use whichever interpretation seems to be most appropriate for the individual.

Es

— **NOTES** —

Lb SCALE
(Low Back Pain — Functional Scale)

In the previous edition of this book (1975), the suggestion was made not to use the **Lb** scale because we (Duckworth & Duckworth) had not been able to discover any useful interpretation of it for college counseling centers or mental health clinic populations. In the process of analyzing the scale according to the content of the items since that printing, we (Duckworth & Anderson) feel we have some leads on the possible interpretation of high scores (above 60 T score points) for this scale.

In the original study by Hanvik (1951) this scale was developed to differentiate between those people with organic low back pain and those with functional low back pain (no organic reason for the pain). The scale has 25 items, twelve of which are claims to being unflappable, seldom angry, and always in control of feelings; for example, answering false to "It makes me angry to have people try to hurry me."

These items alone however would not make any major elevation on the scale. The addition of items which indicate that all is not what it seems to be in this person's professed Eden is what raises the score to interpretable levels (above 60 T score points): "I wish I could be as happy as others seem to be (true);" "I have periods of restlessness when I cannot sit long in a chair (true)." An additional four items indicate the presence of physical complaints, and several items which deny religious beliefs also are included.

The message that the individual seems to be giving is that "I'm a wonderful person. I love people, and they never annoy me, but for some reason I am uncomfortable and not as happy as I should be."

Dynamically, we have a picture of an individual who at one level of awareness feels comfortable with the demands that others place on him or her but who at another more unconscious level is saying "get off my back." Considerable psychic energy maybe going into maintaining a friendly facade.

These personality characteristics are likely to be true even if no back complaints are present. While this seems similar to a conversion reaction which is shown by an elevated **3** scale, an elevation on the **Lb** score represents a more specific reaction to stress than a conversion reaction. When the stress is gone, we hypothesize that the **Lb** score will come down below 60 T score points whereas the **3** scale will not become lower.

We predict that if **Lb** is elevated and the **3** scale is not, the possibility of an isolated conversion reaction exists. If both the **Lb** scale and scale **3** are up, a more general conversion syndrome exists.

In summary, the **Lb** scale seems to be measuring a person's ability to maintain a friendly, non-flustered facade while feeling frustration and discontent at a preconscious level. We hypothesize that this "conversion" or control over psychic pain is less entrenched as a characterological trait than the conversion reaction shown by the **3** scale; and therefore we believe the **Lb** scale will be more mobile, rising and falling more readily than the **3** scale, while showing many of the same characteristics.

GENERAL INFORMATION

1. In Hanvik's (1951) original study, this scale of 25 items differentiated between two groups, each of 30 patients, one group with diagnosed organic low back pain (low **Lb**) and the other group with back pain but no clearcut organic reason for the pain (high **Lb**).

2. The correlation of **Lb** with other scales is minimal.

   a. Hanvik (1951) found the **Lb** scale to correlate highly with scales **1** and **3**; however, we have found **Lb** to have a correlation only of .32 with scale **1** and .39 with scale **3** in a group of 847 normals (Appendix C). Swenson et al. (1973) for a group of 50,000 medical patients found a .21 correla-

Lb   212

tion between **Lb** and scale **1** and a .26 correlation for **Lb** and scale **3** (Appendix C).

    b. The scale does correlate .45 with an anxiety score, .45 with a neurotic score, and .41 with a subtle hysteria scale in Swanson, Pearson, and Osborne's medical population (1973). The correlations with other scales however are minimal.

    c. In our population of 847 normals (Appendix C) the **Lb** scale does not correlate above .40 with any other scale on the MMPI.

3. Swenson et al. (1973) found that the **Lb** scale varied little according to age.

4. The mean T score on this scale was 54 for a medical population (Swenson et al., 1973). This also is the mean T score found in a group of counseling center clients (N = 406) (Anderson and Duckworth, 1970) who had no Clinical scales above 70 T score points with the possible exception of the **5** scale.

5. The original article proposing this scale is in *Basic Readings on the MMPI in Psychology and Medicine* (Welsh & Dahlstrom, 1956).

SUMMARY OF Lb SCALE INTERPRETATIONS*

T Score	Interpretations

60 or below The interpretation is unknown at the present time.

60 or above People with scores in this range may see themselves as not angry and in control of their feelings. Underneath they may be irritated and unhappy with what is happening. They may recognize that they are uncomfortable but not the depth of their unhappiness or anger.

*Where T scores are listed in two categories (i.e., 60 or below and 60 or above) and a score is obtained that is listed for two categories, use whichever interpretation seems to be most appropriate for the individual.

Ca SCALE
(Caudality Scale)

In the 1975 edition of this book, we (Duckworth & Duckworth) suggested not using this scale because we were not sure of its meaning for our populations.

The **Ca** scale originally was developed to differentiate patients with focal cerebral damage in the parietal area from patients with focal lesions in the temporal areas. Because this judgment is better made medically, the scale would seem to have little relevance for the populations with which we are mainly concerned. In a normal college population the scores on this scale tend to be lower than in the original norm group since the mean for the college population is 45 (Anderson & Duckworth, 1970).

As we have worked with the **Ca** scale, we have found that when it is elevated it seems to be measuring the same thing as the **A** scale; that is, a general conscious anxiety. The **Ca** scale correlated .88 with The **A** scale in a group of normals (Appendix C) and .85 with the **A** scale for a large population of medical patients (Appendix C). These high correlations are found even though little item overlap between the two scales exists. Only eight of the 36 items of the **Ca** scale are on the **A** scale.

The **Ca** scale however does not always correlate so highly with the **7** scale, another measure of anxiety. In a group of normals (Appendix C), the **Ca** scale correlated only .57 with the **7** scale. This would seem to indicate that the anxiety shown by this scale may be more a conscious reaction to some stressful situation that is shown also by the **A** scale and is less likely the ruminative, obsessive thinking more characteristic of the **7** scale.

The **Ca** scale has the greatest number of high correlations with other MMPI scales of any of the 24 MMPI scales. For a group of normals (Appendix C), the **Ca** scale correlates in the positive direction with the following scales: **F** (.53), **2** (.62), **7** (.57), **0** (.63), **A** (.84), **Dy** (.80), **Pr** (.61); and in the negative direction with the following scales: **K** (—.65), **Es** (—.61), **Do** (—.57), **St** (—.51). Approximately the same number of high correlations are found in a medical population (Appendix C).

An investigation of the items in the **Ca** scale suggests why the scale correlates so highly with the previous scales. The item groups are as follows:

1. Ten items which suggest a fear of loss of control or decrease in mental ability. (I am afraid of losing my mind.)

2. Nine items which have to do with nervousness and brooding. (Most of the time I feel blue.)

3. Six items dealing with physical concerns, especially tiring easily. (I feel tired a good deal of the time.)

4. Four items indicative of social introversion. (I find it hard to make talk when I meet new people.)

5. Seven miscellaneous items. (I dislike to take a bath.)

Eight of the 36 items overlap with the **A** scale, seven of which suggest an inability to make and stay with decisions. Nine of the items overlap with scale **7** and convey a feeling of unhappiness and discomfort. Nine of the items overlap with scale **2**; five of which also overlap with scale **7** and indicate general unhappiness and dissatisfaction with life.

In summary, an elevated score (60 T score points or more) on the **Ca** scale would indicate an individual who has a great deal of overt, conscious anxiety. He or she has a poor attitude towards self, fears loss of control, and lacks enthusiasm for becoming involved in activities. On the other hand, low scorers (45 T score points or below) would tend to feel in control of their own actions, have little anxiety, and feel comfortable in social situations.

GENERAL INFORMATION

1. This scale consists of 37 items selected by Williams (1952) to discriminate those patients with frontal brain lesions (low scores on the scale) from those with posterior brain lesions (high scores on the scale).

2. In Williams' (1952) original study, high scorers tended to show anxiety, depression, guilt, introversion, feelings of inadequacy, worry about the future, and somatic concern.

   Low scorers tended to deny anxiety and worry; to have attitudes of acceptance, affability, and self-confidence; and to have rather low levels of aspiration.

3. Williams' original article proposing this scale is in *Basic Readings on the MMPI in Psychology and Medicine* (Welsh & Dahlstrom, 1956).

SUMMARY OF Ca SCALE INTERPRETATIONS*

T Score	Interpretations

45 or below A person with a score in this range feels in control of his or her own actions, has little anxiety, and feels comfortable in social situations. This is the range in which most college students usually score.

45 thru 60 This person has a score similar to that of the general, non-college population.

60 or above A person with a score in this range is reporting a great deal of overt, conscious anxiety. Check the **A** and **7** scales to see if they also are elevated as additional confirmation of this anxiety.

*Where T scores are listed in two categories (i.e., 45 or below and 45 thru 60) and a score is obtained that is listed for two categories, use whichever interpretation seems to be most appropriate for the individual.

Dy SCALE
(Dependency Scale)

The dependency scale is a fairly easy one to interpret. The higher the scale score, the more the person would like to or actually is leaning on others. The lower the scale, the more independent the person usually is.

Most mentally healthy persons will have their **Dy** scales below a T score of 50, whereas the typical client's profile has the **Dy** scale above a T score of 55. As the client becomes better able to cope with his or her problems, the **Dy** scale typically will be reduced below 50, thus becoming like the **Dy** scales in the healthy profiles.

Benefits can be obtained by interpreting the **Dy** scale in conjunction with the **Do** (Dominance) scale; therefore, we have included a summary table of **Dy-Do** combinations, pp. 227-228. In general, when dependency is high, dominance is low and vice versa, but occasionally both scales will be elevated above a T score of 55. When this happens, people seem to be ambivalent about whether or not they want to take charge of their own lives. This ambivalence tends to come out as passive-aggressive or passive-demanding behavior. These people may ask others to help them by making decisions for them (dependency), but then they become aggressive about or critical of the decision that is made (dominance). Persons with this **Dy-Do** combination are especially difficult to deal with in therapy because the therapist usually is one of the people the client is passive-aggressive or passive-demanding toward. The prognosis for these clients is not as good as it is for other clients (even those with high **Dy** and low **Do**) because the ambivalence usually gets in the way of therapy, unless it is handled adroitly by the therapist.

GENERAL INFORMATION

1. Navran (1954) developed the **Dy** scale of 57 items to identify people who are highly dependent upon others.

2. He developed the scale by asking 16 judges to specify independently MMPI items they felt reflected dependency. The resulting 157 items were tested and cross-validated on neuropsychiatric patients and a scale of 57 items was derived.

3. The mean for this scale is low (44 T score points) for college students (Anderson & Duckworth, 1969).

4. In addition to interpreting the **Dy** scale alone, in certain instances shown in the **Dy** and **Do** combination summary, pp. 227-228, the **Dy** scale is to be considered in relationship to the **Do** (dominance) scale.

HIGH SCORES
(T = 55 or Above)

See also the **Dy** and **Do** combinations, pp. 227-228.

1. High scores tend to indicate that the person is dependent and somewhat passive.

2. Graham (1977) felt that this scale might be a good measure of self-reported dependency, however other people might not judge the person as dependent.

LOW SCORES
(T = 50 or Below)

See also the **Dy** and **Do** combinations, pp. 227-228.

1. Persons with low scores tend to be independent of others.

2. This level tends to be typical for college students, with the mean score being 44 T score points (Anderson & Duckworth, 1969).

COMBINATIONS

Dy·Do

1. For a summary of selected **Dy·Do** scale combinations, see pp. 227-228.

SUMMARY OF Dy SCALE INTERPRETATIONS*

T Score	Interpretations
50 or below	This person tends to be independent of others; this can be either from choice or necessity. The mean score for college students is 44.
50 thru 55	A person at this level feels a need to be somewhat dependent.
55 or above	This person has a strong need to be dependent at this time; the higher the elevation, the more dependent the person feels. Such a score may be either characterological or situational. These persons also may be somewhat passive. This is the typical range of scores for clients coming in voluntarily with serious problems for which they want some help.

*Where T scores are listed in two categories (i.e., 50 or below and 50 thru 55) and a score is obtained that is listed for two categories, use whichever interpretation seems to be most appropriate for the individual.

Do SCALE
(Dominance Scale)

The **Do** scale is a fairly simple measure of a person's ability to take charge of his or her own life. The higher this scale, the more the person is saying that he or she is able to take charge of his or her own life. The **Do** scale may show domineering behavior when the scale is very high (above 75) and the **4** scale is above 70 T score points. Even then, the person may not always show domineering behavior. The presence of the behavior seems to depend upon certain other scales being elevated with the **Do**. If the **5** scale is elevated 5 or more T score points above the **4** scale for men or is below 40 T score points for women, it may temper the domineering behavior.

The lower the **Do** scale, the more the person is saying he or she does not want to take charge of his or her life. The lower **Do** score usually is accompanied by an elevation on the **Dy** scale. When this happens, the person usually wants other people to take over his or her life and wants to be dependent upon them.

In addition to interpreting this scale alone, its relationship with the **Dy** scale should be considered. The **Dy-Do** combinations have been summarized in the summary on pp. 227-228. We have found an elevation on the **Do** scale to be a good sign of progress in therapy. Also, elevations above a T score of 60 on **Es**, **Do** and **St** usually are signs of a healthy profile.

GENERAL INFORMATION

1. The **Do** scale of 60 items was developed by Gough, McClosky and Meehl (1951) and measures poise, self-assurance, resourcefulness, efficiency, and perseverance.

2. The scale was developed by the "peer group nomination technique." One hundred college and 124 high school students were asked to nominate the members of their group whom they considered to be the most and least dominant. Those items on the MMPI that differentiated between the two groups were used for the **Do** scale.

3. This scale seems to measure a person's ability to take charge of his or her own life.

4. The **Do** scale has been shown to be successful in predicting staff ratings and peer nominations for dominance and in identifying outstanding leaders in high school programs (Dahlstrom & Welsh, 1960).

5. College students tend to score high on this scale with the mean 60 T score points (Anderson & Duckworth, 1969).

6. A group of college achievers scored higher than non-achievers on this scale (Morgan, 1952).

7. An elevated score on the **Do** scale has been found to be significantly related to middle management success (Miles, 1968).

8. In addition to interpreting this scale alone, in certain instances shown in the **Dy** and **Do** combination summary, pp. 227-228, the **Do** scale is to be considered in relationship to the **Dy** scale.

9. The article originally proposing this scale is in the *Basic Reading on the MMPI in Psychology and Medicine* (Welsh & Dahlstrom, 1956).

HIGH SCORES
(T = 60 or Above)

See also the **Dy** and **Do** combinations, pp. 227-228.

1. High scorers tend to be people who take charge of their lives.

When the person has a **Do** score above a T of 75, he or she may be seen as a leader and/or domineering.

LOW SCORES
(T = 50 or Below)

See also the **Dy** and **Do** combinations, pp. 227-228.

1. A person with a low **Do** score usually would like others to take charge of his or her life.

COMBINATIONS

Es-Do-St (T = 45 or below) See p. 208.

E̅s-D̅o-S̅t (T = 45 or below) See p. 208.

Dy-Do

1. For a summary of selected **Dy-Do** scale combinations, see pp. 227-228.

SUMMARY OF Do SCALE INTERPRETATIONS*

T Score	Interpretations

50 or below A person with a score in this range prefers to have others take charge of his or her life at this time. This level is typical for clients in therapy.

50 thru 60 A person with a score at this level is able to control much of his or her life and at the same time is able to be dependent upon others periodically. This range is typical for people who do not have a college education.

60 or above This person tends to take charge of his or her own life. He or she is able to meet deadlines, plan, and organize his or her life. At higher levels (T = 75 or above), a person may be seen by others as imposing or domineering if his or her **4** scale score is above 70 T score points. The mean for college students is a T score of 60.

*Where T scores are listed in two categories (i.e., 50 or below and 50 thru 60) and a score is obtained that is listed for two categories, use whichever interpretation seems to be most appropriate for the individual.

SUMMARY OF Dy and Do SCALE COMBINATION INTERPRETATIONS

If the Dy Scale Score Is	If the Do Scale Score Is	Interpretations
50 or below	45 or below	This combination is found rarely. In a group of over 500 profiles, only 12 had this combination. Ten of these persons were previously long-term dependent persons (**Dy** = 60 or above, **Do** = 45 or below) who were no longer dependent but who had not yet learned to control their own lives. The other two persons were hostile males who were successful in business and who insisted that the significant women in their lives (mothers or wives) maintain a quiet, isolated, womb-like home.
45 or below	60 or above	This person is able to control his or her life. Leaders usually fall in this category. This combination is usual for college students.
60 or above	45 or below	This person feels unable to take charge of his or her life and feels that others must be relied upon at this time. The individual may feel more comfortable being a follower or in a semi-dependent position and may be unable to make major decisions. When the ego strength (**Es**) and status (**St**) scales also are low, the person may feel worthless. Most likely, the person feels the need to lean on someone and will use either the therapist or another person for this purpose. These clients rarely miss appointments and usually try hard to please the therapist.
60 or above	60 or above	A person with these scores controls through weakness. That is, the person appears to be de-

pendent but is actually in charge of the situation. This person usually manipulates others (including the counselor) by appearing to be dependent, when in fact the person is determining the course of his or her own behavior and the counseling sessions.

Re SCALE
(Social Responsibility Scale)

The **Re** scale originally was developed to determine the social responsibility of a person. That is, persons receiving high scores on this scale were seen as socially responsible, willing to accept the consequences of their behavior, trustworthy, and dependable, while persons receiving low scores were seen as socially irresponsible. We have noted however that persons receiving low scores could be equally as socially responsible as persons receiving elevated scores. Instead of social responsibility then, we feel this scale measures the acceptance (high score) or rejection (low score) of a previously held value system.

For persons under age 25, an elevation on this scale (T = 50 thru 65) indicates that they accept in general the value system of their parents. A score in the 40 thru 50 range usually indicates that the person is questioning the parental value system (a typical procedure for college students and for those mental health clients going through a traumatic life change). Scores below 40 usually indicate that the person is not just questioning but actually is rejecting the parental value system.

One caution must be noted. Many people tend to presume that a person is showing acceptance or rejection of white middle class values by his or her score on the **Re** scale. What this scale seems to be showing for this below 25 age group is acceptance or rejection of the *parental* values however which may or may not be those of the white, middle class. For example, Black ghetto-reared college students may receive low scores on this scale because they are rejecting the ghetto values with which they were reared and now are accepting white middle class values. Thus, to tell accurately what values are being accepted or rejected, one must know the person's background.

Re

For persons above the age of 25, interpretation of this scale is based upon the person's present value system which may or may not be similar to the parents. Persons with elevations on the **Re** scale (T = 50 thru 65) tend to accept their present value system and intend to continue using it. Persons with scores of 40 thru 50 are questioning their present value system and those below 40 are rejecting their most recently held value system. An illustration of this is a 40 year old male with a **Re** score of 35. He had been reared with one value system (his parents') which he had rejected in his early 20's. Now at age 40, he was re-evaluating his own value system and felt that the values of his parents (those rejected 20 years previously) now were more valid for him than those he had held more recently.

For people of all ages, the higher a score above 65 on the **Re** scale, the more rigid a person seems to be in his or her acceptance of values and the less willing to explore other values.

As one examines the items and the intercorrelations of this scale with other scales, a consistent picture of a person with a high score emerges.

High scorers report that they had little trouble with authorities as they were growing up. They answer false to such items as "In school I was sometimes sent to the principal for cutting up" and "My parents have often objected to the kind of people I went around with." This self-report receives some support from **Re's** —.48 correlation with the Obvious Psychopathic Deviate Scale (Swenson et al., 1973).

Part of their comfort with authorities may be based on the fact that they seldom admit to taking risks. Seven of the 32 items on this scale indicate a lack of interest in creating excitement. They answer true to "I have never done anything dangerous for the thrill of it" and false to "I enjoy a race or game better when I bet on it."

This conservative approach to life does not appear to be related to fear but rather to a lack of interest in this kind of stimulating situation because they report that they feel comfortable with a variety of other situations that could produce anxiety. They answer true to "I do not dread seeing a doctor about a sickness or injury" and "I usually work things out for myself rather than get someone to show me how."

The items concerning not taking risks seem to support the presence of a control factor in high **Re** people's behavior. This also is supported by a correlation of —.53 with Impulsivity and —.50 with Neurotic Undercontrol scales (Swenson et al., 1973).

High scorers on **Re** also report that they expect others to be positive in their behavior. They answer false to "A large number of people are guilty of bad sexual conduct" and "I have often found people jealous of my good ideas, just because they had not thought of them first." This also is supported by **Re**'s correlation of —.49 with the **Pr** scale and .52 with the **K** scale (Appendix C).

This would seem to be one scale on which a certain type of good student would get high scores. This would be the student who reports liking school since **Re** correlates .61 with academic achievement, .51 with intellectual efficiency, .51 with intellectual quotient, and .51 with teaching potential (Swenson et al., 1973).

All of these factors together indicate someone who is confident, even-tempered, non-pretentious, comfortable with authority, and competent in academic areas, with little need to pursue adventure.

While high scorers have many strong points, several defects are possible. They may be unimaginative and non-creative. This is particularly likely to be true if scales **7** and **8** are below 45 T score points. Their lives may be controlled by a considerable number of "ought to's" with which they are comfortable but which could annoy other people who have to work with them. That is, they may expect others to live up to their standards and be as comfortable with them as they are. Consequently they may have difficulty understanding why others cannot or will not perform as they do.

In addition to interpreting the **Re** scale alone, in certain instances shown in the **Re** and **Pr** combination summary, pp. 241-242, considering the **Re** scale in relationship to the **Pr** (prejudice or rigid thinking) scale is helpful. At first glance the **Re** and **Pr** scales would appear to be positively correlated; that is, those who question their previous values (low **Re**) also would be open to alternate viewpoints (low **Pr**). Similarly, those who wholeheartedly accept their previous values (high **Re**) would not be open to alternate viewpoints (high **Pr**). Certainly these combinations do appear. Other combinations also appear however. Specifically, at least one segment of people who are questioning their previous values (low **Re**) (they usually consider themselves to be "liberal" thinkers) are not tolerant of others (high **Pr**), particularly others who accept the more traditional American value system. Apparently, these people are not as liberal as they believe themselves to be, at least about others who believe differently than they do.

Conversely, some people who accept their middle-class background with all its implications (high **Re**) also are able to listen to alternative beliefs held by others (low **Pr**). These people appear to have taken a position for themselves, but they are able to allow others to have their own positions.

If however the **Re** scale is above 65 T score points and the **Pr** is low, the person's tolerance may be a willingness to let others express their beliefs as long as the others carry out their responsibilities and are "good."

Interestingly, the **Re** scale tends to be correlated with age; the older the person, the higher the **Re** scale tends to be. We usually find the **Re** scale low for college students as they question how they were reared and some of the values of their parents. One other group that tends to receive low **Re** scores is women who are Biblical fundamentalists.

GENERAL INFORMATION

1. The **Re** 32-item scale was developed by Gough (1952) to measure social responsibility.

2. Social responsibility was defined by Gough as the willingness to accept the consequences of one's own behavior, dependability, trustworthiness, and sense of obligation to the group.

3. Gough used the "peer nomination" method with this scale, asking college and high school students to choose the most and least responsible members of their groups. The MMPI items that differentiated between these two groups were the basis for the scale.

4. Instead of measuring social responsibility, the **Re** scale seems to measure how much the person accepts the values with which he or she was reared. Persons below age 25 who score high on this

scale tend to accept their parents' values. When people question or reject the values of their parents, they usually score low on the **Re** scale.

Persons above age 25 who score low on this scale may be rejecting their most recently held value systems which may or may not be the same as their parents.

5. In addition to interpreting this scale alone, consideration of the **Re** scale in relationship to the **Pr** scale is helpful. See the **Re** and **Pr** combination summary, pp. 241-242.

6. The **Re** scale has differentiated "responsible" from "irresponsible" people (school disciplinary problems, people nominated for responsibility, and good school citizenship) (Dahlstrom & Welsh, 1960).

7. A group of college achievers scored higher than non-achievers on this scale (Morgan, 1952).

HIGH SCORES
(T = 50 or Above)

See also the **Re** and **Pr** combinations, pp. 241-242.

1. People under the age of 25 who score high on the **Re** scale tend to accept their parents' values.

Persons over the age of 25 accept their present value system, which may or may not be the same as their parents'.

2. Persons with high **Re** scores tend to have positions of leadership and responsiblity (Knapp, 1960; Olmstead & Monachesi, 1956).

LOW SCORES
(T = 40 or Below)

See also the **Re** and **Pr** combinations, pp. 241-242.

1. When people under the age of 25 reject their parents' values, they tend to score low on the **Re** scale.

Persons over the age of 25 tend to reject their present value system, which may or may not be the same as their parents'.

2. Low scorers may have substituted a new religion, philosophy, or political outlook for their old values.

3. Women who are Biblical fundamentalists also may receive low scores on this scale.

COMBINATIONS

Re-Pr

1. For a summary of selected **Re** and **Pr** scale combinations, see pp. 241-242.

SUMMARY OF Re SCALE INTERPRETATIONS*

Interpretations

T Score	Below Age 25	Over Age 25
40 or below	This person tends to deny the value system of his or her parents. Such a person may have substituted another value system for the parental one.	This person tends to deny his or her most recently held value system (which may be different from the parents').
40 thru 50	People in this range tend to question their parents' values. They may be exploring alternative viewpoints. Their values seem to be in flux.	People in this range tend to be questioning their most recently held value system and are usually exploring different values.
50 thru 65	People with scores in this range tend to accept their parents' values. The higher the score in this range, the more the person has accepted these values.	A person with a score in this range tends to accept his or her present value system. The higher the score, the more the person has accepted these values.
65 or above	The higher a score above 65, the more rigid a person seems to be in his or her acceptance of values and the less willing to explore other values.	

*Where T scores are listed in two categories (i.e., 40 or below and 40 thru 50) and a score is obtained that is listed for two categories, use whichever interpretation seems to be most appropriate for the individual.

Re

Pr SCALE
(Prejudice Scale)

The **Pr** scale was designed originally to measure anti-Semitic prejudice. While the scale does measure prejudice, it appears to be concerned with the much broader concept of rigidity in thinking. That is, elevations on this scale seem to indicate that a person is able to accept only concepts and values similar to his or her own and rejects alternative ways of thinking. Elevations on this scale also may identify persons who are not secure with their present value systems and therefore must shut out alternative viewpoints.

People with low **Pr** scores usually are able to tolerate opinions different from their own. These lower scores also can indicate a person who is secure with his or her values and thus is able to allow others to have theirs. Thus, the **Pr** scale seems to indicate a person's willingness to accept or to look at alternate viewpoints.

The **Pr** scale consists of 32 items. The largest number (12 items) reflects negative, cynical, and contemptuous attitudes toward the motivations of others. "I can't blame anyone for trying to grab everything he can get in this world." Nine items of foreboding or unreasonable fears are included. "Sometimes I feel as if I must injure either myself or someone else."

Seven items indicate uncertainty of self and social skills. "I refuse to play some games because I am not good at them." The remaining four items are miscellaneous types, e.g., "I feel there is only one true religion."

Split half reliability coefficients are .79 and .81 and test-retest reliability is .56 (Jensen, 1957). The scale is thus subject to change or at least is somewhat unstable over a period of time.

Pr   236

Evidence exists that prejudice may be a general response tendency which influences the individual's reactions to a variety of situations and persons. English (1971) pointed out that a sizeable majority of studies seems to confirm the belief that prejudice is a general pervasive attitudinal characteristic of some individuals. These people tend to reject any group they consider significantly different from their own, particulary those with ethnic, racial, or religious differences.

Some interesting correlations were found by Gough (1951a) in his original study. Low scorers had an average I.Q. of 111, whereas high scorers had an average of 98. A later correlation was found (1951b) between **Pr** and Intellectual Quotient of —.70 and **Pr** and Intellectual Efficiency of —.63. Further support for this negative relationship between intellectual ability and prejudice comes from college students who have a mean score of 40 on **Pr** (Anderson & Duckworth, 1969).

Social class also is related to prejudice. Again, in Gough's original study (1951a), the socioeconomic status (SES) scale he used correlated —.60 with **Pr** with higher SES students scoring lower on the **Pr** scale. Thus, an elevated score is not unusual for an individual of lower social status or for one of more limited intellectual potential; but an elevated score for someone of better than average intelligence, such as a college student, needs to be looked at in another way.

Therapists should explore the possibility that their more intelligent clients with high **Pr** scores may be in a period of poor expectations, that is, these clients may have some doubts as to whether or not they can cope with the problems that are bothering them. They may have a pervasive sour grapes attitude which could be temporary and subject to therapeutic intervention. The possibility exists that some resistance to therapy may occur because these clients tend to be blaming others for what has gone wrong in their lives. They also may be very resistive to accepting new ideas during the counseling session.

In addition to interpreting this scale by itself, it should be interpreted in combination with the **Re** scale. The summary of the various combinations of **Re** and **Pr** is found on pp. 241-242.

Pr

GENERAL INFORMATION

1. The **Pr** 32-item scale was devised by Gough (1951a) to differentiate those high school students who scored high on an anti-Semitism test (were more prejudiced) from those who scored low.

2. The scale seems to measure the much broader area of rigidity in thinking with people who are more rigid scoring high on the scale.

3. In addition to interpreting this scale alone, in certain instances shown in the **Re** and **Pr** combination summary, pp. 241-242, considering the **Pr** scale's relationship to the **Re** scale is helpful.

4. The **Pr** scale correlates positively with the California F Scale (Jensen, 1957).

5. College students tend to score in the low range on this scale with a mean of 40 T score points (Anderson & Duckworth, 1969).

6. Gough's original article proposing this scale is in the *Basic Readings on the MMPI in Psychology and Medicine* (Welsh & Dahlstrom, 1956).

HIGH SCORES
(T = 55 or Above)

See also the **Re** and **Pr** combinations, pp. 241-242.

1. High scorers on this scale tend to be rigid and not willing to look at others' points of view.

2. They may not be willing to question their own value systems.

3. The higher the score, the more rigid and adamant these people usually are about their beliefs.

4. This rigidity can either be a permanent attitude ("I am always correct") or the result of situational stress ("I need to maintain my present position so that I don't become disoriented").

5. High scorers in college may have poor academic achievement.

6. High scorers are more likely to come from the lower social classes (Gough, 1951b).

7. They also are likely to have lower IQ scores (Jensen, 1957).

LOW SCORES
(T = 45 or Below)

See also the **Re** and **Pr** combinations, pp. 241-242.

1. Low scorers tend to be open to alternative points of view.

2. The person usually has a positive view of the world and tends to be effective in coping with his or her life.

3. A score in the 45 or below range is helpful in counseling, because the client is receptive to opinions different from his or her own.

COMBINATIONS

Re-Pr

1. For a summary of selected **Re** and **Pr** scale combinations, see pp. 241-242.

SUMMARY OF Pr SCALE INTERPRETATIONS*

T Score	Interpretations
45 or below	Persons in this range usually are seen as openminded and willing to entertain opinions contrary to their own. They are likely to have a positive outlook on life. College students tend to score in this range.
45 thru 55	The majority of people score in this range.
55 or above	Persons with elevations on this scale usually are rigid in their beliefs. That is, they are not open to considering alternative points of view or questioning their own value systems. As the scores increase, the person becomes more rigid and restricted in his or her thinking. He or she also tends to be cynical and distrustful of other people and of the world in general.

*Where T scores are listed in two categories (i.e., 45 or below and 45 thru 55) and a score is obtained that is listed for two categories, use whichever interpretation seems to be most appropriate for the individual.

SUMMARY OF Re AND Pr SCALE COMBINATION INTERPRETATIONS*

If **Re** Is	and **Pr** Is	Interpretations
40 or below	45 or below	A person with this combination usually has rejected a previously held value system and has adopted a new one. He or she is willing to let others express their beliefs however and can tolerate being around people with different opinions.
	55 or above	People with this combination usually have rejected a previously held value system and have adopted a new one. They also tend to be rigid about their new beliefs and cannot tolerate others who have beliefs different from theirs.
40 thru 50	45 or below	People with this combination usually are questioning their value system and are open to exploring other people's ideas and values.
	55 or above	People with this combination are usually questioning their own beliefs and may not be able to tolerate others around them who are not also in the process of questioning their beliefs.
50 thru 65	45 or below	A person with this combination tends to accept the value system with which he or she was reared but is still able to associate with people who have different value systems. A person with this combination may believe very strongly in his or her own values, but is able to appreciate people with different values.
	55 or above	People with this combination usually are accepting of the value system with which they were reared. They also have a difficult time accepting other people who believe differently than they do.

Re-Pr

65 or above	45 or below	A person with this combination may be rigid in his or her beliefs and value system but is willing to let others express different beliefs as long as they are seen as "good" people and carry out their responsibilities.
	55 or above	A person with this combination may be rigid in his or her beliefs and value system. He or she also is intolerant of others who have different beliefs. He or she is likely to reject things that are "different."

---

*Where T scores are listed in two categories (i.e., 40 or below and 40 thru 50) and a score is obtained that is listed for two categories, use whichever interpretation seems to be most appropriate for the individual.

St SCALE
(Status Scale

The **St** scale was developed originally to distinguish those people who had high socioeconomic status from those who had low socioeconomic status. Instead of measuring the socioeconomic status the person has however we feel this scale is measuring the socioeconomic status the person desires. It also may be measuring a liking for some of the finer things of life (books, art, music, clothes, and nice surroundings) which go along with higher socioeconomic status. This last interpretation of a high status score is especially true when the **5** scale is elevated above 60 for males and is below 45 for females. In many respects, the **5** and **St** scales are measuring some of the same aspects of a person's life.

When the **5** scale is low for males or high for females, a high **St** score then may be measuring the strivings of a person to better himself or herself, to achieve recognition, and to improve his or her way of life. It also may be measuring an emphasis which the person has on acquiring some of the materialistic trappings of a better life, i.e., a nicer home, better car, or more material goods. In other words, when the **5** scale indicates that a person has aesthetic interests, the **St** scale also seems to be measuring this. When the **5** scale indicates that a person does not have many aesthetic interests, then the **St** scale seems to be measuring a desire for upward mobility and recognition.

Many times an MMPI profile has problem areas indicated on it, and the **St** scale is elevated. This elevation may be a good sign, because the client is saying he or she desires some of the better things of life and may be willing to improve in order to achieve them. An elevation on the **St** scale may be showing why a person is striving to remain in college or in a good job when everything is collapsing around him or her.

We also find this scale a very useful one to look at in marriage counseling. If the **St** scale is at approximately the same level for both people, usually no problem exists in this area. If one of the couple's **St** scores is high while the other's is low or average, however then this may be an indication of a problem area. One of the couple desires a high status while the other one does not and indeed may see no reason for striving in this way. A frequent occurrence with married couples coming in for counseling is to have a wife scoring high on **St** and the husband not. She wants to better their life (usually by him getting a better job) while he is content where he is. A compounding factor may be that the wife feels unable to specify her ambitions because "a wife should not criticize her husband's work if he's happy with it." Frequently, we have been able to persuade the wife to find a job herself or to go back to school for further education to satisfy her status needs, without necessarily disturbing the husband with his lesser status needs.

The **St** scale frequently is elevated above 60 T score points with the **Es** and **Do** scales. When **St** is, it shows a very normal pattern for college students and people with good psychological functioning.

People with low **St** scores tend to fall into three groups. The first is composed of those people who work in low status jobs, are from a low socioeconomic status background, and are reasonably content with their lot in life. In fact, these people may become uncomfortable in high status situations. The second group of people with low **St** scores is made up of those who have achieved middle status positions but who feel that their upward mobility is ended. The third group of people with low **St** scores is made up of those who also have low **Es** and **Do** scores and high **Dy** scores. These people usually feel that they are not worth much and therefore should not expect much from life including high status. When counseling persons in this third group, we have found that it is usually necessary to build their self-concept before other counseling can be done.

To explore further the implications of the low **St** score, we took a group of college counseling center clients (N = 16) with a low **St** score and examined the case notes for these clients. Some marked consistencies among the clients existed. Almost all of them generally have disturbed profiles, that is, three or more of the Clinical scales are above 70 T score points. All these clients report dissatisfaction with themselves and how they are adjusting to their environment.

St   244

Often the dissatisfaction centers around an inability to make decisions or to deal in a comfortable fashion with people.

All of the case notes for these people report inappropriate social behavior. The clients do not always interpret it as such, but the case notes indicate that the behavior is unusual for the situations in which the clients find themselves. For example, "The client came in and kept his finger in a page of a book he was reading. He would go back to reading after finishing a sentence." And again, "She appeared to come on very strongly as one who desired much closeness and friendship. Whenever anyone came close to her however she would turn her back to them psychologically and refuse to acknowledge them. At this point she would react with surprise and anger when they became upset with her."

Another common behavior for these clients was resistance to counseling, that is, they found it difficult to talk, avoided subjects, and frequently missed sessions. A close corollary to this was the large number of these clients who terminated counseling either by becoming no-shows or by quitting before the counselor felt that they had reached maximum benefit. As a result, these clients generally had poor outcomes although several of them made great gains in terms of changing their behavior. To a lesser extent, some of them seemed to be easily influenced by others.

In summation, this group of individuals in a college counseling center with low social status scores were people who generally had disturbed profiles, were dissatisifed with themselves, and were engaged in some inappropriate social behavior. In spite of their stated desire to change some of the above, they generally were resistive to counseling and were likely to terminate counseling before the counselor felt that any real progress had been made.

These generally unfavorable implications of the *low* status score are borne out in the favorable implications found for the high status scores for a group of normal persons not coming in for counseling (Appendix C). The status scale correlates highly with the following MMPI scales: **0** (—.61), **Es** (.54), **Ca** (—.51), **Dy** (—.53), and **Do** (.61).

GENERAL INFORMATION

1. The **St** scale of 34 items was developed by Gough (1948) to distinguish between two groups of high school students, those with high socioeconomic status and those with low socioeconomic status.

2. These 34 items can be grouped as follows: literacy and aesthetic interests; social poise, security, and confidence in self and others; denial of fear and anxiety; broadminded attitudes toward moral, religious, and sexual matters; and positive, dogmatic, and self-righteous opinions (Gough, 1948).

3. A significant positive correlation exists between this scale and the **K** scale.

4. Gough (1949b) has found an interesting relationship when objective status measures (such as amount of money earned) are compared to the **St** scale score. Persons of low objective status, but upwardly mobile, tend to score relatively higher on the **St** scale than on the objective status scale. The reverse is true of people tending toward downward mobility.

5. Gough's original article proposing this scale is in the *Basic Readings on the MMPI in Psychology and Medicine* (Welsh & Dahlstrom, 1956).

HIGH SCORES
(T = 55 or Above)

1. High scores tend to indicate a desire for the better things of life which usually are associated with education and/or upper socioeconomic status.

2. A person with a high **St** score, as compared to a person with a low **St** score, seems to have greater reserve in connection with personal affairs and problems, fewer somatic complaints, more satisfactory overall adjustment, greater intelligence, high scholastic aptitude, and less social introversion (Gough, 1949b).

3. College students typically score high on the **St** scale, with the mean being between 55 and 60 (Anderson & Duckworth, 1969).

4. A person with **St** scores in this range may be dissatisfied if his or her job is not of high status.

5. If a wife has an **St** score in the high range but her husband does not, she may be dissatisfied because he does not want or strive for higher status.

6. If a person has an **St** score in this range and is coming in for help for serious problems, the elevated **St** score can indicate good motivation for counseling. The client may be willing to work very diligently on these problems in order to achieve higher status.

LOW SCORES
(T = 40 or Below)

1. People with scores of 40 or below tend to have status desires similar to people from the lower socioeconomic levels.

2. Three groups of people tend to make low **St** scores.

   a. Those who work in low status jobs, are from a low socio-economic background, and are reasonably content with their status.
   b. Those who are in middle status positions and feel they have gone as high as they can.
   c. Those who also have low **Es** and **Do** scores and high **Dy** scores. These people usually have low self-esteem and low self-confidence and feel they do not deserve any higher status.

   These people may be unmarried, may stay in a bad marriage, or may have been in a series of bad marriages.

3. If a person with a score in this range is in college, the motivation to remain in college may be lacking unless family pressure helps to keep him or her there.

COMBINATIONS

Es-Do-St (T = 55 or Above) See p. 208.

E̅s̅-D̅o̅-S̅t̅ (T = 45 or Below) See p. 208.

SUMMARY OF St SCALE INTERPRETATIONS*

T Score	Interpretations

40 or below These people have status desires similar to people from the lower socioeconomic levels. They usually have low achievement needs and do not expect or strive for a higher status. If these people are from a lower SE group, they tend to be reasonably content with their lives. If they are from a middle SE group, they may feel their upward mobility is ended and not be so contented with their lives. When the score is elevated and the **Es** and **Do** scores are low, people may have extremely poor self-esteem and no self-confidence. They may feel they do not deserve a better life. These people may be unmarried, may stay in a bad marriage, or may have contracted sequential bad marriages. If people with these scores are in college, they may not really want to be there but may remain in college through family pressure.

40 thru 55 These people have status desires similar to the general, non-college population.

55 thru 60 People at this level have status desires similar to those of the general college graduate. They tend to like having some of the nicer things in life, such as good books and a nice home. They may be dissatisfied if their jobs lack status or the financial rewards are insufficient to provide the material that goes with status.

60 or above People at this level have status desires similar to those of a graduate student or someone from a high socioeconomic level. They usually have high achievement needs and especially like to be recognized for doing a good job at work or school. They may be dissatisfied if they do not have some of the nicer things in life, such as good books or nice homes. They may complain of job dissatisfaction if their status needs are not met by their jobs.

---

*Where T scores are listed in two categories (i.e., 40 or below and 40 thru 55) and a score is obtained that is listed for two categories, use whichever interpretation seems to be most appropriate for the individual.

St

Cn SCALE
(Control Scale)

The control scale is an especially useful one on the MMPI. An elevated **Cn** scale can be a clue as to how much of the behavior indicated by elevations on the Clinical scales will be exhibited in the presence of other people. If the **Cn** scale is elevated with other Clinical scale elevations indicating some problems, the client has some ability to control his or her problem behavior and to show only what he or she wishes others to observe. While these others may not always be the people the counselor wishes would or would not see the client's behavior, the elevation on **Cn** does indicate a strength, because the client has the ability to control problem behavior to some extent. A problem occasionally occurs when the client chooses to hide certain or all problem behavior from the counselor as well as from others.

When the **Cn** scale is above the typical range (55 or above) with no elevations above 70 on the Clinical scales, the client may appear somewhat reserved and non-emotional. This behavior is especially true the higher the **Cn** scale. Many people with this combination have grown up in an environment where emotions were not readily expressed or encouraged. Some of these people may express the wish that they could be freer with other people or at least more expressive of their emotions. In these instances, a sign of therapeutic progress may be a lowering of the **Cn** scale. Elevations on the **Cn** scale can thus indicate client strength (when the Clinical scales are high) or potential problems (when the Clinical scales are low).

A low **Cn** score means that the person tends to show the behavior indicated by his or her Clinical scale score elevations. If the Clinical scores are low (below 70), the person has no behavior that needs to be controlled. This does not mean however that the person cannot control his or her behavior if the Clinical scales should become elevated. The **Cn** scale in this latter instance might also become elevated. However if a person has Clinical scale elevations of 70 or above, a low **Cn** score does mean that the behavior indicated by the elevated Clinical scale scores is not being controlled by the person, and the Clinical scale behavior is exhibited in the presence of others.

Elevations on the **Cn** scale, especially when accompanied by elevations on the **K, 3,** and **R** scales may indicate a type of person who is constricted in many ways. For further discussion of these scales, see the **R** scale commentary, p. 197.

The important thing to remember in interpreting the **Cn** scale is to look at the accompanying Clinical scales and to use their elevations in combination with **Cn** scale placement to get the most accurate interpretation of the **Cn** scale.

A rather wide combination of items make up the **Cn** scale. The items can be divided into seven major categories:

1. The first group of items appear to be an awareness of and an admission to base impulses and behavior. "I sometimes feel like swearing." "I gossip a little at times." This may lead to an openness in counseling interviews which interviewers like.

2. A second group of items indicates that the individual is uncomfortable at the conscious level. "I sometimes feel that I am about to go to pieces." "I wish I could be as happy as others seem to be." In a college population, people with elevated Clinical scales and high **Cn** scores report uncomfortable feelings but seem to see their cause as being situational, that is, a bad marriage situation, lack of vocational choice, or inability to set appropriate goals because of the university structure.

3. A group of manic items is the third major category. "When I get bored I like to stir up some excitement." "At times my thoughts have raced ahead faster than I could speak them." This suggests that a rather high activity level exists for the person with a high **Cn** Scale score.

4. Some religious items are included as a fourth group that appear to be a rejection of some of the more fundamentalistic beliefs such as miracles and the accuracy of prophets.

5. A fifth group of items concern the denial of certain symptoms such as the use of alcohol and fainting spells.

6. Some items referring to family relations compose a sixth group. People with a high **Cn** scale report their relations are poor. They answer false to "I love my mother" and to "Members of my family and my close relatives get along quite well."

7. A final group of items deals with the expectations of others. In this area, some would say that people with high **Cn** scores simply are being realistic because they agree with an item such as "People generally demand more respect for their own rights than they are willing to allow for others."

Seemingly, in looking at these groups of items, people with high **Cn** scores appear to have a tendency to be very aware of their feelings, especially their feelings of discomfort and impulsivity. A hypothesis we would like to suggest is that persons with a high control scale may have a set to admit that these impulses exist and this may raise the pathological scales unduly high. The **Cn** scale then may be picking up a response bias. People with a high control scale and high Clinical scales may overemphasize the pathological feelings they do have and therefore may not truly be as disturbed as individuals with high Clinical scales but lower control scales.

GENERAL INFORMATION

1. Cuadra (1953) developed the 50 item **Cn** scale as a measure of personality control.

2. After identifying 30 pairs of similar MMPI Clinical scale profiles, where one person of the pair was hospitalized and the other was not, Cuadra isolated the MMPI items that differentiated these two groups and developed the **Cn** scale.

3. Cuadra's original article proposing this scale is in the *Basic Readings on the MMPI in Psychology and Medicine* (Welsh & Dahlstrom, 1956).

HIGH SCORES
(T = 50 or Above)

1. A person with a high **Cn** score may have a measure of personal control that can prevent problem behavior (as shown by elevations on the Clinical scales) from being exhibited in the presence of others. This depends upon how close the control scale score is to the highest Clinical scale elevation. Consult the summary table of the **Cn** scale, pp. 255-256 for further information on this scale.

2. People who have high **Cn** scores without elevations on the Clinical scales may appear to be overcontrolled and somewhat unemotional. Their lack of Clinical scale elevations would seem to indicate that no need exists for the amount of personal control shown by the elevations on the **Cn** scale.

LOW SCORES
(T = 50 or Below)

1. A person with a low **Cn** score, but with elevated Clinical scale scores (T = 70 or above), readily shows the behavior indicated by the Clinical scale elevations.

2. A person with a low **Cn** score and no elevated Clinical scale scores (T = 70 or below) has no behavior which needs to be controlled and the **Cn** score reflects this.

These combinations do not mean that the person is unable to control his or her behavior should the Clinical scales go above 70. If the Clinical scales do go above 70, the **Cn** scale also may rise.

SUMMARY OF Cn SCALE INTERPRETATIONS*

If the Highest Clinical Scale Is	and **Cn** Is	Interpretations
70 or below	50 or below	This combination of scores is usual for person with minor or no psychological problems.
	50 thru 60	This person may appear to be somewhat unemotional. He or she may tend to mask feelings.
	60 or above	The person tends to be over-controlled, objective, and detached. He or she tends to suppress outward expression of inner feelings and impulses and probably has difficulty expressing warmth.
70 or above	11 or more below the highest Clinical scale	The person cannot keep the impulses and/or behavior shown by the Clinical scale elevations from being observed by others. If the Control scale is 11 or more points below the highest Clinical scale but still above 60, the person may have some control over the amount of behavior that is shown.
	Within 10 points of the highest Clinical scale	The person is able to conceal and control the impulses and behavior indicated by the Clinical scale elevation, although, if the person chooses to do so, the impulses and behavior may be revealed. If the person chooses not to show the behavior indicated by the Clinical scales, he or she may fantasize about them.
	11 or more points over	The person has much control over the impulses indicated by the Clinical scale elevations. He or she may appear cool or strained and probably fantasizes about the problems shown by

| the highest Clinical Scale | the Clinical scale elevations with little outward manifestation of the behavior. |

---

*Where T scores are listed in two categories (i.e., 50 or below and 50 thru 60) and a score is obtained that is listed for two categories, use whichever interpretation seems to be most appropriate for the individual.

chapter **5**

INTERPRETING THE MMPI

Jane Duckworth and Wayne Anderson

This chapter presents two different methods of interpreting MMPI profiles using the New scales as well as the Validity and Clinical scales. The first section of the chapter was written by Jane Duckworth and the second section was written by Wayne Anderson. In interpreting the MMPI many similarities occur for the two methods as well as many differences. Both approaches are presented to show different ways of doing MMPI interpretations.

MMPI INTERPRETATIONS
by
Jane Duckworth

When I interpret a MMPI, I usually am focusing my attention on two things: (1) what are the current *behaviors* and *feelings* of the individual who took the test, and (2) what are the *underlying reasons* for these behaviors and feelings. If the person is coming in for counseling and/or therapy, I also am interested in *what type of treatment* might prove most effective for the individual.

Some limitations of the applicability of the way I do MMPI interpretations may exist. I have worked mainly with bright people both young (students) and old (faculty) at a university counseling center. If a choice of interpretations for the MMPI is possible, I tend to err on the side of the optimistic one. I have found that the high points of a profile for these two groups do not always have the dire implications that are attached to them in the MMPI interpretations derived from clinical populations. True, the behavior and feelings of these counseling center clients may be maladaptive, but because of the client's intelligence and residence in an environment geared to trying new things, the manifestations of the maladaptive behavior and feelings usually are milder and the liklihood of positive change is much greater than with clients in clinical populations. If the profile being interpreted is from a different population than that found in a counseling center, checking to see if the optimistic approach I use is applicable may be necessary.

Another difference between the way I do interpretations and the way some others do them is that I operate from a philosophy that emphasizes looking for the strengths within a client and building on those while minimizing maladaptive behavior. I tend to ignore maladaptive behavior if it is not causing the client or the people around him or her a great deal of trouble, and I reinforce or try to build upon the adaptive behavior the client is exhibiting. A further difference in the way I do interpretations is that while I am aware of the underlying dynamics of the client's behavior as shown in the MMPI, my main focus in the interpretation is on the client's behavior and the way his or her feelings affect their behavior.

My impression is that this interpretative approach emphasizing client strengths rather than weaknesses, focusing on behavior and feelings rather than underlying dynamics is becoming more applicable to the mental health centers and private clinics populations than it used to be. As state outpatient mental health systems become prevalent and therapy is more available and less stigmatized, my feeling is that more "normal" people (non-neurotic, non-psychotic) are coming for help with everyday problems such as dealing with their children or marriage or divorce concerns. Clients in these agencies resemble the ones seen in college counseling centers more than they resemble patients in mental institutions, and the approaches stressed in this chapter may be very applicable to them.

For a more clinical approach to MMPI interpretation, I suggest Graham's (1977) book on the MMPI in which he discussed his general interpretive strategy. Graham's chapter and the two approaches presented in this chapter give a broad overview of MMPI interpretation.

When working with the MMPI, I divide the interpretation into three parts, those concerning the Validity, Clinical, and New scales. I deal with each section separately at first and then look at them together. In general, I do not pay attention to scales appearing between 45 and 60 T-score points, because scales in this middle range do not tend to indicate unique behavior. I start by individually interpreting the very highest scales in each section and then work down to the scales closest to 60 T-score points. After this, I look at the scales that are the farthest below 45 and work up to the scales closest to 45 T-score points. In most profiles many more high points occur than low points.

I start an MMPI interpretation by looking at the *Validity scales* and use them as an indication of the general test-taking attitude of the individual: for example, is the client saying he or she is feeling good (high **K**) or bad (high **F**) about life on the day he or she took the test. The higher these Validity scales are above 60 T-score points, the more likely the person is to be emphasizing that particular feeling and maybe even exaggerating it: "I feel like I'm overwhelmed with problems" (high **F**); "Life is absolutely beautiful, nothing is the slightest bit wrong with what's happening" (high **K**). Listed on pages 45-47 in this book are some typical combinations of Validity scales and their interpretations.

After getting a general idea about the mood of the person taking the test, I then proceed to the *Clinical scales* and interpret them individually from the highest scale above 60 down to the one closest to 60 T-score points. I look then at the lowest scales and move up to the scales closest to 45 T-score points. If several scales are above 70 T-score points (four or more), I tend to down play the scales between 60 and 70 T-score points, because these may be elevated due to the emotional state of the client.

If only a few scales are above 70, then the scales within the 60-70 T-score range can be very useful for indicating behavior that is present but not necessarily a problem as it might be if the scale were above 70. Instead the behavior may be a way of dealing with life that is adaptive rather than maladaptive. The summary at the end of each Clinical scale section indicates the wealth of information that can be obtained from scale scores in this usually ignored 60-70 T score range.

After looking at the various high and low points of the Clinical scales, I move to the *New scales* and follow the same procedure used with the Clinical scales. I start interpreting the highest scales and work down to those scales closest to 60 T score points. I then interpret the lowest scales and work up to the scales closest to 45 T score points. I do not ignore the ones between 60 and 70 T score points within this New scale group even if a number of scales are above 70. I find that all elevations on these scales are useful regardless of their relative height.

After noting the high and low scales for the Clinical and New scale sections, I then start the much more difficult process of considering the scales in combinations and balancing the information from one scale against the information from another. I do not ignore inconsistencies in the individual scale interpretations but rather try to determine under what conditions these two behaviors could exist in the same person at the same time. This situation is where the New scales are of greatest use. They can help refine the information presented in the Clinical scale elevations so that the most accurate interpretation of the Clinical scales can be given. A high 2 scale may not indicate self-deprecation, for example, if the Ego Strength scale (**Es**) is above 50-T score points. Summaries showing refinements of the Clinical scales by the New scales are at the end of the appropriate Clinical scales.

In addition to the refinements mentioned previously, the New scales indicate strengths that a client may have that temper predictions made from the Clinical scales. The Control scale (**Cn**), if elevated above 60 T-score points, indicates ability of the client to control the outward manifestation of his or her maladaptive behavior shown on the elevated Clinical scales. A client may have a **2-7-8** profile, but if he or she also has a **Cn** scale above 70 that person probably has some control over who sees the depression, anxiety, and confusion indicated by the Clinical scales. He or she also may be able to temper the amount of these behaviors shown. These New scale refinements provide important information for the most accurate interpretation of the Clinical scales.

In addition to examining these refinements of the Clinical scale information, the practitioner should consider the Clinical scales in their various combinations. I have found two point combinations to be the most useful. Occasionally, three point combinations are helpful; but, in general, they do not add more information than what is found in the two point combinations.

I believe that Graham's (1977) work with two point combinations and the work of Gynther et al. (various references in the Reference section) all reported in the Clinical section of this book are some of the best sources of information on the two point codes. Graham's book and Gynther's articles should be consulted for more thorough descriptions of these combinations.

When all this information on a profile has been gathered, the interpretation can be made. When I do an interpretation, I try to say something first about the *test-taking attitude* of the person so that the rest of the information given in the report can be interpreted in the light of how the client was feeling at the time. I proceed then with the body of the report and start by mentioning those *behaviors and feelings* most likely to be overtly shown and expressed by the client, using the two or three highest Clinical scale elevations as my clues. In reference to the 2-7-8 profile mentioned previously, for example, I might say "Mr. R. is most likely to be reporting severe depression and would appear to be highly anxious and confused."

Next I bring in the *refinements* to the Clinical scales that I may have learned from the New scales, or from the Clinical scale combinations. If the 2-7-8 profile has an **Es** scale above 45, I would say "The depression shown by Mr. R. does not however include the self-deprecation typically seen in these cases."

After describing as accurately as I can the behavior and feelings shown by the client, I then proceed to hypotheses, if I have any, concerning why these behaviors and feelings may be present. An interpretation for a woman with a high 2-4-6 in the midst of a divorce might be "The depression, anger, and confusion shown by this woman seem most likely to be her reaction to the pending divorce. It would be helpful to verify this reaction by seeing if her anger is directed specifically toward her husband and the situation she is in or whether it is generalized to many other people and situations."

Following these hypotheses, I then go to *strengths* I may see in the profile. These strengths may be revealed by the New scales or, sometimes by lower Clinical scales elevations.

The report is closed with some predictions concerning *prognosis* and *implications for therapy*. For a 2-8 profile, statements such as the following might be made. "Miss R. should be amenable to therapy because of the amount of psychological pain she is feeling. However,

I recommend that therapy progress slowly and with as many simple, specific suggestions as possible because of the amount of psychological confusion the client is experiencing."

When my students are working on an interpretation, I advise them to get up a work sheet for the profile in the following manner. They are to divide a sheet of paper by drawing a vertical line two-inches from left side; then place the scale number they are interpreting on the left side of the line and the interpretation of it on the right. They do this for all the Validity, Clinical, and New scales above 60 and below 45 T score points starting with the highest scales working down to 60 and then interpreting the lowest scales up to those closest to 45. After doing all the scales individually, they are to look at what they have written and try to fit the various bits of information together as a whole, emphasizing the highest Clinical scales the most and taking into consideration the refinements indicated by the test-taking attitude of the client, the New scales, and the lower Clinical scales. After this preparation is done they are to write a summary for the profile, making sure to cover the client's behavior and feelings, strengths, and so forth.

With these points in mind, Figure 17 is a profile of Mr. J.R. The following is a typical interpretation for a person with such a profile.

The client, Mr. R., is a thirty-four year-old white male with a masters degree in art. He is on the faculty of a small, midwestern college. Mr. R. is coming for therapy because he is upset about his marriage and also because his family doctor has suggested that some of the tenseness he has been experiencing may be because of psychological problems.

This man is doing well as an art professor at the college, but he reports not feeling really good about what is happening in his life. He has the feeling, he says, that something must be better somewhere. He has focused on his wife as the cause of much of his unhappiness because she is "too placid" and, he feels, not interested in discussing anything other than everyday events.

The following is an example of a work sheet and summary (interpretation) as they might be for Mr. R. When the MMPI interpretation is sent to someone, the work sheet material about the individual scales is not sent. Only the summary with the scale

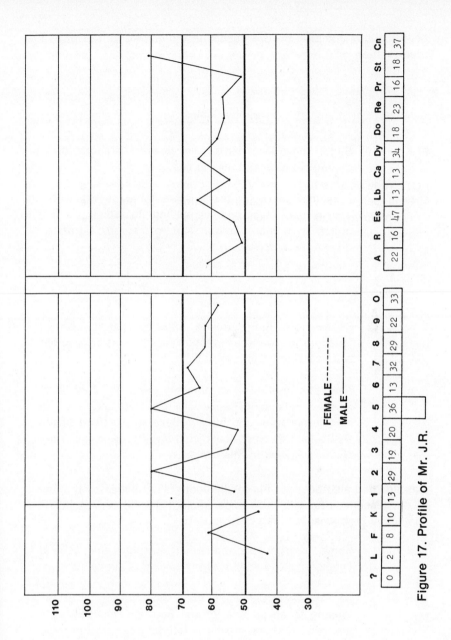

?	L	F	K	1	2	3	4	5	6	7	8	9	O
0	2	8	10	13	29	19	20	36	13	32	29	22	33

A	R	Es	Lb	Ca	Dy	Do	Re	Pr	St	Cn
22	16	47	13	13	34	18	23	16	18	37

FEMALE------
MALE————

Figure 17. Profile of Mr. J.R.

263

identifications (material in parentheses in the summary) is sent as the interpretation.

Validity Scales

F = 62	Slight elevation; perhaps a minimal amount of psychological pain and feeling bad.
L = 43	A typical score for the **L** scale for a person with his educational level. He is willing to admit to some common human faults. Not of much significance unless the **L** score is high.

Clinical Scales

2 = 80	Depression, may include self-deprecation. Check **Es** score in New scale section for clues as to whether self-deprecation is involved.
5 = 80	Aesthetic interests and possible passivity. Very likely this scale is at least partially elevated because this man is an artist and highly educated. Need to check **Dy-Do** in the New scale section to see if passivity also is involved in this elevation.
7 = 69	Anxiety, but at a minimum level (below 70). This anxiety will most likely be seen as occasional tenseness rather than overt anxiety.
6 = 67	Some interpersonal sensitivity without the general suspiciousness seen when the scale is above 70.
8 = 64	At this level the scale may show creativity or belonging to an atypical group. Because this person is an artist, that the creativity interpretation is the most accurate is likely.
9 = 63	An abundance of psychological energy. This is a typical level for a productive person.

0 = 60	Borderline for interpretation. This scale may indicate preference for being by himself, but it does not indicate problems with being around others.

New Scales

Control **Cn = 81**	Great ability to control who sees the behavior shown on the elevated Clinical scales. Because **Cn** is very high and Clinical scores are not greatly elevated, this person may even be too controlled at times.
Low back pain **Lb = 66**	Maybe saying, "I'm a wonderful person. I love people, and they never annoy me, but for some reason I am uncomfortable and not as happy as I should be."
Dependency **Dy = 66**	Psychological dependency. He would like to lean on others at times and have them take care of him.
Anxiety **A = 62**	Some situational anxiety. This score is at about the level to be expected when the **7** scale is between 60 and 70 T score points.
Dy-Do combination **Dy = 66** **Do = 59**	This is sometimes looked at when a small point spread exists (less than 10 T score points) or either scale is within the 50-60 T score range and the other is above 60 T score points.

For this person, it indicates the psychological dependency already mentioned, combined with a strong underlying desire to take charge of his own life. This ambivalence can create problems for this man and those close to him because he may act one way one time and the opposite way very shortly afterwards. Another way this combination may be shown is by passive-aggressive behavior. This man may subtly ask others to take care of him and then subvert that helping by complaining about the results or subverting the effectiveness of them in some way.

F elevation compared to Clinical scale elevations	When the **F** scale elevation is only between 60 and 70 T score points, but the Clinicals (excluding scales **5** and **9**) are above 70 T score points, the person is not complaining as much on the **F** scale as he is on the Clinicals. This may be because he is used to feeling the depression shown by the elevated **2** scale. He reports being definitely depressed (the elevation on **2**), but he is not greatly worried about it nor does he feel really bad about it (lower **F** scale).
2 scale compared to **Es** scale	Mr. R. is feeling depressed but is not self-deprecating. He feels life is somewhat unpleasant (high **2**) but does not necessarily see himself as the cause or as unworthy of a better existence. (**Es** above 50).
5 scale compared to **Dy** and **Do** scales	While showing aesthetic interests, this scale (**5**) also may be showing some passivity (**Dy** = 66). However, this passivity is tempered by some feelings of dominance and/or passive aggressiveness (**Do** = 59 and **Dy** — **Do** spread).

Summary

(Scale identifications are added for clarity. In an ordinary report they are not included.)

This profile depicts a person who was feeling somewhat bad at the time he took the test (**F** scale). He most likely was complaining about feeling depressed (**2**) and also may have shown tenseness (**7**). He is liable to have some passive-aggressive tendencies (**5** and **Dy—Do**) that could be directed at those closest to him, because he has a tendency to be quite sensitive to how others feel about him (**6**).

He has much control (**Cn**) over his behavior, and he can keep people from seeing his depression and tenseness if he wishes. However, this control is at such a high level that he may use it in the therapy situation to keep important feelings and behavior from the therapist as well as from others in the outside world.

Another problem in working with this client could be that he may not have some of the necessary insight into why he is so unhappy (**Lb**). He may feel that he tries hard and loves people, but things still do not feel right nor is he happy.

These feelings of unhappiness and depression probably have been around for a long time, so that the client is not as worried about them as others with similar feelings might be (difference between **F** elevation and Clinical elevations). The prognosis for therapy is mixed. On the one hand, this client does report depression and tenseness and a general feeling of malaise; but, on the other hand, he is not exceptionally worried about these feelings and has such control over the expression of them that he may not be willing or able to show them in their full ramifications to the therapist. Add to this the possibility of some passive-aggressive behavior as the therapist gets closer and the interpersonal sensitivity of the client, and it can be seen that some potential problems are at hand.

This type of client tends to work well with a therapist who goes slowly and helps deal with the overt signs of discomfort before starting to delve into the underlying dynamics of the individual. Frequently a client of this type does well with a woman or a very empathetic man because of the perceived help this type of counselor/therapist can give. This client wants someone to lean on and usually will respond quickly to therapist warmth. What the client does not see and what may take longer to deal with are his underlying aggressiveness and sensitivity. The possibility exists that the client will terminate therapy once the pain is gone but before the more hidden dynamics are worked upon.

MMPI INTERPRETATIONS

by

Wayne Anderson

Interpreting MMPI profiles often takes a considerable amount of time in the beginning because of the need to think through the many possibilities and to check sourcebooks for ideas. With practice, an interpretation can be done quite quickly. As the standard characteristics associated with a certain profile become known, spotting inconsistencies and outstanding characteristics is possible. Even with experience however it does pay to review occasionally the information given in this book, because even an experienced clinician will not always recall all possible interpretations.

A general procedure for developing an interpretation would be as follows:

1. Check the Validity scores to find out what the attitude of the client was toward taking the test; that is, was the client being open, defensive, or admitting to thoughts and behavior of an unusual nature? A frequent profile in a client population is a high **F** (70) and a low **K** (below 45). This would influence me to develop a different interpretation about the profile than if there were an **F** of 45 and a **K** of 70. In the first case, I would suspect that the client might be exaggerating symptoms and thus creating an undue elevation of the Clinical scale scores. In the second case, the client might be striving to present a normal picture and would be much less likely to be open about personal defects.

    I also pay attention to **L** scale scores over 55 although certain features may be present in the profile such as a high **Re** scale score that will allow me to interpret the profile even with a **L** scale score around 65. (See the **Re** section, p. 232.) I would recommend special attention to the patterns of **L, F, K** which are discussed on pp. 45-47.

2. Next I establish the basic characteristics of the high Clinical scales both by themselves and in combination with each other. For example, if a high **4** scale (70 T score points or higher) occurs with the next highest Clinical scale half a standard deviation or more below, I use the interpretation for the marked elevation of the **4** scale. If the profile has both the **4** and **9** scales elevated with the two being within two or three points of each other, I use the **4-9** two point code interpretation.

3. Having established the interpretations of the most elevated Clinical scales, I am now in a position to consider how they are being modified. First, I check those scale which also are elevated but at a somewhat lower level than the very highest ones. If the **4** scale is at 80 T score points and the **8** scale is at 70, for example, the **8** scale adds a bad judgment element to the usual high **4** scale interpretation. The person with a **4-8** profile may engage in bizarre actions or interpret incorrectly what another person is expecting or asking of him (**8** scale) as well as be acting out in some way (**4** scale). The **8** scale indicates more negative behavior than just the **4** scale by itself.

On the other hand, some scales may be positive modifiers of highly elevated scales, that is, elevations on them would allow the tester to interpret the higher scales more positively than usual. An example would be a profile where the **5** scale is elevated (above 60) with the **4** scale (above 70). The **5** scale may act as a suppressor of the acting out usually associated with a high **4** scale. Sometimes the positive interpretation is relative; for example, a **7-8** profile with an **A** scale above 60 T score points indicates a disturbed person. He or she usually is very uncomfortable and characteristics of maladjustment typically are present. However, this is a more positive pattern than if the **7** and **8** scales are high and the **A** scale is low (below 50 T score points) because this combination would suggest the possibility of a more chronic adjustment problem and one less likely to change as a result of therapy.

Beginning interpreters sometimes make the mistake of taking each elevated scale and only interpreting it separately. The MMPI interpreter needs to keep in mind that elevated scores tend to modify and change each other. An elevated scale will not necessarily indicate exactly the same characteristic when other scales or combinations of scales also are elevated. We have attempted to present examples in the previous chapters of some of these scale modifications.

4. The next point in developing an interpretation is to consider the low scales (below 45 T score points) on the profile and to look at the high scale and low scale interpretations together for additional insights. An example would be that an individual with a low **4** scale (45 or below) and an elevated **0** scale (65 or above) would likely be someone who is not only shy and withdrawn (**0** scale) but also someone who is probably sexually inexperienced (**4** scale). A female profile with a low **5** scale and high **4** scale would suggest that she is an individual who uses sex as a way of manipulating and controlling men. A low **2** scale with a high **9** scale on a profile would suggest an unusually buoyant, outgoing individual who may not be appropriately responsive to the problems of other people.

5. Having completed the first four points, the more creative aspect of interpreting the MMPI can be done; that is, interpreting the inconsistencies. Much of what we have discussed up to this point can be done in a more or less routine manner. This step requires experience with the test and some knowledge of the relationships between scales. One must ask what are the inconsistencies in the test, what does not relate in a logical manner? The interpreter then thinks through possible reasons as to why these relationships may exist. For example, what can be made out of a profile in which the **Do** and **Dy** scales are both above 60? Or the **2** scale and **9** scale both above 70? What can one make of a high **Es** scale and low **K**? A study of these inconsistencies will help the interpreter form a clearer picture of the individual who is being considered.

As an example, I have a college student's profile with an **F** scale of 80 and a **K** scale at 45. The Clinical scales generally are elevated with the **8** scale at 80 and the **4**, **6**, and **9** scales at 75. So far the test is quite consistent. In looking at the New scales however I find the **Pr** scale to be at 65 and the **St** scale at 64. This does not fit my expectations. These scores usually are negatively correlated with each other (see Appendix C). In a college population, when the **Pr** scale is low, the **St** scale usually is elevated and vice versa. The mean **Pr** scale score for college students is 40 and the mean **St** scale score for students is 60 (Anderson & Duckworth, 1969). I would like to know why this interesting inconsistency in these profile scores exists. The **Pr** score is consistent with the rest of the test, because it is a sign of general maladjustment and difficulty in relating to others as are the elevated scores on the Clinical scales. The **St** score, on the other hand, seems to correlate more with a healthy outlook on life and with the giving of socially desirable answers. At this point, I may not have a good hypothesis as to how these scores can exist together, but it is a point I can explore with the client.

Occasionally one will have an MMPI profile about which a consistent report can be written, but when talking to the client the report does not match with either the client's overt behavior or with what the client evidently believes about himself or herself. I have found no good explanation for this situation. It is rather rare; but it does occur, and an interpreter should come to expect it occasionally. Some deeper level at which the interpretation is true may exist, but a client should not be forced to fit a particular interpretation if the tester and the client do not view it as applicable.

As examples of how I interpret the MMPI, three brief interpretations will be made of sample profiles.

Profile #1

Profile #1 (Figure 18) is that of an 18-year-old male who was referred to a college counseling center for personal adjustment counseling. The **F-K** index shows that the client is saying that he feels bad, and the possibility exists that he may be exaggerating his symptoms.

The **4-8** would be a fairly frequent two point code in a psychiatric population but is rare in a college population. The **8** scale modifies the **4** scale rather markedly, and the following characteristics could be predicted at a fairly high level of probability for this individual.

271

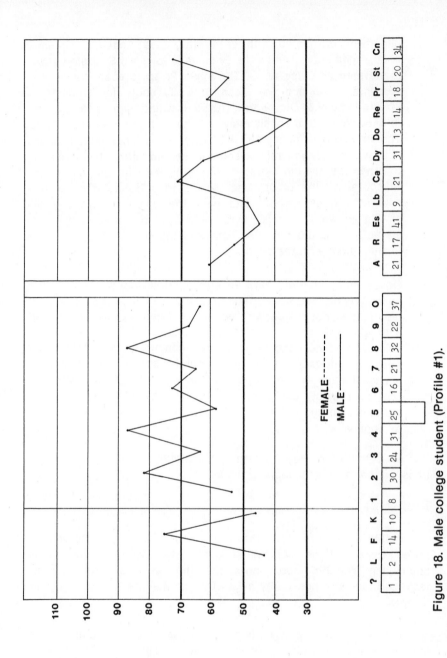

Figure 18. Male college student (Profile #1).

1. He may get into trouble because of bad judgment (**8** scale) as to when to act out against whatever it is he may be fighting (**4** scale). His history probably will show that he has had trouble not only with his family but also with other authority figures such as school personnel and employers.

2. He is likely to distrust others and have problems with close relationships.

3. He probably will engage in unpredictable, impulsive behavior.

4. Because of either his dress or behavior, he will strike others as being strange or odd.

The addition of the elevated **2** scale in this pattern brings in the descriptors "depressed, tense, irritable, and hostile." When the **2** scale is this high, it indicates an individual who has various escape methods in stress situations, such as using drugs, alcohol, or the actual physical avoidance of situations such as dropping out of school.

The **6** scale adds a definite possibility of violence, and as it is over 70, the possibility of delusional thinking also exists. The individual with a **4-8** pattern tends to be suspicious, and the addition of the high **6** scale increases the possibility of increased suspicion and a feeling of being treated unjustly.

These elevations would suggest that the client is coming for therapy because he sees himself as the victim of outside influences or pressures and not because of his awareness of personal defects. I feel this attitude is likely to make him a poor therapy risk.

The New scales in this case add support to the Clinical scale interpretation but not too much new information. The elevated **Ca**, **A**, and **Cn** scales support the general maladjustment hypothesis. The **A** scale may be a bit low for an elevated profile like his, but along with the **Cn** scale suggests that he is likely to be able to hold things together so that hospitalization will not be necessary.

The low **Re** scale is supportive of the tendency toward impulsiveness and trouble with authority indicated by the **4-8** combination. On a student's profile it would suggest also the likelihood of academic difficulties.

The elevated **Dy** scale in conjunction with the elevated **4** scale is an interesting inconsistency; that is, he has a need to fight authority (**4** scale) at the same time that he has a need for a dependent relationship (**Dy** scale). This is not such an unusual pattern, but it is an interesting one to consider. The **Dy-Do** pattern shows that he feels unable to take charge of his life at this time (**Do** scale) and wants to lean on someone (**Dy** scale). Given the other indices in this profile however whether or not a therapist would be able to hold him in therapy is questionable in spite of his felt need for dependency.

We have, then, an impulsive, irritable, hostile person with dependency needs. His bad judgment, difficulty with authority, and probably delusional thinking combine to make him a poor therapy risk.

The actual client was quite delusional in that he felt that others were persecuting him. He thought that he was able to hear people talking about him at long distances because of his very good hearing. He had some real doubts about his masculinity. He took pride in the fact that he was very manipulative and liked things that way. He did many things to draw attention to himself. One of his problems was his inability to get along with other people in the dormitory in which he lived. He also admitted he had trouble interacting with women and that he had a bad temper.

Profile #2

Profile #2 (Figure 19) is that of a female college student. The **L, F, K** pattern suggests a long-standing set of problems to which she has become adjusted, at least to the extent that she feels good about herself (**K** scale) but has some bad feelings about her situation (**F** scale).

On the Clinical scales, Scale **9** frequently is high for college students. The high score on this profile indicates that the client probably is overactive, and makes little progress for the amount of effort expended. We would expect her to be usually good humored but to become irritable at times and have outbursts of temper. Because this profile is of a college counselee, we also would expect her to be aggressive and/or opinionated.

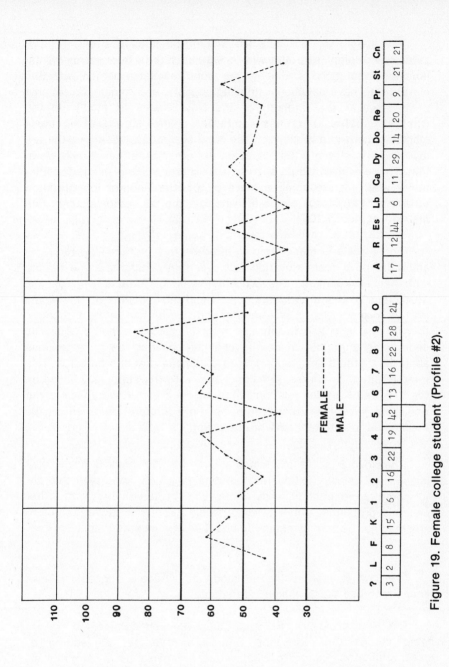

Figure 19. Female college student (Profile #2).

275

The height of the **8** scale would, on the face of it, be a pathological sign. A profile with a **9-8** like this is frequent in mental hospital populations. Ordinarily, we would expect a person with this elevation to have delusional thinking, anxiety, and rumination. At this point however the strength of the New scales in modifying the Clinical scales becomes apparent. The signs of general maladjustment and anxiety on the New scales (scales **A** and **Ca**) are low. The ego strength (**Es** scale), on the other hand, has a mild elevation. This elevation would suggest that she is holding things together rather well. We are going to have to look for another interpretation other than pathology therefore to explain the **9-8** combination in this profile.

The **6** scale is moderately elevated on this profile (T score = 65) and with the **8** scale elevation would certainly suggest some trouble with her environment. She probably is uncomfortable with people, suspicious of them, and feels cut off and misunderstood. This would lead us to predict she has some difficulties with her sense of identity; that is, she is either dissatisfied with her present identity or she is undergoing a period of identity change. She may be quite anxious about how others are responding to the image that she presents. This interpretation, of course, is inconsistent with the statement based on the **L**, **F**, and **K** scales relationship. It seems a better hypothesis about the client, given the total profile, but both interpretations should be considered in an interview with the client.

The low **2** scale in combination with the high **9** scale may indicate a basically extroverted personality which could lead this girl to some corresponding lack of feeling in identifying with other people's problems. When others present problems to her therefore she may not be very sympathetic about what concerns them.

The low **5** scale with the moderate **4** scale suggests some tendency to use sex to manipulate situations.

The New scales, **A**, **Es**, and **Ca**, have been commented on as being inconsistent with the Clinical profile but as adding a meaningful modification to what would otherwise be a pathological profile. Two other scores on the New scales deserve some attention. The low **Lb** scale score suggests that the client is easily angered by people and probably is outspoken about her reactions. This is supported, of course, by the interpretation of the high **9** scale. The low **R** scale score would suggest a willingness to discuss her problems, especially those which she has admitted to in filling out the MMPI.

In summary, what we have is a highly energetic, somewhat irritable individual who is having difficulty relating to others and feels misunderstood by them. The counselor should look for the possibility of identity problems and be prepared to help this individual make some changes in self-concept. The client may at times be somewhat unfeeling about others, and the possibility of sex being used as a manipulative device exists. Given the general features of the profile, the prognosis for this case should be rather good.

Profile #3

Profile #3 (Figure 20) also is for a female college student. The Validity scores indicate the classic "cry for help" pattern. The high **F** and low **K** scales border on indicating that she is exaggerating her symptoms, probably to insure that the therapist will see her problems as serious enough to demand attention.

On the Clinical scales the elevated **2** scale shows gloom, sadness, and dissatisfaction with life, but because of the height of the **7** and **8** scales, we need to consider a modification of the **2** scale. The three scores together suggest a tense, anxious, depressed individual who may exhibit confused thinking and much self-doubt. A not unusual score concurrent with this pattern is a low **5** scale which in college women intensifies what we have just said about tenseness, anxiety, and depression and brings in the strong possibility of lack of skills with the opposite sex. Study problems also are indicated for this combination of scales.

The elevated **0** scale adds emphasis to the shyness and introversion symptoms and again supports the possibility of difficulty in relations with the opposite sex. The general maladjustment of the pattern also is supported by the elevations on the **A** and **Ca** scales in the New scales.

The high **Pr** scale is unusual in a college student; however, as the rest of the profile also is elevated, this scale may be a reflection of some of the difficulties the client is having in adjusting at this time. This scale may reflect a temporary depressed attitude because of her

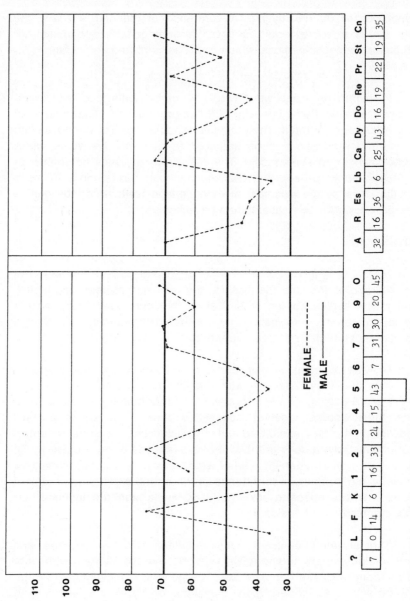

Figure 20. Female college student (Profile #3).

situation; that is, because of her own unhappiness she is feeling that no one is any good, and her prejudice is extended to almost all groups and individuals.

The low **Es** score is certainly not a good therapy indicator; and the **F-K** combination suggests she is hurting, voluntarily seeking help, and is young and intelligent. The elevation of the **Cn** scale suggests that she probably is holding together at least in public. The therapy potential therefore is much better than the low **Es** score would suggest.

A factor which will help in doing therapy with this individual is the elevated **Dy** scale, which shows a strong need to be dependent on someone. If appropriate rapport is established by the therapist, this woman should stay as a client. She will have some tendency toward passivity and permitting the therapist to set the direction and pace. The therapist will need to be aware of this possibility. While using the dependency therapeutically, the therapist should encourage the client to take responsibility for herself and her behavior.

In summary, this test indicates that the client is a depressed, tense individual who is having trouble relating to others. She probably is concerned about relationships with men and has a general negative attitude toward people. Both negative and positive signs are present for her as a therapy risk, although I would suggest that these signs for positive prognosis are stronger at this time.

INTERPRETING THE MMPI TO THE CLIENT

A variety of reasons for interpreting an MMPI exist:
1. a mental health agency may need a diagnostic statement for treatment planning,
2. a rehabilitation agency may need to know a client's potential for a training program,
3. a company may be screening personnel for sensitive positions, or
4. a client may wish to know more about himself or herself.

What is brought into focus by the test interpreter will be different in each of these situations and even the language in which the results are reported is likely to vary.

Most of what has been written about interpreting the MMPI is for its use in the preparation of diagnostic reports in clinical settings.

279

Much of the rest of the previously written material concerns interpretations of the MMPI for screening purposes. Success in a job or in a training program is predictable by interpreting critical scales or specific profile patterns.

Interpretations of the MMPI may be used either as hypotheses for the therapist to test out in therapy or in discussion of the test results with the client.

In interpreting the MMPI to clients, keep certain points in mind:

1. As a therapist interpreting the MMPI, you are trying to create some viable and useful hypotheses about the client and the client's behavior. You are looking for ideas about problem areas and behaviors which may be causing the client difficulties with others and ideas about dynamics which interfere with effective living such as life patterns which may be restrictive of growth. One of the goals of a therapist is to increase the client's awareness of self and of his or her behavior so that control over the behavior is increased.

2. Because you will be dealing with the client directly, the opportunity to verify the accuracy of your hypotheses is greater. If you are wrong about a particular hypothesis, one should be able to determine your error in discussion with the client. Most of the time therefore interpretations should be given to the client as tentative possibilities and not as finalities. A potential problem occurs in that the rejection by a client of an interpretation may not invalidate the hypothesis. On the other hand, ready acceptance on the part of the client of an interpretation does not always indicate that the hypothesis is valid. For an individual with a high **1-3** scale combination to reject the hypothesis that he or she may have psychological factors in his or her physical problems is to be expected, given the dynamics of the high **1-3** combination. The client's rejection does not invalidate the hypothesis.

3. Frequently, as a test interpreter, you can arrive at some generalities about the client and the client's behavior, but the client must be given an opportunity to provide the specifics. A client with a high **2** scale (T = 70 or above) will have the interpretation made that he or she is depressed, for example. The

client should then be able to be more specific about why he or she feels depressed and in what areas of life this is being felt.

4. When several likely interpretations for an elevated score exist, explain to the client that more than one possibility exists and allow the client to sort out which interpretation is the most accurate. For example, an elevated 2-7 combination indicating depression and anxiety may be the result of current difficulties such as current vocational and/or marital dissatisfactions. On the other hand, it may be the result of a long-standing chronic condition. The client should be able to indicate which of two interpretations is more accurate or even whether parts of both interpretations are applicable to him or her.

5. Of necessity, you must be well aware of the norms for the client population. This is particularly true for the New scales with college students where the average scores are not those given on the profile. An "average" score of 50 T score points on scale in a college population, for example, is actually quite elevated, because a score of 40 is the average for this particular group. (Anderson & Duckworth, 1969). An St scale score of 50, on the other hand, is quite low in a college population because scores of 58 and 60 are more the norm.

The need to know special group norms is very important in interpreting profiles for individuals from different racial or cultural backgrounds. The profiles of Northern Europeans tend to be consistent with those found in the United States. However, profiles for people from India or South America are likely to look elevated when in fact the individual's adjustment is quite normal for his cultural group (Butcher & Pancheri, 1976).

6. When working with a new population, you should remember that the interpretation of profiles may vary depending upon the group with which you are working. A profile that looks like that of a relatively acute schizophrenic in a mental hospital population may indicate, for example, an identity crisis in a college student population. The difference in potential for treatment is rather great; therefore, the possibilities of what a particular profile means for one's population needs to be checked with much care.

7. Some counselors interpreting an MMPI to a client worry that the client will see the height of some of the scores on the profile and become upset. Keep in mind that the client does not know what scales height means. If you treat an interpretation calmly, the client will most frequently react similarly.

What is important for the client is to have a meaningful interpretation at a level that is appropriate for the client's present needs. Part of the problem of giving an adequate interpretation revolves around the language the counselor may use in discussing the profile. The interpreter should stay away from using such terms as "schizophrenic," "emotionally disturbed," "passive-aggressive," and as much as possible go back to behavioral references. Such phrases as "You often feel cut off from other people," "People really don't seem to understand you or your intentions," "You find yourself brooding a lot," or "There are times when things feel unreal to you," may be less threatening. Because this is behavior the client has reported and is very close to what the client already feels, most clients accept these interpretations quite readily. They then form the basis for discussion of the problems and reassure the client that the tester is an individual who really understands him or her in a way that others do not.

8. Finally, you should not interpret too much material in one session. The client should be given ample time to deal with, elaborate, or give examples of the behavior that you are presenting. The approach to the client should not be one of an expert laying out or dissecting the client's personality, but rather of two people trying to understand what makes one of the two behave in the way in which he or she does.

Hopefully, this chapter showing two different methods of MMPI interpretation using the three types of MMPI scales (Validity, Clinical, and New) will be helpful in demonstrating the possibilities available in developing a personal style of interpretation.

APPENDICES

APPENDIX A

NEW SCALE ITEM COMPOSITION
Group Booklet Form

The item numbers are from the group form of the test otherwise known as "The Booklet Form".

A Scale (First Factor): 39 Items

True: 32 41 67 76 94 138 147 236 259 267 278 301 305 321 337 343 344 345 356 359 374 382 383 384 389 396 397 411 414 418 431 443 465 499 511 518 544 555

False: 379

R Scale (Second Factor): 40 Items

True: None

False: 1 6 9 12 39 51 81 112 126 131 140 145 154 156 191 208 219 221 271 272 281 282 327 406 415 429 440 445 447 449 450 451 462 468 472 502 516 529 550 556

Es Scale (Ego Strength): 68 Items

True: 2 36 51 95 109 153 174 181 187 192 208 221 231 234 253 270 355 367 380 410 421 430 458 513 515

False: 14 22 32 33 34 43 48 58 62 82 94 100 132 140 189 209 217 236 241 244 251 261 341 344 349 359 378 384 389 420 483 488 489 494 510 525 541 544 548 554 555 559 561

Lb Scale (Low Back Pain): 25 Items

True: 67 111 127 238 346

False: 3 45 98 109 148 153 180 190 230 267 321 327 378 394 429
483 502 504 516 536

Ca Scale (Caudality): 36 Items

True: 28 39 76 94 142 147 159 180 182 189 236 239 273 313 338
343 361 389 499 512 544 549 551 560

False: 8 46 57 69 163 188 242 407 412 450 513 523

Dy Scale (Dependency): 57 Items

True: 19 21 24 41 63 67 70 82 86 98 100 138 141 158 165
180 189 201 212 236 239 259 267 304 305 321 337 338 343 357
361 362 375 382 383 390 394 397 398 408 443 487 488 489 509
531 549 554 564

False: 9 79 107 163 170 193 264 369

Do Scale (Dominance): 28 Items

True: 64 229 255 270 368 432 523

False: 32 61 82 86 94 186 223 224 240 249 250 267 268 304 343
356 395 419 483 558 562

Re Scale (Social Responsibility): 32 Items

True: 58 111 173 221 294 412 501 552

False: 6 28 30 33 56 116 118 157 175 181 223 224 260 304 419
            434 437 468 469 471 472 529 553 558

Pr Scale (Prejudice): 32 Items

True: 47 84 93 106 117 124 136 139 157 171 186 250 280 304 307
            313 319 323 338 349 373 395 406 411 435 437 469 485 543

False: 78 176 221

St Scale (Social Status): 34 Items

True: 78 118 126 149 199 204 229 237 289 430 441 452 491 513 521

False: 136 138 180 213 249 267 280 297 304 314 324 352 365 378 388
            427 448 480 488

Cn Scale (Control): 50 Items

True: 6 20 30 56 67 105 116 134 145 162 169 181 225 236 238
            285 296 319 337 382 411 418 436 446 447 460 529 555

False: 58 80 92 96 111 167 174 220 242 249 250 291 313 360 378
            439 444 483 488 489 527 548

APPENDIX B

NEW SCALE ITEM COMPOSITION
R Form

A Scale (First Factor: 39 Items

True: 32 41 67 76 94 138 147 236 259 267 278 301 305 321 337
343 344 345 356 359 368 370 372 376 414 418 431 443 461 462
465 482 499 511 518 544 549 555

False: 450

R Scale (Second Factor): 40 Items

True: None

False: 1   6   9 12 39 51 81 112 126 131 140 145 154 156 191
208 219 221 271 272 281 282 327 375 377 380 382 383 384 387
394 429 445 447 468 472 516 529 550 556

Es Scale (Ego Strength): 68 Items

True: 2 36 51 95 109 153 174 181 187 192 208 221 231 234 253
270 355 400 410 421 430 451 458 513 515
False: 14 22 32 33 34 43 48 58 62 82 94 100 132 140 189
209 217 236 241 244 251 261 341 344 349 359 420 449 462 482
483 488 489 494 510 525 541 544 548 554 555 559 561

Lb Scale (Low Back Pain): 25 Items

True: 67 111 127 238 346

False: 3 45 98 109 148 153 180 190 230 267 321 327 394 429 449

483 504 516 521 536

Ca Scale (Caudality): 36 Items

True: 28 39 76 94 142 147 159 180 182 189 236 239 273 313 338
         343 361 398 482 499 512 544 551 560

False: 8 46 57 69 163 188 242 383 407 412 513 523

Dy Scale (Dependency): 57 Items

True: 19 21 24 41 63 67 70 82 86 98 100 138 141 158 165
         180 189 201 212 236 239 259 267 304 305 321 337 338 343 357
         361 362 370 372 373 393 398 399 408 440 443 461 487 488 489
         509 521 531 554

False: 9 79 107 163 170 193 264 411

Do Scale (Dominance): 28 Items

True: 64 229 255 270 400 432 523

False: 32 61 82 86 94 186 223 224 240 249 250 267 268 304 343
         356 419 483 547 558 562

Re Scale (Social Responsibility): 32 Items

True: 58 111 173 221 294 412 501 552

False: 6 28 30 33 56 116 118 157 175 181 223 224 260 304 388
         419 434 437 468 471 472 529 553 558

Pr Scale (Prejudice): 32 Items

True: 47 84 93 106 117 124 136 139 157 171 186 250 280 304 307
313 319 323 338 349 375 376 388 435 436 437 485 543 547

False: 78 178 221

St Scale (Social Status): 34 Items

True: 78 118 126 149 199 204 229 237 289 396 430 441 452 491 513
False: 136 138 180 213 249 267 280 297 304 314 324 352 365 378 448
449 480 481 488

Cn Scale (Control): 50 Items

True: 6 20 30 56 67 105 116 134 145 162 169 181 225 236 238
285 296 319 337 376 379 381 418 447 460 461 529 555

False: 58 80 92 96 111 167 174 220 242 249 250 291 313 360 439
444 449 483 488 489 527 548

APPENDIX C
VALIDITY, CLINICAL, AND NEW SCALES
Intercorrelations for Two Normal Populations*

	Validity			Clinical Scales									
	L	F	K	1	2	3	4	5	6	7	8	9	0
L		—.10	.38	—.01	.05	.07	—.20	.11	—.05	—.29	—.27	—.22	—.07
L		—.06	.26	.14	.07	.19	—.03	—.05	.04	.00	.06	—.17	—.02
F	—.10		—.25	.36	.31	.06	.40	—.05	.28	.34	.54	.25	.27
F	—.06		—.44	.24	.45	.11	.34	.08	.29	.43	.60	.23	.36
K	.38	—.25		—.21	—.15	.13	—.15	.02	—.00	—.62	—.54	—.30	—.45
K	.26	—.44		.14	—.25	.27	.20	.12	—.02	—.04	—.02	—.13	—.51
1	—.01	.36	.—21		.51	.29	.24	.19	.21	.44	.43	.13	.25
1	.14	.24	.14		.45	.66	.33	.14	.24	.47	.47	.06	.12
2	.05	.31	—.15	.51		.28	.39	.23	.33	.62	.52	—.03	.52
2	.07	.45	—.25	.45		.35	.30	.06	.32	.64	.48	—.14	.57
3	.07	.06	.13	.29	.28		.16	.13	.17	.12	.13	.03	—.00
3	.19	.11	.27	.66	.35		.44	.15	.37	.42	.39	.06	—.08
4	—.20	.40	—.15	.24	.39	.16		—.05	.43	.47	.56	.42	.13
4	—.03	.34	.20	.33	.30	.44		.17	.31	.44	.53	.33	—.08
5	.11	—.05	.02	.19	.23	.13	—.05		.07	.16	.08	—.06	.12
5	—.05	.08	.12	.14	.06	.15	.17		.03	.18	.19	.19	—.18
6	—.05	.28	—.00	.21	.33	.17	.43	.07		.39	.44	.20	.13
6	.04	.29	—.02	.24	.32	.37	.31	.03		.44	.45	.10	.11
7	—.29	.34	—.62	.44	.62	.12	.47	.16	.39		.83	.32	.61
7	.00	.43	—.04	.47	.64	.42	.44	.18	.44		.72	.16	.36
8	—.27	.54	—.54	.43	.52	.13	.56	.08	.44	.83		.44	.48
8	—.06	.60	—.02	.47	.48	.39	.53	.19	.45	.72		.33	.21
9	—.22	.25	—.30	.13	—.03	.03	.42	—.06	.20	.32	.44		—.14
9	—.17	.23	—.13	.06	—.14	.06	.33	.19	.10	.16	.33		—.31
0	—.07	.27	—.45	.25	.52	—.00	.13	.12	.13	.61	.48	—.14	
0	—.02	.36	—.51	.12	.57	—.08	—.08	—.18	.11	.36	.21	—.31	
A	—.30	.39	—.71	.37	.52	.05	.42	.14	.31	.90	.79	.32	.61
A	—.15	.58	—.71	.19	.61	.06	.14	.02	.29	.59	.48	.11	.64
R	.32	—.00	.40	.13	.39	.18	—.06	.18	.10	—.07	—.11	—.42	.30
R	.30	—.05	.34	.27	.32	.26	.03	.07	.09	.17	.06	—.41	.29
Es	—.10	—.09	.14	—.25	—.24	—.09	—.02	—.39	—.07	—.25	—.20	.03	—.19
Es	—.07	—.42	.45	—.37	—.51	—.24	—.03	—.01	—.29	—.49	—.39	.03	—.51
Lb	.19	.06	.36	.21	.28	.26	.20	.10	.20	—.01	.00	.05	.14
Lb	.17	—.01	.29	.32	.18	.39	17	—.03	.14	.14	.09	—.04	—.09
Ca	—.25	.39	—.61	.47	.63	.13	.42	.14	.30	.86	.74	.23	.66
Ca	—.13	.53	—.65	.32	.62	.13	.18	.05	.24	.57	.44	.12	.63
Dy	—.06	.16	—.21	.17	.22	.04	.13	.21	.13	.32	.27	.07	.25
Dy	—.16	.49	—.66	.17	.54	.00	.08	.06	.28	.56	.40	.08	.63
Do	—.03	—.10	.15	—.10	—.13	—.02	—.10	—.04	—.06	—.18	—.19	.01	—.19
Do	—.09	—.38	.44	—.17	—.46	.00	.00	.12	—.15	—.44	—.29	.07	—.57
Re	.39	—.25	.52	—.06	—.01	.11	—.29	.19	—.07	—.37	—.38	—.31	—.12
Re	.29	—.41	.51	.07	—.11	.18	—.14	.05	—.07	—.12	—.20	—.32	—.15
Pr	—.16	.34	—.67	.24	.26	—.07	.27	—.02	—.00	.59	.59	.31	.47
Pr	—.13	.53	—.69	.09	.35	—.13	.02	—.00	—.00	.26	.30	.19	.46
St	—.05	—.12	.38	—.16	—.23	.06	—.00	—.26	.14	—.38	—.31	.17	—.53
St	—.02	—.23	.41	—.14	—.33	.03	.08	.14	—.11	—.29	—.19	.18	—.61
Cn	—.54	.24	—.42	—.14	.20	.01	.38	.08	.21	.45	.43	.44	.13
Cn	—.40	.36	—.46	—.01	.25	—.06	.20	.11	.11	.20	.23	.32	.14

*Bold figures—847 graduate students from Ball State U. and non-student volunteers from the community. No known clinical patients included.

Light figures—50,000 medical outpatients at the Mayo Clinic. No psychiatric patients included (Swenson, Pearson, & Osborne, 1973).

290

APPENDIX C
VALIDITY, CLINICAL, AND NEW SCALES
Intercorrelations for Two Normal Populations*

New Scales

	A	R	Es	Lb	Ca	Dy	Do	Re	Pr	St	Cn
L	−.30	.32	−.10	.19	−.25	−.06	−.03	.39	−.16	−.05	−.54
	−.15	.30	−.07	.17	−.13	−.16	−.09	.29	−.13	−.02	−.40
F	.39	.00	−.09	.06	.39	.16	−.10	−.25	.34	−.12	.24
	.58	−.05	−.42	−.01	.53	.49	−.38	−.41	.53	−.23	.36
K	−.71	.40	.14	.36	−.61	−.21	.15	.52	−.67	.38	−.42
	−.71	.34	.45	.29	−.65	−.66	.44	.51	−.69	.41	−.46
1	.37	.13	−.25	.21	.47	.17	−.10	−.06	.24	−.16	−.14
	.19	.27	−.37	.32	^2	.17	−.17	.07	.09	−.14	−.01
2	.52	.39	−.24	.2C	⋅⊙	.22	−.13	−.01	.26	−.23	.20
	.61	.32	−.51	.18	⌐⌐	.54	−.46	−.11	.35	−.33	.25
3	.05	.18	−.09	.26	.13	.04	−.02	.11	−.07	.06	.01
	.06	.26	−.24	.39	.13	.00	−.00	.18	−.13	.03	−.06
4	.42	−.06	−.02	.20	.42	.13	−.10	−.29	.27	.00	.38
	.14	.03	−.03	.17	.18	.08	−.00	−.14	.02	.08	.20
5	.14	.18	−.39	.10	.14	.21	−.04	.19	−.02	−.26	.08
	.02	.07	−.01	−.03	.05	.06	.12	.05	.00	.14	.11
6	.31	.10	−.07	.20	.30	.13	−.06	−.07	−.00	.14	.21
	.29	.09	−.29	.14	.24	.28	−.15	−.07	−.00	−.11	.11
7	.90	−.07	−.25	−.01	.86	.32	−.18	−.37	.59	−.38	.45
	.59	.17	−.49	.14	.57	.56	−.44	−.12	.26	−.29	.20
8	.79	−.11	−.20	.00	.74	.27	−.19	−.38	.59	−.31	.43
	.48	.06	−.39	.09	.44	.40	−.29	−.20	.30	−.19	.23
9	.32	−.42	.03	.05	.23	.07	.01	−.31	.31	.17	.44
	.11	−.41	.03	−.04	.12	.08	.07	−.32	.19	.18	.32
0	.61	.30	−.19	−.14	.66	.25	−.19	−.12	.47	−.53	.13
	.64	.29	−.51	−.09	.63	.63	−.57	−.15	.46	−.61	.14
A		−.16	−.32	−.12	.85	.31	−.19	−.39	.64	−.38	.49
		−.10	−.68	−.13	.84	.88	−.60	−.41	.66	−.49	.45
R	−.16		−.09	.33	.00	.00	−.07	.37	−.18	−.15	−.33
	−.10		−.12	.31	−.03	−.08	−.09	.36	−.16	−.21	−.37
Es	−.32	−.09		.00	−.23	−.57	.56	.00	−.15	.20	.09
	−.68	−.12		.03	−.61	−.64	.60	.25	−.53	.54	−.02
Lb	−.12	.33	.00		−.05	−.04	.07	.22	−.17	.29	.08
	−.13	.31	.03		−.10	−.20	.10	.12	−.15	.14	−.04
Ca	.85	.00	−.23	−.05		.30	−.19	−.33	.58	−.40	.41
	.84	−.03	−.61	−.10		.80	−.57	−.38	.61	−.51	.44
Dy	.31	.00	−.57	−.04	.30		−.55	−.09	.20	−.16	.11
	.88	−.08	−.64	−.20	.80		−.63	−.39	.61	−.53	.35
Do	−.19	−.07	.56	.07	−.19	−.55		.08	−.18	.21	−.14
	−.60	−.09	.60	.10	−.57	−.63		.33	−.54	.61	−.02
Re	−.39	.37	.00	.22	−.33	−.09	.08		−.49	.20	−.43
	−.41	.36	.25	.12	−.38	−.39	.33		−.54	.17	−.47
Pr	.64	−.18	−.15	−.17	.58	.20	−.18	−.49		−.30	.27
	.66	−.16	−.53	−.15	.61	.61	−.54	−.54		−.48	.30
St	−.38	−.15	.20	.29	−.40	−.16	.21	.20	−.30		.20
	−.49	−.21	.54	.14	−.51	−.53	.61	.17	−.48		.06
Cn	.49	−.33	.09	.08	.41	.11	−.14	−.43	.27	.20	
	.45	−.37	−.02	−.04	.44	.35	−.02	−.47	.30	.06	

*Bold figures—847 graduate students from Ball State U. and non-student volunteers from the community. No known clinical patients included.

Light figures—50,000 medical outpatients at the Mayo Clinic. No psychiatric patients included (Swenson, Pearson & Osborne, 1973).

REFERENCES

REFERENCES

Adams, J. Defensiveness on the MMPI as a function of the warmth of test introduction. *Journal of Consulting and Clinical Psychology,* 1971, *36,* 444.

Altman, H., Gynther, M., Warbin, R., & Sletten, I. A new empirical automated MMPI interpretive program: The 6-8/8-6 code type. *Journal of Clinical Psychology,* 1972, *28,* 495-498.

Altman, H., Warbin, R., Sletten, I., & Gynther, M. Replicated empirical correlates of the MMPI 8-9/9-8 code type. *Journal of Personality Assessment,* 1973, *37,* 369-371.

Anderson, W. The MMPI: Low Pa scores. *Journal of Counseling Psychology,* 1956, *3,* 226-228.

Anderson, W., & Duckworth, J. New MMPI scales and the college student. University of Missouri Testing and Counseling Service Report, 1969, 23(7).

Apostal, R. Personality descriptions of mental health center patients for use as pre-therapy information. *Mental Hygiene,* 1971, *55,* 119-120.

Arnold, P. Marriage counselee MMPI profile characteristics with objective signs that discriminate them for married couples in general. Unpublished doctoral dissertation, University of Minnesota, 1970.

Barger, B., & Hall, E. Personality patterns and achievement in college. *Educational and Psychological Measurement,* 1964, *24,* 339-346.

Barron, F. Creative persons and creative process. NY: Holt, Renehart, and Minston, 1969.

Barron, F. Ego strength and the management of aggression. In Welsh, G.S. & Dahlstrom, W.G. (Eds.) *Basic readings on the MMPI in psychology and medicine.* Minneapolis: U. of Minnesota Press, 1956.

Barron, F. An ego-strength scale which predicts response to psychotherapy. *Journal of Consulting Psychology*, 1953, *17*, 327-333.

Benton, A.L. The MMPI in clinical practice. *Journal of Nervous and Mental Diseases*, 1945, *102*, 416-420.

Bier, W.C. A comparative study of a seminary group and four other groups on the MMPI. *Catholic University Studies in Psychology and Psychiatry*, 1948, *7*, 1-107.

Black, J.D. The interpretation of MMPI profiles of college women. Unpublished doctoral dissertation, University of Minnesota, 1953.

Blazer, J. MMPI interpretation in outline: II. The L scale. *Psychology*, 1965, *2*, 2-7. (a)

Blazer, J. MMPI interpretation in outline: III. The F scale. *Psychology*, 1965, *2*, 2-9. (b)

Blazer, J. MMPI interpretation in outline: IV. The K scale. *Psychology*, 1966, *3*, 4-11.

Block, J., & Bailey, D. Q-sort item analyses of a number of MMPI scales. Officer Education Research Laboratory, Technical Memorandum, OERL-TM-55-7, May, 1955.

Blum, L.P. A comparative study of students preparing for five selected professions including teaching. *Journal of Experimental Education*, 1947, *16*, 31-65.

Booth, L.G., Jr. Personality traits of athletes as measured by the MMPI. *Research Quarterly of the American Association of Health and Physical Education,* 1958, *29*, 127-138.

Briggs, O.F., Wirt, R.D., & Johnson, R. An application of prediction tables in the study of delinquency. *Journal of Consulting Psychology*, 1961, *25*, 46-50.

Brill, N., Crumpton, E., & Grayson, H. Personality factors in marihuana use. *Archives of General Psychiatry*, 1971, *24*, 163-165.

Browher, D. The relation between intelligence and MMPI. *Journal of Social Psychology*, 1947, *25*, 243-245.

Brown, F.G., & DuBois, T.E. Correlates of academic success for high ability freshmen men. *Personnel and Guidance Journal*, 1964, *42*, 603-607.

Butcher, J. Manifest Aggression: MMPI correlates in normal boys. *Journal of Consulting Psychology*, 1965, *29*, 446-454.

Butcher, J. (Ed.) *MMPI: Research developments and clinical applications.* New York: McGraw-Hill, 1969.

Butcher, J., Ball, B., & Ray, E. Effects of socio-economic level on MMPI differences in Negro-white college students. *Journal of Counseling Psychology*, 1964, *11*, 83-87.

Butcher, J. & Pancheri, P. *A handbook of cross-national MMPI research.* Minneapolis: University of Minnesota Press, 1976.

Butcher, J., & Tellegen, A. Objections to MMPI items. *Journal of Consulting Psychology*, 1966, *30*, 527-534.

Caldwell, A. Families of MMPI code types. Paper presented at the Twelveth Annual Symposium on the MMPI, Tampa, FL, 1977.

Caldwell, A. Families of MMPI pattern types. Paper presented at the Seventh Annual Symposium on the MMPI, Mexico City, Mexico, 1972.

Caldwell, A. Characteristics of MMPI pattern types. Paper presented at the Ninth Annual Symposium on the MMPI, Los Angeles, California, 1974.

Canter, A. A brief note on shortening Barron's ego strength scale. *Journal of Clinical Psychology*, 1965, *21*, 285-286.

Canter, A., Day, C.W., Imboden, J.B., & Cluff, L.E. The influence of age and health status on the MMPI scores of a normal population. *Journal of Clinical Psychology*, 1962, *18*, 71-73.

Carkhuff, R.R., Barnette, L., & McCall, J.N. *The counselor's handbook: Scale and profile interpretation of the MMPI.* Urbana, Illinois: R.W. Parkinson and Associates, 1965.

Carson, R. Interpretative Manual to the MMPI. In J. Butcher (Ed.), *MMPI: Research developments and clinical applications.* New York: McGraw-Hill, 1969, pp. 279-296.

Carson, R. MMPI profile interpretation. Paper read at the Seventh Annual Symposium on the MMPI, Mexico City, Mexico, 1972.

Chance, J. Some correlates of affective tone of early memories. *Journal of Consulting Psychology,* 1957, *21,* 203-205.

Chyatte, C. Psychological characteristics of a group of professional actors. *Occupations,* 1949, *27,* 245-250.

Clark, J.H. Interpretation of the MMPI profiles of college students: A comparison by college major subject. *Journal of Clinical Psychology,* 1953, *9,* 382-384.

Clark, J.H. The interpretation of the MMPI profiles of college students: Mean scores for male and female groups. *Journal of Social Psychology,* 1954, *40,* 319-321.

Clippinger, J., Martin, C., Michael, V., & Ingle, J. Personality characteristics of a Los Angeles college population. *Corrective Psychiatry and Journal of Social Therapy,* 1969, *15,* 27-37.

Cooke, M.K., & Kiesler, D.J. Prediction of college students who later require personal counseling. *Journal of Counseling Psychology,* 1967, *14,* 346-349.

Costello, R., & Tiffany, D. Methodological issues and racial (Black-white) comparisons on the MMPI. *Journal of Consulting and Clinical Psychology,* 1972, *38,* 161-168.

Cottle, W.C. *The MMPI: A Review.* Lawrence, Kansas: University of Kansas Press, 1953.

Crites, J.O. Ego-strength in relation to vocational interest development. *Journal of Counseling Psychology,* 1960, *7,* 137-143.

Crumpton, E., Cantor, J.M., & Batiste, C. A factor analytic study of Barron's ego-strength scale. *Journal of Clinical Psychology,* 1960, *16,* 283-291.

296

Cuadra, C.A. A psychometric investigation of control factors in psychological adjustment. Unpublished doctoral dissertation, University of California, 1953.

Cuadra, C.A., & Reed, C.F. *An introduction to the MMPI.* Downey, IL: Veterans Administration Hospital, 1954.

Dahlstrom, W.G., & Welsh, G.S. *An MMPI handbook: A guide to use in clinical practice and Research.* Minneapolis: University of Minnesota Press, 1960.

Dahlstrom, W.G., Welsh, G., & Dahlstrom, L. *An MMPI handbook: Volume I. Clinical interpretation.* Minneapolis: University of Minnesota Press, 1972.

Davies, J., & Maliphant, R. Refractory behavior at school in normal adolescent males in relation to psychopathy and early experience. *Journal of Child Psychology and Psychiatry and Allied Disciplines,* 1971, *12,* 35-41.

Davis, K. The actuarial development of a female 4'3 MMPI profile. Unpublished doctoral dissertation, St. Louis University, 1971.

Davis, K., & Sines, J. An antisocial behavioral pattern associated with a specific MMPI profile. *Journal of Consulting and Clinical Psychology,* 1971, *36,* 229-234.

Dean, R.B., & Richardson, H. Analysis of MMPI profiles of forty college-educated overt male homosexuals. *Journal of Consulting Psychology,* 1964, *28,* 483-486.

Drake, L.E. MMPI profiles and interview behavior. *Journal of Counseling Psychology,* 1954, *1,* 92-95.

Drake, L.E. Interpretation of MMPI profiles in counseling male clients. *Journal of Counseling Psychology,* 1956, *3,* 83-88.

Drake, L.E. MMPI patterns predictive of achievement. *Journal of Counseling Psychology,* 1962, *9,* 164-167.

Drake, L.E., & Oetting, E.R. An MMPI pattern and suppressor variable predictive of academic achievement. *Journal of Counseling Psychology,* 1957, *4,* 245-247.

Drake, L.E., & Oetting, E.R. *An MMPI codebook for counselors.* Minneapolis: University of Minnesota Press, 1959.

Drake, L.E., & Thiede, W.B. Further validation of the social I.E. scale for the MMPI. *Journal of Educational Research,* 1948, *41,* 551-556.

Drasgow, J., & Barnette, W.L., Jr. F-K in a motivated group. *Journal of Consulting Psychology,* 1957, *21,* 399-401.

Dvorak, E.J. Educational and personality characteristics of smokers and non-smokers among university freshmen. *Journal of American College Health Association,* 1967, *16,* 80-84.

Edwards, A., & Abbott, R. Further evidence regarding the R scale of the MMPI as a measure of acquiescence. *Psychological Reports,* 1969, *24,* 903-906.

Ellinwood, E.H., Jr. Amphetamine psychosis: I. Description of the individual and process. *Journal of Nervous and Mental Disease,* 1967, *144,* 273-283.

English, R.W. Correlates of stigma towards physically disabled persons. *Rehabilitation Research and Practice Review* 1971, *2(4),* 1-17.

Evans, R.R., Borgatta, E.F., & Bohrnstedt, G.W. Smoking and MMPI scores among entering freshmen. *Journal of Social Psychology,* 1967, *73,* 137-140.

Exner, J.E., McDowell, J., Stockman, W., & Kirk, L. On the detection of willful falsification in the MMPI. *Journal of Consulting Psychology,* 1963, *27,* 91-94.

Feldman, M.J. The use of the MMPI profile for prognosis and evaluation of shock therapy. *Journal of Consulting Psychology,* 1952, *16,* 376-382.

Fowler, R.D., & Athey, E.B. A cross-validation of Gilberstadt and Duker's 1-2-3-4 profile type. *Journal of Clinical Psychology,* 1971, *27,* 238-240.

Fowler, R.D., & Coyle, F.A. Collegiate normative data on MMPI content scales. *Journal of Clinical Psychology,* 1969, *25,* 62-63.

Fowler, R.D., Teal, S., & Coyle, F.A. The measurement of alcoholic response to treatment by Barron's ego strength scale. *Journal of Psychology*, 19, *67*, 65-68.

Gallagher, J.J. MMPI changes concomitant with client-centered therapy. *Journal of Consulting Psychology*, 1953, *17*, 334-338.

Getter, H. & Synderland, D.M. The Barron ego strength scale and psychotherapy outcome. *Journal of Consulting Psychology*, 1962, *26*, 195.

Gilbert J., & Lombardi, D. Personality characteristics of young male narcotic addicts. *Journal of Consulting Psychology*, 1967, *31*, 536-538.

Gilberstadt, H., & Duker, J. *A handbook for clinical and actuarial MMPI interpretation*. Philadelphia: W.B. Saunders, 1965.

Gloye, E., & Zimmerman, I. MMPI item changes by college students under ideal-self response set. *Journal of Projective Techniques and Personality Assessment*, 1967, *31*, 63-69.

Good, P., & Brantner, J. *The physician's guide to the MMPI*. Minneapolis: University of Minnesota Press, 1961.

Good, P., & Brantner, J. *A practical guide to the MMPI*. Minneapolis: University of Minnesota Press, 1974.

Gough, H.G. A new dimension of status: II. Relationship of the St scale to other variables. *American Sociological Review*, 1948, *13*, 534-537.

Gough, H.G. Studies of social intolerance: III. Relationship of the Pr scale to other variables. *Journal of Social Psychology*, 1951, *33*, 257-262.

Gough, H.G. A short social status inventory. *Journal of Educational Psychology*, 1949, *40*, 52-56. (b)

Gough, H.G. Studies of Social Intolerance: III. Relationship of the Pr scale to other variables. *Journal of Social Psychology*, 1951, *33*, 257-262. (a)

Gough, H.G. Studies of social intolerance: III. Relationship of the Pr scale to other variables. *Journal of Social Psychology*, 1951, *33*, 257-262. (b)

Gough, H.G. A personality scale for social responsibility. *Journal of Abnormal and Social Psychology*, 1952, *47*, 73-80.

Gough, H.G., McClosky, H., & Meehl , P.E. A personality scale for dominance. *Journal of Abnormal and Social Psychology*, 1951, *46*, 360-366.

Gough, H.G., McKee, M.G., & Yandell, R.J. Adjective check list analyses of a number of selected psychometric and assessment variables. Officer Education Research Laboratory, Technical Memorandum, OERL-TM-55-10, May, 1955.

Graham, J. *The MMPI: A practical guide.* NY: Oxford University Press, 1977.

Graham, J., Schroeder, H., & Lilly, R. Factor analysis of items on the Social Introversion and Masculinity-feminity scales of the MMPI. *Journal of Clinical Psychology*, 1971, *27*, 367-370.

Gravitz, M. Self-described depression and scores on the MMPI D scale in normal subjects. *Journal of Projective Techniques and Personality Assessment*, 1968, *32*, 88-91.

Gravitz, M. Use of a short form of Barron's ego-strength scale with normal adults. *Journal of Clinical Psychology*, 1970, *26*, 223. (a)

Gravitz, M. Validity implications of normal adult MMPI "L" scale endorsement. *Journal of Clinical Psychology*, 1970, *26*, 497-499.

Gravitz, M. Declination rates on the MMPI validity and clinical scales. *Journal of Clinical Psychology*, 1971, *27*, 103.

Grayson, H.M. & Olinger, L.B. Simulation of "normalcy" by psychiatric patients on the MMPI. *Journal of Consulting Psychology*, 1957, *21*, 73-77.

Gulas, Ivan. MMPI 2-pt. codes for a "normal" college male population: A replication study. *Journal of Psychology*, 1973, *84*, 319-322.

Gulas, Ivan. MMPI low-point codes for a "normal" young adult population: A normative study. *Journal of Clinical Psychology*, 1974, *30*, 77-78.

Guthrie, G.M. A study of the personality characteristics associated with the disorders encountered by an internist. Unpublished doctoral dissertation, University of Minnesota, 1949.

Gynther, M. The clinical utility of "invalid" MMPI F scores. *Journal of Consulting Psychology*, 1961, *25*, 540-542.

Gynther, M. White norms and Black MMPI's: A prescription for discrimination? *Psychological Bulletin*, 1972, *78*, 386-402.

Gynther, M. Actuarial MMPI interpretation. Paper read at the Ninth Annual Symposium on the MMPI, Los Angeles, California, 1974.

Gynther, M., Altman, H., & Sletten, I. Replicated correlates of MMPI two-point code types: The Missouri actuarial system. *Journal of Clinical Psychology*, 1973, *29*, 263-289.

Gynther, M., Altman, H., & Warbin, R. A new empirical automated MMPI interpretive program: The 2-4/4-2 code type. *Journal of Clinical Psychology*, 1972, *28*, 598-501.

Gynther, M., Altman, H., & Warbin, R. Behavioral correlates for the Minnesota Multiphasic Personality Inventory 4-9/9-4 code types: A case of the emperor's new clothes? *Journal of Consulting Psychology*, 1973, *40*, 259-263. (a)

Gynther, M., Altman, H., & Warbin, R. Interpretation of uninterpretable Minnesota Multiphasic Personality Inventory profiles. *Journal of Consulting and Clinical Psychology*, 1973, *40*, 78-83. (b)

Gynther, M., Altman, H., & Warbin, R. A new actuarial-empirical automated MMPI interpretive program: The 4-3/3-4 code type. *Journal of Clinical Psychology*, 1973, *29*, 229-231. (c)

Gynther, M., Altman, H., & Warbin, R. A new empirical automated MMPI interpretive program: The 6-9/9-6 code type. *Journal of Clinical Psychology*, 1973, *29*, 60-61.(d)

301

Gynther, M., Altman, H., & Warbin, R. A new empirical automated MMPI interpretive program: The 2-7/7-2 code type. *Journal of Clinical Psychology*, 1973, *29*, 58-59. (e)

Gynther, M., Altman, H., Warbin, R., & Sletten, I. A new actuarial system for MMPI interpretation: Rationale and methodology. *Journal of Clinical Psychology,* 1972, *28*, 173-179.

Gynther, M., Altman, H., Warbin, R., & Sletten, I. A new empirical automated MMPI interpretive program: The 1-2/2-1 code type. *Journal of Clinical Psychology*, 1973, *29*, 54-57.

Gynther, M., Fowler, R., & Erdberg, P. False positives galore: The application of standard MMPI criteria to a rural, isolated Negro sample. *Journal of Clinical Psychology*, 1971, *27*, 234-237.

Gynther, M., & Shimkunas, A. Age, intelligence, and MMPI F scores. *Journal of Consulting Psychology*, 1965, *29*, 383-388. (a)

Gynther, M., & Shimkunas, A. More data on MMPI F > 16 scores. *Journal of Clinical Psychology*, 1965, *21*, 275-279. (b)

Halbower, C.C. A comparison of actuarial versus clinical prediction to classes discriminated by MMPI. Unpublished doctoral dissertation, University of Minnesota, 1955.

Hampton, P.J. The MMPI as a psychometric tool for diagnosing personality disorders among college students. *Journal of Social Psychology*, 1947, *26*, 99-108.

Hanvik, L.J. MMPI profiles in patients with low-back pain. *Journal of Consulting Psychology*, 1951, *15*, 350-353.

Harmon, L.R., & Wiener, D.N. The use of the MMPI in vocational adjustment, *Journal of Applied Psychology*, 1945, *29*, 132-141.

Hathaway, S.R., & McKinley, J.C. *The minnesota multiphasic personality inventory Manual*. Revised. New York: The Psychological Corporation, 1951.

Hathaway, S.R., & McKinley, J.C. *The Minnesota Multiphasic Personality Inventory manual*. Revised. New York: The Psychological Corporation, 1951.

Hathaway, S.R., & Monachesi, E.D. MMPI studies of ninth-grade students in Minnesota schools. Unpublished materials, 1958.

Hathaway, S.R., Reynolds, P.C., & Monachesi, E.D. Follow up of the later careers and lives of 1,000 boys who dropped out of high school. *Journal of Consulting and Clinical Psychology*, 1969, *33*, 370-380.

Haun, K.W. A note on the prediction of academic performance from personality test scores. *Psychological Reports*, 1965, *16*, 294.

Heilbrun, A.B. The psychological significance of the MMPI K scale in a normal population. *Journal of Consulting Psychology*, 1961, *25*, 486-491.

Heilbrun, A.B. Revision of the MMPI K correction procedure for improved detection of maladjustment in a normal college population. *Journal of Consulting Psychology*, 1963, *27*, 161-163.

Himelstein, P., & Lubin, B. Relationship of the MMPI K scale and a measure of self-disclosure in a normal population. *Psychological Reports*, 1966, *19*, 166.

Himelstein, P., & Stoup, D. Correlation of three masculinity-feminity measures for males. *Journal of Clinical Psychology*, 1967, *23*, 189.

Hiner, D., Ogren, D., & Baxter, J. Ideal-self responding on the MMPI. *Journal of Projective Techniques and Personality Assessment*, 1969, *33*, 389-396.

Hokanson, J.E., & Calden, G. Negro-white differences on the MMPI. *Journal of Clinical Psychology*, 1960, *16*, 32-33.

Holmes, D. Male-female differences in MMPI ego-strength: An artifact. *Journal of Consulting Psychology*, 1967, *31*, 408-410.

Hoper, R. MMPI in a counseling service setting. Paper presented at the Eleventh Annual Symposium on the MMPI, Minneapolis, MN, 1976.

Horton, M., & Kriauciumas, R. MMPI differences between terminators and continuers in youth counseling. *Journal of Counseling Psychology*, 1970, *17*, 98-101.

Hovey, H., & Lewis, E. Semi-automatic interpretation of the MMPI. *Journal of Clinical Psychology*, 1967, *23*, 123-134.

Hundleby, J.D., & Connor, W.H. Interrelationship between personality inventories: The 16PF, the MMPI, and the MPI. *Journal of Consulting and Clinical Psychology*, 1968, *32*, 152-157.

Jensen, A.R. Authoritarian attitudes and personality maladjustment. *Journal of Abnormal and Social Psychology*, 1957, *54*, 303-311.

Jensen, V.H. Influence of personality traits on academic success. *Personnel and Guidance Journal*, 1958, *36*, 497-500.

Jurjevich, R.M. Short interval test-retest stability of MMPI, CPI, Cornell Index, and Symptom Check List. *Journal of General Psychology*, 1966, *74*, 201-206.

Kahn, H., & Singer, E. An investigation of some of the factors related to success or failure of School of Commerce students. *Journal of Educational Psychology*, 1949, *40*, 107-117.

Kanun, C., & Monachesi, E.D. Delinquency and the validating scales of the MMPI. *Journal of Criminal Law, Criminology, and Police Science,* 1960, *50*, 525-534.

Karson, S., & Pool, K. The construct validity of the Sixteen Personality Factor Test. *Journal of Clinical Psychology*, 1957, *13*, 245-252.

Kleinmutz, B. An extension of the construct validity of the ego-strength scale. *Journal of Consulting Psychology*, 1960, *24*, 463-464.

Kunce, J. & Anderson, W. Normalizing the MMPI. *Journal of Clinical Psychology*, 1976, *32*, 776-780.

Laforge, R. A correlational study of two personality tests. *Journal of Consulting Psychology*, 1962, *26*, 402-411.

Lair, C.V., & Trapp, E.P. The differential diagnostic value of MMPI with somatically disturbed patients. *Journal of Clinical Psychology,* 1962, *18*, 146-147.

Lanyon, R. Simulation of normal and psychopathic patterns. *Journal of Consulting Psychology*, 1967, *31*, 94-97.

Latta, W. Projected set and MMPI scale changes. Unpublished doctoral dissertation, University of Cincinnati, 1968.

Lebovits, B.Z., & Ostfeld, A.M. Personality, defensiveness and educational achievement. *Journal of Personality and Social Psychology*, 1967, *6*, 381-390.

Lewandowski, D., & Graham, J.R. Empirical correlates of frequently occurring two-point MMPI code types: A replicated study. *Journal of Consulting & Clinical Psychology*, 1972, *39*, 467-472.

Lieberman, L., & Walters, S. Self-ratings and inventory scores in the measurement of social introversion. *Journal of Clinical Psychology*, 1971, *27*, 363-366.

Loney, J. An MMPI measure of maladjustment in a sample of "normal" homosexual men. *Journal of Clinical Psychology*, 1971, *27*, 486-488.

Loper, Rodney. MMPI in a counseling service setting. Paper presented at the Eleventh Annual Symposium on the MMPI. Minneapolis, MN 1976.

Lough, O.M. Women students in liberal arts, nursing and teacher training curricula and the MMPI. *Journal of Applied Psychology*, 1947, *31*, 437-445.

Lough, O., & Green, M. A comparison of the Minnesota Multiphasic Personality Inventory and the Washburne S-A Inventory as measures of personality of college women. *Journal of Social Psychology*, 1950, *32*, 23-30.

MacKinnon, D.W. The nature and nurture of creative talent. *American Psychologist*, 1962, *17*, 484-495.

Malmquist, C., & Kiresuk, I.J., & Spano, L.M. Mothers with multiple illegitimacies, *Psychiatric Quarterly*, 1967, *41*, 339-354.

Manosevitz, M. Early sexual behavior in adult homosexual and heterosexual males. *Journal of Abnormal Psychology*, 1970, *3*, 396-402.

Manosevitz, M. Education and MMPI Mf scores in homosexual and heterosexual males. *Journal of Consulting and Clinical Psychology*, 1971, *35*, 395-399.

Marks, P. An assessment of the diagnostic process in a child guidance setting. *Psychological Monographs*, 1961 (75, Whole No. 507).

Marks, P., & Haller, D. Adolescent profiles: A new typology. Paper read at the Ninth Annual Symposium on the MMPI, Los Angeles, California, 1974.

Marks, P., & Seeman, W. *The actuarial description of abnormal personality.* Baltimore: The Williams and Wilkins Co., 1963.

Marks, P., Seeman, W., & Haller, D. *The actuarial use of the MMPI with adolescents and adults.* Baltimore: The Williams and Wilkins Co., 1974.

McAree, C.P., Steffenhagen, R.A., & Zheuttin, L.S. Personality factors in college drug users. *International Journal of Social Psychiatry,* 1969, *15*, 102-106.

McDonald, R., & Gynther, M. MMPI differences associated with sex, race and class in two adolescent samples. *Journal of Consulting Psychology*, 1963, *27*, 112-116.

McKenzie, J.D., The dynamics of deviant achievement. *Personnel and Guidance Journal,* 1964, *42*, 683-686.

McKinley, J.C., & Hathaway, S.R. The MMPI: V. Hysteria, hypomania, and psychopathic deviate. *Journal of Applied Psychology*, 1944, *28*, 153-173.

Meehl, P. Profile analysis of the MMPI in differential diagnosis. Journal of Applied Psychology, 1946, *30*, 517-524.

Meehl, P. *Research results for counselors.* St. Paul, Minnesota: State Department of Education, 1951.

Mello, N., & Guthrie, G. MMPI profiles and behavior in counseling. *Journal of Counseling Psychology*, 1958, *5*, 125-129.

Mitler, C., Wertz, C., & Counts, S. Racial differences on the MMPI. *Journal of Clinical Psychology*, 1961, *17*, 159-161.

Morgan, H.H. A psychometric comparison of achieving and non-achieving college students of high ability. *Journal of Consulting Psychology*, 1952, *16*, 292-298.

Murray, J.B. The Mf scale of the MMPI for college students. *Journal of Clinical Psychology*, 1963, *19*, 113-115.

Murray, J.B., Munley, M.J., & Gilbart, I.E. The Pd scale of the MMPI for college students. *Journal of Clinical Psychology*, 1965, *21*, 48-51.

Nance, R.D. Masculinity-feminity in prospective teachers. *Journal of Educational Research*, 1949, *42*, 658-66.

Navran, L. A rationally derived MMPI scale to measure dependence. *Journal of Consulting Psychology*, 1954, *18*, 192.

Nelson, S.E. The development of an indirect objective measure of social status and its relationship to certain psychiatric syndromes. Unpublished doctoral dissertation, University of Minnesota, 1952.

Norman, R.D., & Redlo, M. MMPI personality patterns for various college major groups. *Journal of Applied Psychology*, 1952, *36*, 404-409.

Nyman, A.J., & LeMay, M.L. Differentiation of types of college misconduct offenses with MMPI subscales. *Journal of Clinical Psychology*, 1967, *23*, 99-100.

Oetting, E.R. Examination anxiety: Prediction, physical response, and relation to scholastic performance. *Journal of Counseling Psychology*, 1966, *13*, 224-227.

Osborne, R.T., Sander, W.B., & Young, F.M. MMPI patterns of college disciplinary cases. *Journal of Counseling Psychology*, 1956, *3*, 52-56.

Palau, N. Aggression and hostility in Mexican women as measured by the MMPI. Paper presented at the Seventh Annual Symposium on the MMPI, Mexico City, Mexico, 1972.

Panton, J.H. MMPI profile configurations among crime classification groups. *Journal of Clinical Psychology*, 1958, *14*, 305-308.

Panton, J.H. The identity of habitual criminalism with the MMPI. *Journal of Clinical Psychology*, 1962, *18*, 133-136.

Parsons, O.A., Yourshaw, S., & Borstelmann, L. Self-ideal-self-discrepancies on the MMPI: Consistencies over time and geographic region. *Journal of Counseling Psychology*, 1968, *15*, 160-166.

Perlman, M. Social class membership and test-taking attitude. Unpublished master's thesis, University of Chicago, 1950.

Persons, R., & Marks, P. The violent 4-3 MMPI personality type. *Journal of Consulting and Clinical Psychology*, 1971, *36*, 189-196.

Pothast, M.D. A personality study of two types of murderers. Unpublished doctoral dissertation, Michigan State University, 1956.

Rankin, R.J. Analysis of items perceived as objectionable in the MMPI. *Perceptual and Motor Skills*, 1968, *27*, 627-633.

Rapfogel, R., & Armentrout, J. Inner-versus other-directedness and hypomanic tendencies in a nonpsychiatric population. *Journal of Clinical Psychology*, 1972, *28*, 526-527.

Rice, D.G. Rorschach responses and aggressive characteristics of MMPI F   16 scorers. Journal of Projective Techniques, 1968, *32*, 253-266.

Robbins, P., Tanck, R., & Meyersburg, H. Psychological factors in smoking, drinking and drug experimentation. *Journal of Clinical Psychology*, 1971, *27*, 450-452.

Rose, A. A study of homesickness in college freshmen. *Journal of Social Psychology*, 1947, *26*, 185-202.

Rowley, V.N., & Stone, F.B. MMPI differences between emotionally disturbed and delinquent adolescents. *Journal of Clinical Psychology*, 1962, *18*, 481-484.

Schwartz, M., & Krupp, N. The MMPI "conversion V" among 50,000 medical patients: A study of incidence, criteria and profile elevation. *Journal of Clinical Psychology*, 1971, *27*, 89-95.

Schwartz, M., Osborne, D., & Krupp, N. Moderating effects of age and sex on the association of medical diagnosis and 1-3/3-1 MMPI profiles. *Journal of Clinical Psychology*, 1972, *28*, 502-505.

Sheriff, A., & Boomer, D.S. Who is penalized by Re penalty for guessing? *Journal of Educational Psychology*, 1954, *45*, 81-90.

Simon, W., & Hales, W.M. Note on a suicide key in the Minnesota Multiphasic Personality Inventory. *American Journal of Psychiatry*, 1949, *106*, 222-223.

Simono, R. Personality characteristics of undergraduate curricular groups. *Psychology in the Schools*, 1968, *5*, 280-282.

Singer, M. Comparison of indicators of homosexuality on the MMPI. *Journal of Consulting and Clinical Psychology*, 1970, *34*, 15-18.

Smart, R., & Jones, D. Illicit LSD users: Their personality characteristics and psychopathology. *Journal of Abnormal Psychology*, 1970, *75*, 286-292.

Spero, J.R. A study of the relationship between selected functional menstrual disorders and interpersonal conflict. Unpublished doctoral dissertation, New York University, 1968.

Spiaggia, M. An investigation of the personality traits of art students. *Educational and Psychological Measurement*, 1950, *10*, 285-293.

Stone, F.B., & Rowley, V.N. MMPI differences between emotionally disturbed and delinquent adolescent girls. *Journal of Clinical Psychology*, 1963, *19*, 227-230.

Sutker, P. Personality differences and sociopathy in heroin addicts and non-addict prisoners. *Journal of Abnormal Psychology*, 1971, *78*, 247-251.

Swenson, W. Structured personality testing in the aged: An MMPI study of the geriatric population. *Journal of Clinical Psychology*, 1961, *17*, 302-304.

Swenson, W., Pearson, J., & Osborne, O. *An MMPI source book.* Minneapolis University of Minnesota Press, 1973.

Tamkin, A.S. & Klett, C.J. Barron's ego strength scale: A replication of an evaluation of its construct validity. *Journal of Consulting Psychology*, 1957, *21*, 412.

Thumin, F. MMPI scores as related to age, education and intelligence among male job applicants. *Journal of Applied Psychology*, 1969, *53*, 404-407.

Tsubouchi, K., & Jenkins, R. Three types of delinquents: Their performance on the MMPI and PCR. *Journal of Clinical Psychology*, 1969, *25*, 353-358.

Ungerleider, J.T., Fisher, D., Fuller, M., & Caldwell, A. The "bad trip" — the etiology of the adverse LSD reaction. *American Journal of Psychiatry*, 1968, *124*, 1483-1490.

Vaughan, R.P. The influence of religious affiliation on the MMPI scales. *Journal of Clinical Psychology*, 1965, *21*, 416-417.

Warbin, R., Altman, H., Gynther, M., & Sletten, I. A new empirical automated MMPI interpretive program: 2-8 and 8-2 code types. *Journal of Personality Assessment*, 1972, *36*, 581-584.

Welsh, G.S. Factor Dimensions A and R. In G.S. Welsh and W. Grant Dahlstrom (Eds.) *Basic readings on the MMPI in psychology and medicine.* Minneapolis: University of Minnesota Press, 1956, pp. 264-281.

Welsh, G. MMPI profile and factor scales A and R. *Journal of Clinical Psychology*, 1965, *21*, 43-47.

Welsh, G.S., & Dahlstrom, W.G. (Eds.). *Basic readings on the MMPI in psychology and medicine.* Minneapolis: University of Minnesota Press, 1956.

Wiggins, J.S., & Rumrill, C. Social desirability in the MMPI and Welsh's factor scales A and R. *Journal of Consulting Psychology*, 1959, *23*, 100-106.

Williams, H.L. The development of a caudality scale for the MMPI. *Journal of Clinical Psychology*, 1952, *8*, 293-297.

Wilson, D.L. Interpretive hypotheses for the MMPI in a Veteran's Administration setting. Pre-doctoral clinical paper, University of North Carolina, 1965.

Wolking, W.D., Quast, W., & Lawton, J.J. MMPI profiles of the parents of behaviorally disturbed children and parents from the general population. *Journal of Clinical Psychology*, 1966, *22*, 39-48.

Yeomans, W.N., & Lundin, R.W. The relationship between personality adjustment and scholarship achievement in male college students. *Journal of Genetic Psychology*, 1957, *57*, 213-218.

ABOUT
THE AUTHOR AND
CONTRIBUTOR